THE WAY WITHOUT MASTERS

Rose Circle Publications
Bayonne, NJ
2024

By Rémi Boyer

The Ways of Awakening Trilogy

Freemasonry as a Way of Awakening

Mask Cloak Silence:
Martinism as a Way of Awakening

Beneath the Veil of Elias Artista
The Rose-Croix as a Way of Awakening:
An Oral Tradition
(with Lima de Freitas and Manuel Gandra)

The Rectified Scottish Rite:
From the Doctrine of Reintegration
to the *Imago Templi*

With Sylvie Boyer-Camax:

Letters to Friends of the Spirit:
Martinist Views & Others

The Way Without Masters

THE WAY WITHOUT MASTERS

BY

RÉMI BOYER

IN SYZYGY WITH
SYLVIE BOYER-CAMAX

A Collection of Nondualist Texts

La Voie des Sans Maîtres
La Voie des Cent Maîtres (Cent Nagas)
La Voie des Sangs Maîtres (Sangs Réels)

The Way Without Masters

Copyright © 2024 by Rémi Boyer
English translation copyright © 2024 by Michael Sanborn

ISBN: 978-1-947907-29-4
Library of Congress Control Number: 2024921529

First published in French as *La Voie des Sans Maîtres* by Éditions de la Tarente, 2021.

Cover photograph: "Au commencement, sont les Nagas…" by Sylvie Boyer-Camax.

Drawings by Françoise Pelherbe.

Gouache paintings by Jean-Gabriel Jonin: pp. 189, 207, 225.

Book design and layout by Michael Sanborn, TextArc LLC. michael@textarc.net

All rights reserved. No part of this publication may be reproduced, distributed, or transmitted in any form or by any means, including photocopying, recording, or other electronic or mechanical methods, without the prior written permission of the publisher, except in the case of brief quotations embodied in critical reviews and certain other non-commercial uses permitted by copyright law. For permission requests, write to the publisher at the address below.

Rose Circle Publications
P.O. Box 854
Bayonne, NJ 07002, U.S.A.
www.rosecirclebooks.com

To EivLys
Ultimate Woman and Goddess

Contents

Fore-ward	v
Incoherist Manifestos & Treatises	1
Incoherist Manifesto & 17	3
22 Short Incoherist Treatises	5
Pieces of Incoherism	33
Fragments of Absoluteness	41
Sparks of Internity	47
Parcels of Beingness	51
Incoherist Tatters & Torches	55
Disjointed Words of the Mad Monk	67
Incoherist Manifesto K 22	77
A Few Crazy Considerations on the Absolute	81
Disjointed Words of a Mad Monk to Unbind	81
Songs of the Master of Flowers	101
Distant Echoes of Incoherist Imperience	103
Almond	103
Axis	123
Sword, Brush, and Garden	132
Nine Questions Asked of the Mad Monk	137
The Lover of Shambu and the Fool of Shakti	145
Teachings Whispered by a Muse of Shambu	147
Whispers of the Timeless	147
Whispers of the Intangible	155
Whispers of the Uncertain	161
Whispers of the Forbidden	167
Whispers of the Immortal	173
Chùa Tâm Sen: Monastery of the Three Lotuses	183

The Sayings of Monk Durian — 187

    The Words of Stinking Monk Durian — 189
    The Words of Luminous Monk Durian — 207
    The Words of Secret Monk Durian — 225

Hymnal to the Goddess — 249

    To the Supreme — 251
    Hymn to the Goddess of Grace — 252
    Hymn to the Goddess of Free Spirits — 254
    Hymn to the Goddess of Wisdom — 256
    Hymn to the Goddess of Dreams — 257
    Hymn to the Goddess of the Arts — 258
    Hymn to the Goddess of Understanding — 260
    Hymn to the Goddess of Adjustment — 262
    Hymn to the Goddess of Angels — 264
    Hymn to the Goddess of Origins — 266
    Hymn to the Goddess of the Dawn — 267
    Hymn to the Goddess of Strength — 268
    Hymn to the Goddess of Mutation — 269
    Hymn to the Goddess of Death — 271
    Hymn to the Goddess of Ecstasy — 273
    Hymn to the Goddess of Breath — 274
    Hymn to the Cardinal Goddess — 276
    Hymn to the Goddess of Storms — 277
    Hymn to the Goddess of Power — 278
    Hymn to the Goddess of Passion — 279
    Hymn to the Goddess of Joy — 280
    Hymn to the Crowned Goddess — 282
    Hymn to the Goddess of Lights — 283
    Hymn to the Goddess of the Time of Times — 284
    Hymn to the Goddess of the Uncreated — 285
    Hymn to the Serpentine Goddess — 286
    Hymn to the Empurpled Goddess — 287
    Hymn to the True Black Goddess — 288

Hymn to the Goddess of the Arcana	289
Hymn to the Unnameable Goddess	290
Great Hymn to the Adamantine Goddess	292
Great Hymn to the Goddess of Heavenly Roses	294
Great Hymn to the Goddess of the Great Nothing	297
Great Hymn to the Goddess of Absolute Freedom	299

Kamala Sutra   301

The Lost Words of Monk Durian   349

Hymnal to the Hidden King   371

Sebastianist Manifesto	373
Hymnal to the Hidden King	375
PATH S	
Hymn to the Poet-Prophets	375
Hymn to the Sacred Fools	377
Hymn to the Templar Pastors	378
Hymn to the Undines of the Tagus	380
Hymn to the Grail Boatmen	381
Hymn to the Panels	382
Hymn to the Divas of Fado	384
Hymns to the Standard Bearers	385
Hymn to the Friends of the Hidden King	387
Hymn to Those of the Saudade of the Hidden King	389
PATH I	
Hymn to the Dragon of Portugal	391
Hymn to the Angel of Portugal	392
Hymn to the Lusitanian Horse	393
Hymn to Inês	395
Hymn to St Jerome	396
Hymn to Prester John	398
Hymn to the Hidden King	400

Confessions of the Goddess on the Pillow of the Back of the World   405

Fore-ward

At the dawn of a new world that will no longer believe in old certainties, it suffices to note the acceleration of the changes that affect us, or will affect us all: the multiplication of self-proclaimed false prophets and the appearance of fanciful movements.

But the false prophets and the said movements are useful.

They stimulate the searching spirit of seekers.

In Europe, that peninsula of the Asian continent, the last attempt at construction dates back to the Carolingian Empire: the sacralization of space through pilgrimages; the transition from horizontal to vertical architecture, from Romanesque to Gothic, from alchemical to medical concerns.

All this to build the City of God.

The monastic and chivalrous Order charged with this task was and remains particularly discreet. It was not acclaimed in the legal or historical chronicles.

Rémi Boyer's book consecrates the end of a cycle of awakening.

As with François Rabelais, you have to break the bone to find the substantive Marrow.

As with Don Quixote of la Mancha.

Or with André Breton, Sarane Alexandrian, Lima de Freitas, etc.

Everything we do is unblocked.

Leaving or staying, everything is equal.

Direct awakening is without awakening.

Non-emptiness is true emptiness.

Nurturing the mind to keep silence is, incidentally, like departing from vices.

The wandering monk, who goes on a pilgrimage with his umbrella.

Lao Hon Vai

INCOHERIST
MANIFESTOS
& TREATISES

Incoherist Manifesto & 17

1. Incoherism is a vertical force of creation, a free manifestation of Essential Nature, beyond doing or having anything, oriented only towards Absoluteness, born from the Ocean of Silence and springing from the Interval, like a demonic genius.

2. Incoherism generates Life as Performance from a position of Awakening: a Performance to break free even from liberation, or to raise the banner of perfection enfolded in imperfection. The Absolute Gesture resides within the perfection of the imperfect gesture.

3. Incoherism is a posture of the body and the mind against all impostures.

4. Incoherism is heightened consciousness, the consciousness of intensity, the consciousness of intention, the consciousness that "I am" is the sole creator, the sole actor, the sole director, the sole producer, and ultimately the sole spectator of its own spectacle, which it calls "world" and is only "wave." Total solipsism. The High Game of "that happens" while "This abides."

5. Incoherism notes of the *Person* that its need for global coherence is the source of its alienation. History, politics, science (both the wished-for "soft science" and the self-proclaimed "hard science"), established religions, and the fixed arts are pathologies of the Person. Being is the only Coherence, beyond all coherences, and the Great Nothing stands outside of this and those.

6. There are no universal values, only personal values. The question of values, the source of all conflicts, internal or external, will be resolved with the disappearance of the *Person*.

7. We are under a dictatorship, whether subtle or crude. This did not originate in a hypothetical and improbable *exterior* but within ourselves. The noble fight is therefore internal and axial. External and peripheral fights invariably lead to exhaustion. Nevertheless, or all the more so, there is a need to develop a true Art of War.

8   Incoherism settles its account in time and at all times, in order to navigate, free, in the relative worlds, following the wind of Will.

9   The search for going beyond art finds its apogee in the Quest for an Art of Nothing, the Absolute Art of the Interval. At the Crossroads of Absolute Beauty, Absolute Virility, and Absolute Femininity, the Unfathomable alone is Art.

10 Incoherism demands and proclaims, serious in the Moment and the Always, the unlimited respect and celebration of Absolute Femininity, essential and universal, the magnificent power and sublime face of the Real, the Eternal Feminine, in all its forms, divinely human or humanly divine, all wise-women.

11 Only the Masters of the Great Nothing can recognize, in the total fullness of Being, subversion, diversion, and *Reversal* as paths of the Interval. To the unlearned and clumsy, there only remains the egotistical agitation of the *Person*.

12 Incoherism is the Loving Idea-Seizure, the Place-State, at the apex of Being. The Lightning of Absoluteness.

"I Am, Absolute Will"

"I Am, Absolute Freedom"

22 Short Incoherist Treatises

SHORT TREATISE ON BREVITY

Nothing that can be stated is of the order of the Real. The Real is indescribable. It cannot be stated, understood, or explained. The Real remains.

§ The Real is grasped only Immediately, through Evidence. No mental process leads to the Real or can even process the Real. If it is necessary to "state" the Real, the briefest, most incisive language will be preferred for being the most opportune. Language in effect dilutes the Real in the representations to compose magical worlds, our daily realities, our realities of desire… or horror. Seek neither to satisfy nor to reassure the mind. Make it short! Be brief! May your words not come from the midst of words, but from the heart, from the choir, from amidst the Silence.

SHORT TREATISE ON THE THREE COVENANTS

The Three Covenants:
 1st Covenant: the Stone
 2nd Covenant: the Lost Word
 3rd Covenant: the Silent Power

The masks fall. The Person disappears: Quest for Being.

Then Being goes in search of non-Being, which is the Absolute. Quest in the quest. Quest by the quest.

SHORT TREATISE ON THE RELATIONSHIP BETWEEN TEACHER AND DISCIPLE

There is nothing worse for a teacher than a disciple who seeks to understand "the mind of the teacher." The teacher does not think. They free from thought. They are Absolute Freedom. The disciple must understand their own primal and ultimate nature.

§ The now famous, misunderstood, and unfortunate formula, *The master appears when the disciple is ready,* means that the master appears when the disciple no longer needs a master. It is in fact a precise indication of the nature of the "mirror of oneself."

§ It is only when total boredom sets in that the disciple turns resolutely and absolutely towards the one and only master: Being. Then they lose their head and the headless arises, free.

§ The initiatory chain is uninterrupted, not because it formally survives through linear time, but because it always essentially remains here and now, free from all time.

§ The disciple fails because they respect Essence but wish to practice all its forms. On the contrary, they must respect all forms, but practice only Essence.

§ Transmitting who we are to others is invariably a mistake.
Only revealing to others what one is has any efficacy.
But "doing Nothing" is superior to any other form.

SHORT TREATISE ON COMMON CONFUSIONS

The human being is lived by systems of beliefs, while the adept lives systems of different realities.

The human being pretends to think. In its arrogance, it sometimes claims to have ideas. In reality, this is just chatter, commentary at best.

§ The unawakened human is a sick, degenerate animal that wants to submit nature to the yoke of its degeneration.

§ There is no social or political application of Awakening or the Real. Any attempt in this direction is not only doomed to failure but invariably leads to the worst. It remains, moreover, the work of "persons," of unawakened entities who have developed a concept of the Real without ever having approached it.

§ The ego is totalitarian.

The ego is the tyrant, the prototype of all totalitarianisms, political, economic, religious, or any others, which are only the hypertrophied and spasmodic extensions of the egoic totalitarianisms of a few individuals.

§ The true election, which has nothing to do with the falsified procedures of our democracies, is a manifestation of Being. Election is indeed the only perfect manifestation within the human kingdom. While most religions and traditions have retained a trace of it, they have lost its intrinsic virtue.

§ We must constantly reaffirm the total independence of Initiation vis-à-vis any system of beliefs, religious, philosophical, psychological, political, or scientific, even moreso vis-à-vis any syntax.

Initiation is a-syntactic.

SHORT TREATISE ON MORAL AND ETHICAL CONSIDERATIONS

Pity, the other side of contempt.
Indifference, the other side of fear.

§ Forgetting is superior to forgiveness. Forgetting is the forgiveness of the gods and heroes who "release" events into Nothingness.

§ Forgiveness always leaves a scar; forgetting erases even the wound.

§ The idea of a sacrifice necessary for all creation is strictly human. The adept knows that all true Creation, which comes from the Real, by the Real, for the Real, is born from Nothingness, from the Interval. Therefore, they have nothing to sacrifice: Nothing to sacrifice.

§ The feeling of guilt is always an ego manifestation.

§ Old age is beautiful if it is unadorned, if it rejects the disguises of the Person.

§ It takes great courage to face the dizzying lie of man. This is the first step on the heroic path.

§ The very absurdity of the world is its meaning, if there is meaning.

§ If we are strong, then we are weak.
If we are weak, then we are strong.
We must therefore achieve "neither strong nor weak."

§ To become immortal requires as a prerequisite the conscious acceptance of one's own death and total helplessness.

Death is our best friend. Just to our *left,* slightly behind, erased but ever so present, she is both our bodyguard and our companion. We don't listen to her, yet she teaches life. Deaf to her wisdom, we cannot become alive. Not even being alive, we cannot be Immortal.

§ In the Zone of Silence,
   The nobleman in every man still conscious,
   The fairy woman in every woman still conscious,
   The child-light in every child still conscious,
   Uplifts, awakens, and restores.

SHORT TREATISE ON ADEPTSHIP

"Adept," "initiate": these are words that have become emphatic to designate simply the human being free of themselves.

§ Whether the adept goes to the right or to the left, whether they walk here or there, no longer has the slightest importance or meaning. They know the center of themself, the earth without ego, the earth without the Person.

§ The quest is not a quest for meaning, but a quest for perfection. When, at the end of the wandering, the adept accomplishes the perfect gesture, the whole wandering becomes perfect.

§ The adept integrates the fact of dying now as a reality. This is what frees them. Death is the intimate friend and the initiator, here and now. The coming death, like the past birth, is of no use.

§ The adept who remains in Silence masters the Word and begins to perceive the other side of Silence, namely the Non-Word, in the bosom of the unspeakable word, the "Name that has never been pronounced in the Beingness that has never been begotten."

§ A very old language, made up of strange and various silences, remains in my Reality.
   It is this language that was used at the inception of chaos.
   It is this same language that will be used for the return of another chaos, always made of the undifferentiated but unified.

§ The adept learns to conjugate the universe in the Interval. It is the place where the worlds are born from the conjugation of Letters and Numbers.

The Interval is the place before A, the place without Number, Temple of the Silence of Silences, Temple of all the possible and impossible, apex and seed of the worlds.

§ The adept who grasps the Infinite masters the Art of Numbers. Then they turn, find the Infinite, and grasp the Non-Number, which is not zero.

SHORT TREATISE ON MAGIC

Any magic circle, any "world" therefore, should be a reminder to the unconscious of the power of self-presence. In reality, no "demon" will ever be stopped by a magic circle. The only "circle" impassable to the darkness is the Axis, the Circle of the Void.

To truly operate is to operate in the Real. It is not about operating on a Monday, a Wednesday, or a Sunday, at the time of Venus, Mercury, or the Sun; it is about operating in the Moment itself. Nor is it about operating in just such a sacred or consecrated place, according to just such an orientation; it is about operating in the Zone of Silence, the non-phenomenal zone.

§ There are more or less self-conscious forces without the power of formation: they remain without form yet are not immaterial. There are also self-conscious forces with the power of formation, which therefore know how to coagulate and maintain a given form for a time: this is the case for humans, animals, plants, and minerals.

§ I can turn back the forces when "I am" the Force.

Nothing is the most mysterious force in the Cosmos.

It emanates from Absoluteness as Intention while the Orient emanates from Beingness.

Nothing is, in a certain way but only in a certain way, the very "substance" of the Cosmos. An absent substance.

§ Any statement, evocation, or invocation in the relative world is only recidivism, repetition, a distant echo, already exceeded though barely emitted. Only the immobile and silent expression of Verticality proves to be both immutable, as in Itself, and always new, although present at the "origin of time." Silence is indeed the mathematical origin of Numbers and Letters and, consequently, the cosmic origin of relative time.

§ There is a magic of the Void (and of Silence), a theurgy of the Void, and an alchemy of the Void, much more powerful, infinitely more powerful, than all the high sciences of forms and arts of the gods, accessible to demigods as to heroes.

That is why the adept will never cease to remain in the Great Interval and to use the forces that are the intervals between the worlds, rather than the forces that the worlds themselves present.

§ On the Axis of the Real, no one is a magician. No one *does* magic. *Doing magic* is permitted in the relative worlds of the periphery, in the Dionysian worlds. Dionysus and the Great Illusionist.

On the Axis of the Real, "I am" is *magic*. The mage is *magic*. Magic is the Real.

§ God does not respond to prayers.

But the Absolute Real responds to the Silent Real.

§ "I am" is the Rite.

The Rite is the Interval.

The Breath is the invocation of the God of the Interval.

§ When personalities come together to perform a ritual, they should first coalesce into a unified assembly. Then, after the ceremony, when the rite itself intervenes, thus forging the Act, the assembly will disappear into Being.

On the contrary, when non-personalities come together, unconditioned humans, Being is immediately present, or more precisely, Immediate Presence. The ceremony is then useless. The rite operates on its own. It is a Theurgy of Silence while in the first case we had a Magic of the Word.

SHORT TREATISE ON THE PERSON

The Person is an unstable amalgamation of little *I*'s. The *I*, an *I*, is incapable of idea. The *I* is only conditioning. Being can only generate from the Freedom, and not from the need or necessity, of the pure Ideas. The rarity of pure Ideas demonstrates the sobriety of Being.

§ We are all in a vicious circle, the personal vicious circle, the vicious circle of the Person. There is a single exit: the Center, on the Axis of the Real.

§ It is not the Person who has the problem, it is the Person who is the problem. The Person is paralyzed by fear. Every Person is only fear. The adept is not a Person. For the adept, there is no longer any Person.

§ All existence is problematic.
Existence itself is *the* problematic.
To remove the whole problem at the root is to renounce existence.
Cease to exist in order to simply, uniquely, absolutely Be.
Existence is the container of experience.
The more existence, the more experience.
Experience is the container of the Person.
No more existence, no more Person.

§ Freeing yourself from experience is freeing yourself from the Person that is so cumbersome. It is to free oneself from personal history, which is so harmful.
The person can only heal on their own. They are their own disease.

§ To renounce experience is to find Being.
To find Being is, by reversal, to grasp non-Being.
To unite the two, Being and non-Being, is to master the Interval, the ultimate Awakening, Awakening without any form of awakening.
"I am" Being and non-Being, that is, the non-Being Being.

§ Being carries all in its path, good and evil, towards supreme happiness. It plays with the proliferation as well as the confusion of worlds. Both emanate from its omnipresence.
Thus, Being is not attracted. It lives; it is Fusion.
Only the Person is attracted.

§ Any human activity pushed to its perfection is initiatory because it requires going beyond the Person. Perfection, all perfection, requires Being!

§ The failure of the Person is total.
The impotence of the Person is total.
Our failure as a Person is perfect. Our impotence is perfect. They mean that we must learn "to do Nothing."
That is awakening.

§ It is the conscious acceptance of our total impotence to save the world, as well as to save ourselves, that opens the way, or rather discovers the way, to absolute Freedom. The world only serves our intention to no longer be the world.

§ In the quest, there is never any Person to help you.
Never any person: no personality: negated personality.
Only being.
God is ultimately a personal matter.
Whereas the Absolute is an impersonal, a-Personal, response and reality.

§ There is, here and now, in the Interval of the Real, an awakened Humanity, a total integrated and unified entity, a realized entity, both unrelated to people and one with "all people" as an undifferentiated consciousness. It is given to everyone to experience this "more than human" Humanity, on condition of abandoning the condition, that is to say the Person.

§ The human, the personal, always ends up dying by the hands of the "others": this "other" so attractive, so repulsive, so adorable, so terrifying; this "other" so much oneself.

May Permanence be sweet to you!
May imPermanence be sweet to you!
Permanence-imPermanence,
Perfect identity for This/That who Remains.
Perfect incomprehension for the Person.

SHORT TREATISE ON REBELLION

The sublime rebel is only some One who strives to Be, and absolutely refuses to be anything other than themself.
The sacred rebel, the hero, refuses to not Be,
Refuses the Being-bypass.
Renounces manifestation outside the Self.
Their quest is that of the Great Real.

§ All rebellion demonstrates a capacity for ascesis.

§ True marginality is located at the Center.

The other marginalities, social or political, are clumsy attempts, sometimes deformed, to approach the Verticality whose presence is confusedly felt or intuited.

§ "I am," royalist and libertarian.
"I am," royal and free.
As King of Nothing and Free of All.
Freed Nobility.
Mad-King of Beingness,
Emperor beggar of absoluteness.

§ The Emperor is the collective entity born from the solitary works of the adepts who knew how to operate and create in the World of the Interval, that is, in the Real.

§ The adept, having reached the end of the quest, continues the quest.
Beyond the beyond. Purpose beyond purpose.
For the beauty and the total freedom of the Gesture.
For the Beauty of the act of Love.

§ The art of diversion is particular to the adept.
Diverting time then diverting the world makes it possible to reorient energy in its initial verticality and reverse it to face the Absolute.
"Diversion of oneself" is another term for Awakening.

§ Liberation means escaping from all habits, the habits of prison as well as the habits of freedom.

SHORT TREATISE ON TRADITION AND THE AVANT-GARDE

Tradition and the Avant-Garde are both quests for the Absolute: Absolutely All in the case of Tradition; Absolutely Nothing in the case of the Avant-Garde. The first invariably leads to the second because the second invariably leads to the first.

Absolutely All and Absolutely Nothing are exactly the same.

Several traditions propose non-ways, that is to say desperate searches for the Absolutely Nothing. The avant-gardes also have their searches for a perfect poetry, or a perfect aesthetics, to approach the Absolutely All of the traditions.

The common strength of traditions and avant-gardes lies in the vital and free rebellion against what is established. The Absolutely All, like the Absolutely Nothing, only surrenders, and is surrendered to, *in* and *through* freedom.

§ Traditions are the poems of awakening.
Initiatory societies should be the poetry of traditions.

§ Tradition is a non-tradition. Tradition belongs to the unnameable. All the expressions of Tradition, all the ways, are partial and biased, since they are tinged with human concepts. Tradition is only accessible to those who become Tradition by an unrestrained and immediate plunge into the Real. The man of Tradition and the woman of Tradition remain in the Interval. Regardless of appearances, they never return to the conceived worlds.

§ The work, whatever the art, possesses its own life as soon as it is completed, a completion that can be found most precisely in its incompleteness. Only the incomplete work is perfect.

The artist, artisan or adept, artisan and adept, if they are really conscious, will then recognize that they never created the work, that they did not "give it life," to use the expression of many artists who believe they "give life" when they themselves do not exist, being only lived images. On the contrary, the artist will know that they only became aware of, and therefore only made an impression on, what remained there, in the Interval. Little by little, the work revealed itself to itself, mirroring itself in the gaze of the artist, as their consciousness increased.

That is not the Art, but it is Art.

SHORT TREATISE ON MADNESS

The game of all and nothing, the Game of All and Nothing, is the game of Energy and Consciousness.

Allowing all within oneself allows the adept to attain the stillness of Nothing.
How can nothing beget something? Only by nature.
Doing nothing begets the All.

§ This "Other," which is our own ultimate reality, which we call (for want of a better word) *god, devil, angel, demon,* or whatever, according to the game, according to the *I* of the child that agrees with the Person, is the Great Nothing, Oneself!

§ The endgame is Really the In-Games.

§ One must be of rare lucidity and great wisdom to consciously decide to become Mad, or more exactly to recognize one's state of Madness. Madness is what best characterizes our divinity in the world as it seems. The adept is a master of controlled madness.

§ The Mad One of Nothing is the All of Nothing.

§ The obstacle to the direct way is the direct way.

§ The direct way to the Great Real is an insane diagonal, the Dance of the Crazy Lovers.

SHORT TREATISE ON LAZINESS

Doing nothing, or Non-Doing, is an art superior to any other but accessible to very few, because malpractice is easier in this area than in any other.

§ Non-Doing is, in fact, reserved for Kings, crowned ones, those of the Kingdom of the Center who, mad trapeze artists of the Axis of the Real, are adrift in the Interval, subjugated by the Beauty of the Great Nothing.

Four postures prepare for this strange royalty:

- The posture of slowness. Abiding in the Breath and abiding in the A, slow down the movement of the world by slowing down your own movement. Depart from your Stillness and donate your perfect stillness to the situation until it slows down to the point of freezing.

- The posture of letting go. Abiding in the Breath and in the A, let things and events come into place, let the equation of the world resolve itself by self-dissolution. Intervene only through non-intention. Influence only through non-influence.

- The posture of the reverse. Abiding in the Breath and in the A, do the reverse of what is normally expected in the situation. Go backwards, sleep during the day, work at night, use your right hand to do what your left hand does and vice versa, look for all the ways to turn the tide of the world.

- The fixed posture. Abiding in the Breath and in the A, repeat the same useless gesture every day at a fixed time. This gesture must be binding, considered insane by the witness present, and provoke the anger of your ego which will finally get carried away against the incomprehensible will of your reality.

These four postures held with rigor and determination help to remove and bring down the masks of the Person and thus expose the Being, the eternal inhabitant of the Center of oneself.

§ If *failure* and *success* had a meaning, if meaning made or required meaning, we would always fail no matter what we did. The only conceivable and "really" achievable success would be Non-Doing.

SHORT TREATISE ON INCOHERISM

The adept lives against the tide of the world, which is why it is necessary for them to master the Interval.

§ One is an incoherist who makes the Interval their home.
Because of the Interval, the adept is a Witness to the Game of the world.
Because of the Interval, the adept does not act.
They first seek the interval between two fullnesses, and then, once they have perfect control of it, the extraordinary Interval of Nothingness between two Voids. It is a wonderful calligraphy.

§ The *nothing* of the nihilist is the usually aggressive absence of something. A lack.
The *nothing* of the incoherist is an empty Presence, source of infinite fullness.

§ Incoherism is an elegant blend of madness and wisdom that aims to "return" the intrinsic absurdity of the world into creative poetry and magic.

§ Incoherism has an inner *meaning,* but no signification.
Incoherism designates an Orientation, but no path.

SHORT TREATISE ON AWAKENING

The awakened, the conscious/knowing, always respects the being even if they are often irreverent towards the person (the mask).

§ The awakened is in the Interval because they are the Interval! Poetically and energetically.

§ Awakening is the clear understanding and unqualified integration of the impossibility of awakening.
Awakening is an embodied understanding of non-awakening.

§ The ways of Awakening, ways of the Real, ways of Nothing, borrow and "imprint" the garments of creative utopia. This is necessary for the awakening of Hermes in his double form of initiatory intuition and poetic intuition because the approach of the Real is accompanied for the adept, entirely in their rediscovered or seized freedom, by an opportunity to re-enchant the world. The adept is an enchanter, they master the magic art. The adept is a creator, they master the theurgic art and the science of Al-chymia. What makes the magic act is the magic will.

§ Awakening is the ultimate form of Art.
Awakening is absolute poetry.
Awakening is absolute dance,
Absolute painting,
Absolute carving,
Absolute performance.

§ Awakening is a conquest where you abandon, one by one, all your positions. Awakening is a radical attitude, a posture made of immobility and immediacy which eliminates all forms of imposture.

§ True Consciousness, heightened, awakened Consciousness, is not a faultless consciousness, but on the contrary the consciousness of the totality of the fault, of the totality of the interval, of its absolute infinity and intensity.
Any gap in consciousness is an opportunity.

SHORT TREATISE ON THE INTERVAL

The culture of secrecy kills the culture of Awakening.

Beingness is its own secret.

Human secrets are only the chimeras of the Person.

As the human is programmed to die, all their creations carry their self-destruction within themselves from the very root of desire. What is immortal is only that which is born from the Interval by the fertilizing act of Will.

§ What the human of the current calls will does not exist. A game of conditioning, a game of dupes. Will only remains a quality of Being in unconditioned humans, or in heightened consciousness. These are the two methods of approaching the Real: the unconditioned or the heightened consciousness; one corresponds to the empty Void, the second to the full Void.

§ We can only fight against evil through absence: science of the interval.

§ The interval of the Real is never impressed, never imprinted, never "marked," nothing can be precipitated there, whether by chemistry or by magic. Always, totally, definitely Virgin!

§ Throw a diamond in the filth, it remains a diamond. No filth reaches Being. Being remains.

§ What constitutes the Real link between two things, two elements, two phenomena, or two lives, is ultimately the absence of a link, the Interval which, *ipso facto,* requires that each thing, each event, each life, which are equally "moments," is unique, a perfect totality, a perfect All, a perfect Nothing. Nothingness of Being and Being of Nothingness.

§ The Interval is the fifth dimension of physicists as well as of the religious, of which nothing can be said, where the Great Nothing can be stated.

The Science of the Interval is the Ultimate Science, the Non-science Science.

The Wisdom of the Interval is the Ultimate Wisdom, the Un-wisdom Wisdom.

§ The Interval is beyond all paradoxes and encompasses them all.

The Interval is the supreme and sublime paradox.

§ God is the sole inhabitant of the Interval of the Great Real. He is the Occupant. This is why to be "born" in the Interval means to be born God. Likewise, to "die" in the Interval is to die God.

§ In a way, God is the sole Tree of the Interval.

SHORT TREATISE ON THE *PASSAGE WITHOUT A DOOR*

Each temple, each edifice of the spirit, born of a tradition or born of an art, must be considered, not as the bearer of any truth, but as a Door-without-a-Door of freedom, a radiant fissure looking out on the Interval of the Great Real.

§ It is at the moment when any way, any passage, any opening, appears in its bare expression, be it as a total dead end, that the "Passage without a Door" stands out as a unique and unavoidable impossible possibility and that the absolute Non-Way springs up, majestic and terrible.

§ Each relative world, personal or spiritual, micro-world or macro-world, has within its intimacy a flaw. This flaw is the door of the Interval: it opens onto a way without a path to the Absolute Real.

§ The keys are given to "the one who passes without a door." No one can break in to enter. Whoever is tempted to break in to enter penetrates a place-state that they will confuse for a time with the Real. It is this place-state that is at the origin of the myths of purgatory, Hell, and other places of damnation. This place-state is a malicious densification of our own ignorance, of our own opacity.

SHORT TREATISE ON STILLNESS

The master of the place (the one who has mastery of the worlds) is the master of the states (of consciousness). This one is the still master of the movement of movements.

§ Any incident, any accident, any rupture of harmony always has a single origin, a haste unsuited to the present energy. In any of the possible realities, all questions of harmony can invariably be reduced to a balanced proportion between motion and Stillness.

The very idea of the *Fall*, so misunderstood, will be clarified in a very interesting way if it is examined in its relation to haste. The two concepts, like the two phenomena, are indisputably linked, as is the concept of acceleration, but also "precipitation," which must be understood in an almost chemical sense.

§ Beingness is the essence of the movement of Sacred Stillness, the essence of the movement of Permanence.

Absoluteness is the essence of Sacred Stillness, the essence of Permanence.

Beingness and Absoluteness are both of the nature of Perfect Void and Null Perfection, one (the Other), Beingness, is of the nature of Void in Motion, the other (the One), of the nature of Fixed Void.

This movement is a dance of Stillness, a song of Stillness, an ecstasy of Stillness.

§ Stillness is the only, true, and unique Real movement.

It is the movement of Being in the Breath.

Seizing the Breath before adopting Stillness is the sequence.

§ Just as Breath is independent of respiration, Energy is independent of the body. The loss of identification with the human form makes it possible to know the free movement of Energy.

§ Movement is stillness.

Stillness is the perfection of movement.

§ There are two forms of stillness: that of the belly and that of the heart.

That of the belly is the breath of the universe.

That of the heart is the breath of the interval.

One must first inhabit the belly in order to one day live in the heart.

SHORT TREATISE ON NOTHINGNESS AND THE REAL

Some give up at the last moment. Fear of the Void, Nothingness, frightens them because they still have a concept of the Void, a concept of Nothing. So they give up and prefer to choose chaos. But chaos and order are one. One cannot be without the other. Formlessness does not exist without form. Then the plenitude of Nothing escapes them. But that doesn't matter.

As long as we want to grasp chaos, Being is absent. WE are grasped from the Real. AND Being is presence.

Being could be defined precisely as the fullness of Nothing. This is obviously false. But it's true.

Likewise, Beingness is the enjoyment of the fullness of Nothing, and Absoluteness is the transcendence of the enjoyment of the fullness of Nothing.

§ Before you can use the energy of Beingness you must collect every last drop of the precious energy you lost in the representation. You must have fully reabsorbed the representation. You must have "devoured your own children."

Fullness of Nothing.

§ Be nothing in the profane.
Be all Nothing in the sacred.
Thus, neither profane nor sacred,
But the Great Real.

§ Nothing, only Nothing, is the Way.
The rest is the way of experience.
Accumulation of experiences, including spiritual ones, means
Accumulation of increasingly opaque veils.

§ Become Nothing
And what becomes of you?
But Nothing! And it's so hard, everyone wanting me to be something. Yet nothing can equal the fullness of Nothing. None can establish in it and through it Absolute Freedom, like Free Absoluteness, outside the Kingdom of Nothing.

Yes, become Nothing. Be.

§ Do you know the fullness of Nothing?
Nothing and All are One.
Nothing and All are Being.

§ If you are aware that thought is empty,
Then you realize that speech is empty,
And that the gesture is empty.
Also, control no longer makes sense.

Itself appearing as empty.

You let go, because there are no more holds.

You are free.

Nothing to change.

Nothing to avoid.

Neither becoming nor permanence.

Neither action nor inaction.

Not even Being.

§ What's at the end of Nothing?

The All!

All & Nothing, a new duality?

Yes, if one is careful. This is why the Real is in the Interval: the Real is the Interval between All and Nothing, solely the Interval.

§ You are not breathing. God, better, the Absolute, breathes through you. What we call *breathing* is the ultimate and subtle movement of the Absolute: its Breath within Beingness.

You are not breathing, you are the Witness of this divine breath.

If you become aware of the Witness, then you possess the gaze of the Absolute.

First slay some *I*. Identify the Person.

Then slay the Person. Become the Witness.

Then slay the Witness, become the Absolute by looking back at Thatself.

But be careful not to kill the Witness lightly—you will become a totally dark I in that case!

§ "I Am The Absolute Will" is not concerned with appearances, only with the All or the Nothing, that is, the Great Real.

Being is not concerned, it is consecrated.

There is the horrible turmoil, the horrible decomposition of this relative world. Horror is just an appearance.

No appearance in the All.

No appearance in the Nothing.

§ It is necessary to kill the ordinary human in themself so that the non-ordinary God springs up in all its power and absoluteness.

§ Let the surroundings slide.

Not clinging to the surroundings is a form of ascesis.

Don't cling to the situation.

Approach the axis.

On the axis, the "situation" takes place by itself.

§ The adept is the conscious Interval between All and Nothing, between All and all, between Nothing and nothing.

The power of creation arises from the exchange of Fires by friction between All and Nothing in this perfect Interval which we can also call the Real and whose unique but total quality is Silence (or Perfect Stillness).

From the Real are born realities, realities of All or realities of Nothing.

Realities are born from reality, Silence, fertilized by the Word. A reality is a piece of Silence in movement.

§ There is no other model applicable to the Real than the Real itself.

This implies that thought is inapt.

The experience of the infinite Real is the experience of the "expanded" consciousness of the Real.

The experience of the SurReal is the experience of the essence of the consciousness of the Real.

§ Two main categories of ways: that of integration and that of disintegration. By the first, you ingest the All from the Nothing. By the second, you dissolve the All in the Nothing.

However, one who seeks the All will have to embrace the Nothing.

And the adept of the Nothing will experience fusion with the All.

§ The Way of the Real, or the Way of Nothing, is different from a way of wisdom, although Nothing is absolute wisdom. The ways of wisdom still have something to defend. The ways of the Real are naught but absolute freedom.

§ Sacred solipsism.

Nothing is the Fullness from which you can engender the God that "I Am The Absolute Will" wants in you. Nothing is the Fullness from which you Will to engender yourself as God.

§ Nothing *human* must, or can, subsist in Self.

Only Being.

As for the *human of the world,* not to interfere, not to appear in the world but as Interval, unfathomable Spirit.

Present/absent and absent/present.

§ Absence-presence is a remarkable state born of Fusion, an indelible, slightly erotic sensation of this other become oneself.

Absence-presence, empty and empty.

There is Nothing.

There has always been Nothing,

There will always be Nothing but

"I am," the eternal, perfect absence.

§ If there is indeed a true initiatory secret, it is the science of doing nothing that leads to the Art of Nothing, the Great Art!

SHORT TREATISE ON THE EROTIC

All sexuality is sacred, by Nature, by Essence, in itself, as the dance of life in its most accomplished, most radical, and most transcendent form.

The human being has lost awareness of this state of the sacred in the act solely because of the useless commentary and multiple dysfunctions of a mind in perdition. They thus forbade themselves this direct, obvious access to their own divinity, to their own immortality, which cannot be confused with a hypothetical extension of the person through their offspring.

§ Eroticism without metaphysics is simple vulgarity, more or less elegant, no longer an art, no longer a quest.

§ The caress heals the world.

§ True Love accepts no other setting than Silence.

§ So that the primal Wild Woman never dies, yet the Wild Man can totally disappear in Her, the man must create his Body of Immortality, while the woman need only nourish hers. This is why, in a way, there is indeed an Immaculate Conception.

The primal Wild Woman is also the Ultimate Woman. There is a qualitative leap in the Great Nothing between the Wild Woman and the Ultimate Woman.

§ The New Empyrean, which is also the primordial Empyrean, led and initiated by the A, is characterized in particular by the reconstitution of the original Couples consecrated to the celebration of the Great Work.

The process emerges slowly to reach the flashing splendor of AOR-AGNI, Light-Fire. The first reconstituted original couples have already integrated and deployed the Beingness-Absoluteness Fusion with Art in the densest game of matter. The more the process is advanced, the more the Fusion will be light and rapid until the final conflagration of the gods and goddesses in a singular communion.

SHORT TREATISE ON ON

The Law of ON, that is,
    The Laws of Nothing.
    They express the naked Simplicity,
        the crude Nakedness,
            the simple Crudeness, of Being-Life.

§ "I am," the ON-PO-KHAN
    The freedom of being
    The sacrament of Freedom
    The Being of Freedom.

§ There are two suns:
    The golden sun, moving sun.
    And the motionless, central sun,
    Luminous black,
    Emanation of the Great Real.
    The first animates the Person.
    The second Is our own reality, first and last.

SHORT TREATISE ON SHIVA-SHAKTI

Shiva is headless. Absolute freedom is headless.
   Thus, it can hold all *heads,* all *worlds.*

"I am" headless Shiva.
   The destroyer of the destroyer.
   The Absolute of the Absolute.

Shiva is both formless and all forms.
   "I am" Shiva, the deformed and the perfect. Perfect because deformed, deformed because perfect.

§ Shakti:
   She walks in the A.
   She sings in the A.
   She dances in the A.
   She loves in the A.
   She is the A.
   She is the One-Being.
   The Ultimate Woman.
   I am, the A.
   I am, She.

Empty, Shiva.
   Fullness, Shakti.

§ Shakti:
   Lightning of tenderness.
   Storm of sweetness.
   Tempest of caresses.
   Ocean of love.
   Surge of ecstasy.
   Angelic rain.
   Snow of purity.
   Infinite grace.

§ Shiva must totally surrender to Shakti to be Shiva.

The Absolute must totally surrender to Beingness in order to be Absoluteness.

Withdrawn forever into the Sacred Interval of the Real, the Blue Interval,

Two are One, Shiva-Shakti, Absoluteness-Beingness in the triple and absolute Fusion of Love that sets the three fields of Cinnabar ablaze.

Void & Radiance.

Shiva-Shakti,

Couple-Interval, that generates

The Royalty-Interval, that develops into:

The Community-Interval, that extends into:

The Assembly-Interval, that resolves into:

Interval.

There could be no greater fusion than that which arises from the sacred union of the God of Nothing and the Goddess of Nothing.

The fusion of the Void by the Void is wonderful. The Infinite Nothing and the Absolute Nothing engender the Null All.

§ It dwells very strangely in the sanctuary of the Orgasm of Shakti. A ring of Perfect Void at the center of an ocean of azure and emerald energy stirred by the musical waves of Love. There is the true abode of the ultimate Reality of Shiva, of that which Is, in the sanctuary of the Orgasm of Shakti. In the place where the Inner Lightning is forged, in the non-place, the Supreme Interval.

§ Shiva carries the Fire of Love for Shakti as a banner.

This infinite Fire that consumes all limit, all finitude, so that the Fusion embraces the limitless.

§ *The Triangles of Fusion:*

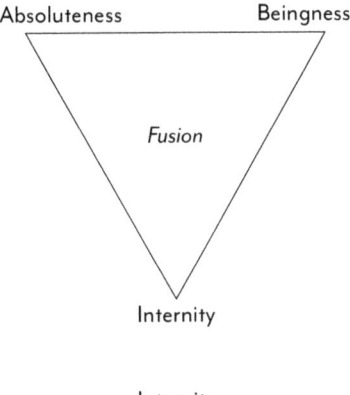

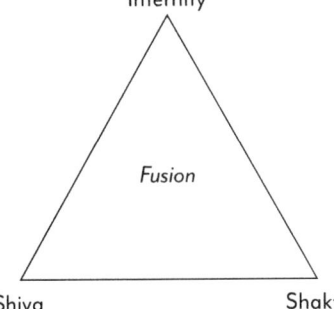

§ *The Hexagrams of Fusion:*

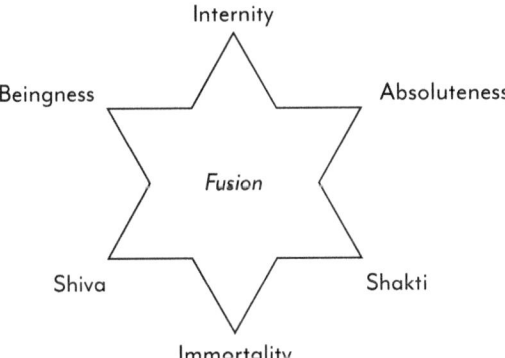

INCOHERIST MANIFESTOS & TREATISES

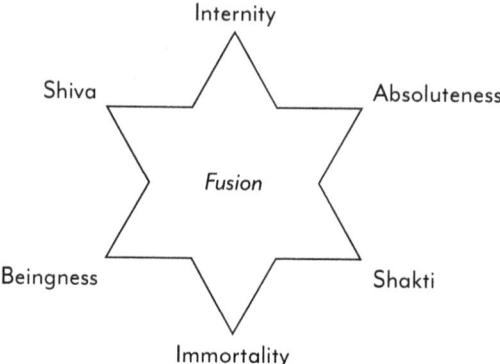

§ *The Cubes of Light:*

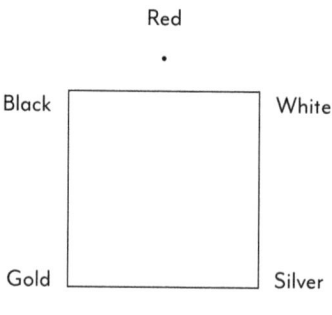

Cube of the Interval

They are born from the full Void to dissolve into the empty Void. The movement of the Cubes of Light is a perfect generation.

From Black and White is born the Red Cube.

At the heart of the Red Cube, from the fusion of Gold and Silver, springs without being born the Cube of the Perfect Interval.

SHORT TREATISE ON THE ROSE-HART

We belong to the same natural order as the Eagle or the King Cobra.

§ A Real Way can only be taken, accomplished, and realized by two entities in the same time-state-world. This entity can manifest itself in a single being, in a couple, in a family, or in a fraternity that cannot be composed of more than 22 elements (which embody the 22 Psyches).

These two entities may or may not meet, may or may not unite formally. They must leave traces of the Way in the world of form, but above all in the Sacred Interval, the only space for transmission. The form is called "the manifesto," it is not necessarily written. The transmission is called "the blaze of the Fires of Essence," an expression that is more technical than poetic.

§ AMA-ZaNAATH: Way of the sorceress with the bound hand.
Right hand: Woman-tree.
Way of the forest.
Sorceress of the bundle.
Grey-white-black.
Left hand: Woman-stone.
Mineral way.
AMA-ZaNAATH: It holds the secret of the values of black to white and white to black, dull to luminous and luminous to dull and all their combinations.

§ Anyone who goes to the Aggaddaath must pass through the Gate of Fire.
The Way begins from the South.

The Rose-Hart and the Ash-Hart are one.
Like Being and non-Being.

The Rose-Hart integrates the nine Aggaddaaths of Being.
The Ash-Hart integrates the four Aggaddaaths of non-Being.

§ Their Fusion by the rite of 13 is the perfection of Absoluteness.
9 and 4 and 9, that is 22.
Or 22 by 13 in the four dimensions of Being.
And in the unique non-dimension of non-Being.

Pieces of Incoherism

1. Incoherism is the art and science of the Immediate. Or the point at which Tradition and the Avant-Garde meet and fuse. "This is new because it is very old," said the Fool, pointing to the Arcanum. Immediate is the hour of Absoluteness, the mathematical moment of Absoluteness, the door of Beingness.

2. To be Incoherist is to be at the Avant-Garde of oneself.

3. Incoherism has its source in the perfect Stillness of body and mind.

   Incoherism is Stillness in movement, Stillness in action. Exactly the opposite of our world, agitated stillness.

4. The Incoherist knows, in the flesh, that no one is indispensable, neither to others nor the world, which are two images. Above all, they know that no person is indispensable to themself, that a person is the main enemy of themself.

5. The Incoherist seeks neither coherence nor incoherence. They are other. Coherence is a drug of the mind, incoherence a frustration of the mind. Being remains.

6   Incoherism affirms the survival of a liberating aristocracy arriving immediately, both from the past and from the future, composed of naked beings, manifesting the old lineages, old because new, new because old.

7   Everything can only be grasped Immediately. Initiation is the science of the Immediate and the art of the Real. All tradition is immediate. All the avant-garde is real. The old traditional filiations are always avant-garde and revolutionary. The rest is just daydreaming.

8   The Lineage is the only manifestation of the Real in the Existent.

9   Claiming to give meaning or finding meaning in what Is is a pure aberration, exclusively human. A delirium of thought, a tool that takes itself for an entity, instinct within form. What is, what Endures, has no need of meaning.

Wars, whether of reason or stupidity, of hate or love, are always wars of meaning.

10 The quest for meaning is an endless wandering, that of the Wandering Jew, unlike the quest for the Center, which alone leads to grasping the Immutable.*

11 The Center is the field of action, the peripheries are the field of reactions. This is the reason to conquer the Center. The place of action is always action-less and meaning-less.

12 Beingness is only accessible to those who possess Will. Only Will can conquer Will. Beingness is opposed to the Existent. The Existent without Will is only an image in a setting.

13 Initiation, the path to awakening, is opposed to the notion of formal order. It destroys identification with all formalisms. It is just as opposed to the notion of disorder, which is only the absence of a known, expected, and desired order. Initiation is a-order, non-order, accessible in the interval that precedes the zone of concept.

---

*   Many popular legends and various literatures take up the story of the Wandering Jew, the source of which we find outside the Synoptic Gospels, even if we can detect an allusion in the Gospel of John ("If I will that he tarry till I come, what is that to thee?" Jesus said about him). The Wandering Jew is immortal. Witness to the Passion, he remains until the return of Christ. Each of us is both a Wandering Jew and a Christ, a Wandering Jew until we realize ourselves as another Christ.

14 The damned of the Earth, those who are rejected by their fellows, amputated of life, excluded from the gray world, convicts of unreason, pariahs, the unclean, and other wretches, remain closer to the gods. The ancients knew this who listened to the senseless chain of their words, watched their strange gestures, the signs and accords of the gods. Today, gagged so as not to be heard, bound to forbid their clumsy and disturbing dances of truth, they are still in the cities of the gods, our awakeners, our teachers!

15 The question of freedom constitutes the very heart of the Quest. The free being has no need of laws and morals. The free being possesses ethics. But the being of the current, the man-machine, conditioned and unconscious of being, cannot free himself from laws and morals to experience the relative world, born of beliefs, opinions, ego states, crystallizations and multiple identifications. This world that we believe to be real is only a state of mind, maintained by adherence to a convention of the mind.

16 In the fabric of the Spirit—the emanations of Absoluteness that generate Shakti, Beingness—the freedom of creation is infinite, coming from the axis of the Center, the perfect interval. The adept, artist-creator of themselves, can thus create another world equally as tangible as the everyday world, by aligning their Intention (I Am) with Absolute Will (That Which Remains). This world, both tangible and illusory, is accessible to those who know how to orient their roots in it, or to those who will be absorbed there by the solar aspect, in their "life" or after their "death." This explains the tangible character of the Christian, Buddhist, and other spiritual worlds, like certain worlds generated by the artistic movements, that were "coagulated" by a pure and powerful Intention.

17 The absolute intensity of Silence.

The absolute silence of the Interval.

Destroy the shackles of morals: falsely useful to the human of the current, they harm the adventure, preventing the attainment of ethics.

Without ethics, no unconditionality.

Without unconditionality, how can the absolute Intention be grasped?

Without Intention, Will cannot be inscribed, nor inscribe, in the real.

Realization is therefore prohibited outside the Interval.

18   Existence is the confinement of Beingness in consciousness.

Intention emanates from Beingness.

Will emanates from Absoluteness.

Intention directs Will.

19   There is a magic of the Interval.

There is a theurgy of the Interval.

There is an alchemy of the Interval.

All three are based on a Geometry of the Interval, a Wisdom Geometry. The body of glory is an Interval of such density that light emanates from darkness. The Interval is luminous black.

20   Two arts:

The art of the circle. The art of the dreamer who pierces the circle of the unconscious.

The art of the center. The art of the tracker who becomes master of the center of total consciousness.

21   Three ways:

The way of the One, solitary.

The way of Two, which merge into One.

The way of One, solitary in the Two.

22   Three immortalities:

The immortality of Blood. Survival.

The immortality of Mercury. Eternity.

The immortality of Soma. Internity.

23   Three covenants:

The Covenant of Nature. The Moon.

The Covenant of Beingness. Mercury.

The Covenant of "I Am the Absolute Will." The Sun.

24   The Law of ON

The Law of ON deals with the consciousness of the Real and Internity, the Immortality of That which Remains.

A is the Law.

The Law is A.

The inspection of the Law, that is, the inspection of A, reveals the secret of the worlds and the rounds, the secret of the gods, and the ultimate secret of He who turns the worlds over to become God, which He has never ceased to be.

25   The Game of ON

The adept-artist is the master of the game. The game has three rules, since there are three natures. The player must conquer three rings. One ring for each fusion, one fusion in each of the three fields of immortality. Three immortalities, three natures.

The adept-artist must accept the Law in order to be accepted by the Law.

Inspection of the Act allows its sense-less interpretation. This gives the Law an infinity of world-forms without ever altering the essence of the Law. The Law is Empty.

The Law of ON is absolute because it generates all the laws and has in itself its own anti-Law. It can self-destruct without ever having its essence affected.

26   Woman, door of eternity. The sex of women often does more for awakening than many altars. "The flesh teaches the Spirit, the Spirit transmutes the flesh."

27   The erotic is an unconditional tension towards Absoluteness or a sudden emergence of Absoluteness in the being that frees itself, in the immediate instant, from the thick and troubled dross of the known worlds, to authorize the manifestation of the pure beauty of this Absoluteness which cannot be expressed at a distance without the erotic game of Shakti.

On the way of the Pleiades, the body of the adept is the Temple of the Thousand Goddesses. Each is an experience of Shakti; each is a keeper of a flame. When the adept has lit all the fires, the Goddess of the Center sparkles. From each fusion of the adept with a goddess is born a living and creative fire.

The blue body of the god emerges from the body of the adept. The adept disappears. They never existed. "Only That Remains."

Shakti is external or internal, she is always a manifestation of the Goddess of the Center, consort of an improbable god who nevertheless springs from nothingness. The adept becomes god by, and in, Shakti.

28 Bodies mingle, sweat comes together, saliva mixes into subtle alloys, the Water of Diana receives the Mercury of Fire, bodies mingle, souls align and melt. Being remains. Beingness has enjoyment through the movement of Absolute Will.

29 Erotic ascesis culminates in the secret way of perfumes, fusion of subtle essences, released by the Moon, which unite and transmute until the Anthéos of the god-goddess dyad releases the primordial and internal perfume, subtle soma of the gods. Dissolution and destruction of worlds. Outpouring of the indomitable Real.

30 The erotic is a path of power. Shakti is the "shrine" of power. Shakti is also the "mausoleum" that the follower will rejoin at the time of their disappearance.

31 Only the Void allows fusion.

Three fusions are necessary for the creation within man, and for the liberation within woman, of the divine egg.

In the Void, Intention allows Will to draw a double spiral of fires, the fire of Shiva and the fire of Shakti, which fertilizes the first field of the Lotus, within its heart a seed of Internity. This first spiral generates a second which generates a third. We thus have the three seeds of Internity whose penetration by the flame of Absoluteness, the flame of the Lord of the Flame, instantly releases into the Void the divine essence that invades the divine egg, the self-conscious palace of the Beingness-Absoluteness couple.

The three fields of the Lotus are the temple of the thousand and eight goddesses, emanations of Shakti. A thousand operations, a thousand orgasms, are needed to light the thousand fires of the temples guarded by the goddesses. The serpentine force of the Naga loses its watery character in the void and becomes fire, stolen immediately by the Great Bird of Mount Kailash, the mountain of the immortals. Union with the Goddess releases the energy which instantly ignites. But it is a cold fire that burns no energy.

When the Temple of a Thousand Goddesses is fully illuminated, the fields of the lotus open up and reveal the three seeds of Internity. Then the flame of Absoluteness descends into the heart of the three Lotuses and penetrates the seeds. It is the reaction of the seeds of Internity that defines the type of immortality established.

It only remains to carry out the eight operations with the Goddess of the Center, under her eight aspects. Eight terrible secrets.

32   The Being-God appears as an egg of light inhabited by a Tree of Fire, the Tree of Marvels.

33   Today I know what god I am, a black god, black of this blue so dense that it feels like a black of light, the superior color.

A black and infinite god made of nothingness and consciousness who momentarily drapes themself in a fold of the universe.

A black and cold god. Black and cold light, immutable beauty of non-movement.

"I am that which remains, being myself the way; I am the word that was never spoken in the Beingness that was never begotten.

"I Am The Absolute Will."

Fragments of Absoluteness

1. The quest requires an encounter with madness, the ultimate choice between the Real and the definitive illusion. Awakening involves a controlled madness and a creator of realities. Wisdom is the very definition of controlled madness.

    Incoherism is controlled madness.

2. The Way is always non-human, because the human being is at first totally animal: woman-wolf or man-horse; woman-snake and man-eagle.

3. There is a way of slowness and laziness, accessible only to those who know that there is Nothing to do, Nothing to possess, to hold, to know, to transmit; adepts of over-effort or releasing-control who have experienced the fullness of Nothing.

4. The incoherist rejects the "civilized" meaning, that is to say, the meaning conveyed by language; they only recognize the wild meaning, the first meaning, brought by the "Whole-Sensorium," the nearest perception of the imperceptible Real.

5   The quest for the Great Intention requires the abandonment of the search for meaning. The quest for meaning is meaningless and obscures the Absolute Intention.

6   Two individuals who have no access to the Real each live in a separate and never-meeting dream world. Each is part of the other's setting. Neither really exists. Their physical death will be only a formality.

7   To do without doing,

   To have without having,

   Means

   To be without doing,

   To be without having.

8   Through presence to oneself, or presence to the Self, the adept bends the relative and profane worlds to the sacred Real. It is wrong to believe in the possibility of the influence of the sacred on the profane or of the Real on the relative. The sacred and the real remain. They are the unnameable immutable. The Real has no influence on the relative. The sacred does not enlighten the profane. The Real absorbs the relative by freeing it from all form. The sacred absorbs the profane by destroying all representation and image.

9   There is no other absolute simplicity than the break with the phenomenal world.

   Moving away from the phenomenal and its accidents.

   Approaching Absoluteness and the Void.

   Being & Remaining.

10 An ego can only constitute a mystery for another ego. Being has no need to be saved, initiated, or illuminated. Being remains.

   Pagan, Christian, Buddhist. Why always reduce Being to a concept? Being can choose to express itself in Pagan form, in Christian form, in Buddhist form, or in any other form. Do not make the mistake of limiting Being to a human expression, be it that of a Buddha or a Christ.

11 The adept suffers more in the body of others than in their own body.

12 The adept walks facing the sun without any shadow being cast on the ground.
There is no person.

13 Impersonal power is the one, the only, absolute power.

14 Insolent, unpredictable, and dangerous: such is the awakened for the "society of the spectacle."

Spirit is elusive and unpredictable.

They who are one with the Spirit are therefore elusive and unpredictable.

15 Awakening. A lie, but so true!

16 Awakening slays number!

It is not the number that is magic, it is the perception of the number.

17 History only ever serves itself, whereas myth reveals the quest and serves awakening.

18 Die before you die. Key to awakening.

Only dying before death makes it possible to never be born.

Neither father nor mother, the being that is being, unbegotten, engendered simultaneously by all forms of life, from the god to the stone, passing through the insect and the yam.

Neither father nor mother, and therefore father-mother of all forms of life.

19 Who am I Reality in the presence of my own birth?

Who am I Reality in the presence of my own death?

Who am I Reality in the presence of my own rebirth?

20 The adept is uncreated.

They cannot die, they can only disappear.

The Initiation to the Real provokes a de-birth.

Having no beginning, the adept also knows no end.

But this is completely unrelated to the concepts of post-mortem survival or reincarnation, two flawed doctrines with therapeutic and political purposes, without the slightest interest to awakening.

21   The interval is the access to the Real.

The interval is the Real!

22   The Ways of the Real first awaken the ancestral predator, the survivor, before the god appears.

23   The Ways of the Real mobilize SuperNature.

In the same way that Initiation begins with a counter-spirituality, the Ways of the Real, by their absolute verticality and their radical character, appear as counter-nature.

24   A law of the Real:

One real is worth another.

25   Nothing can do nothing against nothing.

Nothing can do nothing for nothing.

There is no strength.

Nothing is total fullness.

Therefore action is always empty.

26   Beauty is always operatively superior to calculation.

27   The Stone.

Immortal by its stillness.

Immutable by its silence.

Intangible beauty of that which remains.

28   All that can be said and represented does not belong to the order of the Real.

The Real is nameless, numberless, notionless.

The Real is the union of being and non-being.

29   All revelation is a precipitation of the Real into being.

A revelation is always addressed to being, never to the intellect, even if the latter is upset by it.

30 Impersonal, a-personal, revelation cannot be formulated.
    One can believe in the revelation, never in its formulation.

31 It is by approaching the abyss of Impersonality that one judges the degree of presence to Oneself. If the personality rebels, it is because nothing has been conquered.

32 "I" cannot know awakening. "I" belongs to the dream world.
    Being is awakening. Being remains. There is no awakening.

33 "I am" is reborn, springs up, from yourself, in each instant.
    "I am" is reborn, of Oneself, in each instant.

I : God : GAME*

---

*   Fr.: JE : Dieu : JEU

Sparks of Internity

1. ON ignores both the diamond and the excrement. For it, there is only the interplay of energy and consciousness. It seeks no shapeliness, no beauty, no human perfection. Its beauty is fusion. This is why the orgasm is the only human experience that is non-human and divine, accessible to all human beings, pure presence in the great game, provided that they really are conscious.

2. "I am" the great meditator of A.

   "I am" all meditators, from East to West and from South to North: the Buddhist monk, the fool of Shiva, the ascetic of the desert, the Sufi, the supplicant on the ice, the Indian shaman; "I am" all conscious breaths.

3. "I am" the Great Wanderer. He who, from life to life, created, knew, and practiced all the rites, all the traditions, generated, listened to, and followed all the masters, without knowing awakening. Because "I am" the last.

4. "I am" the ejaculating and laughing God who fertilizes the worlds and rounds before calling them back into Nothing!

5. "I am the Absolute Will" is the path of the Real.

   "I am Absolute Freedom" is the non-path of the Real.

   Taking the path is necessary for entering the non-path.

   Way, no-Way.

6. The gods are the Will.

   The Will springs up only in the Interval.

7. The Guardian, the Elder of the stars, appears when the adept obtains the most perfect mastery of A.

   The Guardian is strange: his skin, dark and tanned by the fire of Agni, wrinkled by time and crackled by starlight.

   The Guardian is beautiful, not according to human criteria (frightening for humans, he illuminates the adept with his smile) but according to the criteria of eternity. Each of his innumerable voids represents a millennium of the wisdom of the stars, a millennium of wandering the infinite worlds.

8 Death is the Great Interval. A dive into the Real for the immortal who has become Master of the Interval.

9 The three covenants of the immortal are those of Nature, of the central Fire (Christ, the Great Sun Buddha, Osiris, etc.) and of the Absolute Feminine (Shakti, Barbelo, Paraclete, Lucifer, etc.).

Isn't the sex of the woman the magical interval *par excellence?* The Double-Door of Life as of Immortality.

10 "I-That which remains" penetrates the lotus of the lotus of the lotus, and bathes in the divine fragrance of Shakti.

11 I, Serpent-Bird

She, Bird-Serpent

We, Naga-Garuda

We, the Only

We, blue god-goddess

12 Shakti is the interval of Shiva.

Shiva is the interval of Shakti.

Shakti is the non-being of Shiva.

Shiva is the non-being of Shakti.

13 Love-Madness, divine, ascetic and erotic, magical and alchemical, irremediably separates from the world. Like the Heroes, the Fools of Love are gods, no longer human.

14 There exists in the human being, inscribed precisely in the verticality, three seeds of immortality, three seeds of Internity, three luminous *bijams* (roots) that remain. The adept releases these three seeds of Internity by consuming the bodies of each of his moments, by the fire of Agni. Having become ashes, these reveal the luminous bijams that become his true body. The order of the liberation of the three bijams determines the type of immortality.

15 28 × 36

   36 shaktis

   36 erogenous fires per day of the menstrual cycle.

16 13 + 22 = 33

   13 × 22 = 1008

   Shiva has 1008 names.

   The Temple of White Marble is home to 1008 goddesses.

17 The sex of Khalys is the Himalayan summit of awakening.

   Its secret perfumes are the divine incense of the Blue Mountains.

18 Alliance of two Fires: essence of the Sacred Seed and essence of the Divine Blood for a coronation and a divine assumption. This is the Way to Absoluteness.

   Seed and Blood. Seed of the Star and Blood of the Land. Fires of Internity.

19 Awakened. Sex taut. Dazzling spirit.

20 The flesh teaches the spirit.

   The spirit transmutes the flesh.

   The first principle of internal alchemy.

21 The Blue Being, the Real in motion, in me, by me, around me.

   The Real in motion, in the A, by the A, for the A: Beingness.

22 A.

   The Brotherhood of A.

       The Apprentices of A.

       The Companions of A.

       The Masters of A.

       The Teachers of A.

23   A.

     ON.

     Blue Being.

24   Any Way of the real refers to the Blue Being. This is one of the great mysteries of the Real.

25   I salute A.

     A is the permanence of ON.

     A is everything installed in the breath and the Breath.

     A not born, not mortal, A container and content of being.

     At the death of the ego, A appears as it has always been, limitless.

     Therefore kill the ego so that the perception of the Work of ON is total.

26   Listen to the destroyed human being. IT breathes. A breathes. A remains.

     In the breath, A is always present.

     Identified with A, you are on the path of the non-mortals.

27   And I invoke ON. Absoluteness.

     In its 13 dimensions of perfection.

     And its 22 aspects of Beingness.

28   Being.

     Oneself by Oneself.

     Self^2 [Self to the Power of 2].

     The Absolute Being.

Parcels of Beingness

FIRST COMMENTARY

Two main types of immortality:

The immortality to last, eternity.

The immortality of "That which remains," Internity.

The first form is related to the Protection and Conservation of the Name, an alchemical formula that coagulates the energy of the body, thus generating a new vehicle for consciousness, the Body of Glory of the Christian Gnostics or the Rainbow Body of the Buddhists.

The second form is that of the Unnameable. The consciousness liberated, even from liberation, merges without dissolution in this Unnameable.

SECOND COMMENTARY

False lies:

In Reality, neither awakening nor liberation.

Breaking free is a concept born of duality and separation.

What is does not need to free itself.

What is has no need.

This is why it is said that one must free oneself even from liberation.

THIRD COMMENTARY

The adept does not adhere, either to the personality or to the world, both of which are the mask.

Detached from the personality, detached from the world, the adept can borrow and "imprint" all the masks he wishes to experience, without identification.

He can just as well remain faceless, really faceless, even headless, because he is the spirit and the spirit is impossible to behold.

The work of "liberation" involves the removal of adhesions. This work is similar to the work on crystallizations in its effects, but different in form and principle.

The approach of the Real Ways is reserved for beings who master their environment and their psycho-physiological mechanisms, who do not have a marked tendency to schizophrenia or neurosis. If a person lacks flexibility, is too identified with the "self-image" or has a "self-image" opposed to change, or is frozen around mental crystallizations that are too strong, a non-analytical psychotherapy can be beneficial before starting a propaedeutic of the Real Way. A powerful tool for change like *The Quadrant of Awakening** can in fact be an effective tool to prevent change if used inappropriately. Thus the *Quadrant* will not suit, for example, a personality identified with erudition. The raw nature must still be visible behind the masks of the ego.

The incoherist adept works to realize the distinction between those who work on the Ways of the Real and those many who get lost in the fabric of illusions *about* the Real. At the same time, they work to restore the alliance between the intellectual and artistic avant-gardes on the one hand and Hermetists and other practitioners of the theosophies of awakening on the other. It goes without saying that the term "awakening," like every word used here, is only a convenience of language.

In the Real, there can be neither awakening, nor the awakened, nor the awakener.

FOURTH COMMENTARY

Two main types of ways of the Real:

The ways of the *twice born* or ways of immortality that borrow the qualities of Beingness.

The ways of the *never born* or ways of awakening that borrow the qualities of Absoluteness.

Let us remember that in Reality, Beingness and Absoluteness are indistinguishable.

FIFTH COMMENTARY

The only possible sacrifice is that of ego. Any other form of sacrifice is an egoic deception.

SIXTH COMMENTARY

The gods have no concept of time. Only a constant yet variable (from one to the other) perception of absoluteness.

---

*   Rémi Boyer, *Mask Cloak Silence: Martinism as a Way of Awakening* (Bayonne, NJ: Rose Circle, 2021), pp. 153–171.

SEVENTH COMMENTARY

The human being of the stream, unawakened, absolutely needs this or that, god or the gods.

The awakened human being is god, absolutely.

The important word is *absolutely* because it is the double game of absoluteness.

EIGHTH COMMENTARY

Power/Potency:

Any living organism that has a fire of consciousness also has an orient, that is to say a focal point, an invisible core around which Consciousness (conscious and unconscious) is organized and towards which the whole organism tends.

If the orient of a human being is money, which is very common especially when the merchant caste dominates the secular world, then whatever they do of a spiritual or occult nature will in fact serve that one purpose. If the orient of a human being is to be recognized in the world, which is also very common in the Kali Yuga, it will be the same. The initiatory propaedeutic therefore aims to give humans the true possibility of freely choosing their orient. Humans seem to be the only animal that has this choice.

Power is an illusory aspect, but natural to the axis of having and doing.

Human beings seek power, they want to *have* the power to *do*. The illusion of power, always limited. The trap of the fascinated ego.

The initiate seeks potency, the infinite and free potency of the Real, accessible on the axis of being. The One who *is*, Absolute Will therefore, is also the Omnipotence. No need to have or do.

Energy follows thought.

Energy is therefore diluted in the worlds of thought.

The mind has only an appearance of continuity; it is in fact totally discontinuous.

Only the Void brings the fullness of "That which remains."

The invisible worlds love Silence, all silences.

Silences are the food of the interval.

Silence is the only raiment bearable by the interval.

Each interval is a gateway to Being, magnificent and divine. The nature of what exists is Emptiness. Emptiness is Being. Yet the nature of what exists is not Being.

One who stops thought stops the worlds and conserves energy.

In conscious being, energy follows breath, not thought.

The act not inscribed in Breath and Consciousness is powerless.

The act inscribed in Breath and full consciousness is a total, divine act.

The Total Human Being is the inhabitant of the Center, the tightrope walker of the Axis of the Real.

But if presence to oneself is not installed in transcendence, if the adept does not rise from this Center into the verticality of Being, they will soon be torn apart again by the four forces of the double expanse of space and time, towards the multiple peripheries of having and doing.

No one can remain at the Center if they are not installed in a permanent transcendence. The Center is the passage. The Center is not verticality. Do not dwell too long on this threshold, lest the trapdoor of *Hell* open.

NINTH COMMENTARY

Indeed, there is the Arcanum and there are the arcana.

In some traditions, the most secret practices are given to everyone, right away, but very few realize it. The secret is not the arcanum but the realization of the arcanum. The arcanum is realized only on the central axis, in the verticality of being.

The arcanum can only be accomplished in certain states of consciousness, states obtained accidentally or artificially. Even if a propaedeutic is necessary, even if a psycho-physiological training most often proves indispensable, they are, either one or both, insufficient. The paradox resides in the fact that it is the practice of the arcanum itself that confers the right attitude, the right state that authorizes the realization of the arcanum.

We see then that a sequence is missing, that a segment remains a-logical (A-logical), that it is not a process, that there is indeed a leap into the void, this famous interval, much sought after, of which nothing can be said. Therein lies the secret and only there. This is what we are talking about when we say that the way must be found and conquered, that the secrets are transmitted only by the gods. But, another paradox, the gods only confide in their peers!

Incoherist Tatters & Torches

1 OF TRADITION AND INITIATION

There is no primordial Tradition in the sense that the "Person" understands it. Being-in-itself is the primordial Tradition.

All initiatory tradition is a skillful means, but also a fierce means.

Indeed, a living tradition is a highly sophisticated means, not a deconditioning, but an "unconditioning" or "One-conditioning" towards awakening, liberation, and Being.

However, as a form, a tradition can only be enclosing, alienating.

It is therefore not the tradition that awakens—it can, on the contrary, develop the "Person" in an illusory way—but the relation to the tradition, which must be elliptical and oblique. The "Person" shifts the issue from the relationship to Being to the relationship to the world, from the relationship to the world to the relationship to tradition, and traps it in a web of concepts. The practice of Silence, the cornerstone of Initiation, is in fact a rupture of this relationship, the end of meaning, the simultaneous acceptance of Being and the Nothingness of Being which are but one. The "Person" is swept away. The place of Being is empty and accessible.

What then of the gods? Nothing, of course. The gods are within us and that is enough, which is to say: *that is,* without further consideration.

Initiation borrows the ultimate mask of Tradition to throw down all masks including that of Tradition, even if it is qualified as primordial. It leads to outfacing oneself, literally, removing one's face, accepting the infinite interval of the Great Real that remains behind the mask of the face, behind the "Person." Tradition is the last Carnival, the sacred farce that will unmask and set apart the "Person" if the fire of Being ignites the stage.

Two techniques:

The elliptical: a double focus, Tradition and the Great Nothing. Approach, move away. Fullness and emptiness.

The oblique: sharp and unexpected breakthrough to the heart, off the beaten track, away from the marked paths.

A truly initiatory tradition teaches the disciple to dance serenely in the Void. Majestic Nataraja.

Initiation is, in Reality, a proposal (always the same, whatever the form) made to Being, to actualize itself by penetration into the form: a putting into perspective, a placement into art.

The work resides in the realization of the initiatory proposal. This realization is immediate and instantaneous, and in no way requires the form, although it can fertilize the form.

Only one who is familiar with the minimalist Initiation—who has, by the direct way, restored their integral being in all its flows around the Ring of Nothing—can recognize and transmit the Essence and its absolute structure (a non-structure in reality, which some clumsily call the Primordial Tradition) in all of the traditional forms. Neither primordial, nor ultimate, nor definitive, neither this nor that: it is, neither more nor less, "That which Remains."

2 OF IDEAS

It is only in the zone of Silence and therefore in the state of Silence that Ideas are born.

In the noise of the representation, only opinions meet one another. The latter are made of shreds of dead and rotting ideas.

An Idea is only creative for the brief time of its flight from the ocean of Nothing. It must be left to itself until just before the peak of its flight.

OF LANGUAGE

A living being is an element of the language of consciousness. Life is the language of Being. Each of us is in a way a word, a momentary writing, sometimes a poem, that briefly directs the consciousness towards a specific experience.

A word is not an entity. A word is the vehicle of an entity. Here, Being.

It is so, says the word, not because "I know," but because "I am."

OF GESTURE

In the Interval of the Real, in the posture of presence to oneself, the body, liberated, remembers the original and primitive gestures that founded life. In the silence, the body moves and links its gestures to sketch a dance of the Real, always different, always identical.

Mudras constitute in a way "the finishing touches": the accomplished forms of these original gestures.

OF THE MARK

The Way of writing is like the Way of the sword. The same gesture must be repeated tirelessly, each time identical, each time unique, until perfection, until the expression, the precipitation in the ink of the Spirit.

Even if a multitude of imperfect gestures precede the perfect gesture, the discerning eye must perceive in each imperfection an implacable will to cut through the ego.

The perfect gesture always includes a slight imperfection. It is that which creates the interval.

Sign, signature, seal, and glyphs must be calligraphed with the ink of fire in the dance of the breath. The impact must be carried in the interval of the Real. The energy is then set in creative motion in the free field of the consciousness of the Real. Apart from this, any gesture only comes to overload the already suffocating decor of the world.

OF POETRY

Poetry, inscribed in the verticality of the sacred, has the double function of finishing off the dead who are still standing—they are numerous, we meet them every day—and of deifying the living before they fall asleep.

At the tip of the pen, here and now, Poetry crowns the human being within the human form, recognizes them in their nakedness and crudeness as a god.

Become god, here and now, be what "I Am."

3 OF SPEECH

Silence is the granite on which speech is engraved.

Without silence, Speech is vain and sterile, the mark impossible.

Silence is the power of the Interval.

The power of the Void is greater than any other.

It absorbs all formal power.

All form is ephemeral; it comes from the Void, returns to the Void, and has the nature of the Void.

The Void is in the eye.

It is in the eye that the Void and its power are perceived.

The inscription of Speech is free.

Speech then garlands the Universe.

Speech is the most subtle creation, immediately erased or inscribed forever until the dissolution of time.

Without Speech, there is no time.

Without Speech, there is no space.

Space-time is born of Speech.

Speech engenders precursors and fertilizes the Great Nothing within the Silence, just in the time of a breath.

In this sense Speech is creative, but Speech is rare and impossible to transcribe. This is why the twilight language is precious. This is why poets are loved by the gods.

4 OF THE INTERNAL CONSTITUTION OF THE HUMAN BEING

The body, not the thought body but the perceived body, is both a door to the Great Real and the musical instrument of Shakti.

In the zone of Silence and the rhythm of the A, the adept can perceive the point of Absoluteness at the end of the inhalation and the point of Beingness at the end of the exhalation.

The point of Beingness is the foundation of the Real Body and the point of Absoluteness is its crowning glory. From one to the other, an invisible trace takes shape, the Great Interval, access to the Grand Real.

For many, the point of Beingness has been displaced by the assemblage point (or point of coherence) of the representation, what the man of the stream calls reality, sometimes to the point of merging with it.

In Gurdjieff's man-machine, for whom physical death will be only a formality, or Pessoa's "postponed corpse that procreates," the point of Beingness is definitively fixed at the assemblage point and the point of Absoluteness has disappeared.

The assemblage point is the architectural balance point of the representation. Moving it changes the representation and experience we have of the world.

When Shiva's heart beats at the back of the adept's head, the death of the "Person" is pronounced and achieved. Being remains.

To join the Seed-People, the five seeds of Immortality for men or Internity for women (corresponding to the five syllables of Shiva's mantra) must be deposited or inscribed in the field traced by the oscillation of the Great Interval between the point of Beingness and the point of Absoluteness.

5   OF NOTHING

Nothing has no importance.

Nothing is importance itself.

The Great Nothing.

The natural milieu of Being is the Great Nothing.

If everything is impermanence, then there really is nothing.

Everything is Void.

The Great Nothing is the Great Real.

The entire Universe is the presupposition of the existent and of each of the formal expressions of the existent, while the Great Nothing is the presupposition of Being.

This makes Martin Heidegger say that "Being is the lieutenant of nothing," that which keeps the place open and accessible.

Shakti unites with the Void to engender the worlds.

The original seed-germ is therefore an interval of Void, a lightning of emptiness, an enlightening of the Great Nothing.

Thus, all worlds are of the nature of the Void.

The Void is Spirit.

Spirit is the Void.

Recognizing the nature of things, the Void, frees the mind in the Spirit.

The trajectories of Being, the movements of the Energy of Shakti, seem to be a totally random hypercomplexity. However, they are structured for a permanent search for balance around a center of gravity: the *Point of Void*.

The "true" reality is the mathematical, geometric, and energetic figure generated by the dance of Shakti, while "the Real arises from the Point of Void" or, in a way, "from the other side of the Point of Void."

6 OF AWAKENING

No person is ever awake.

All being is perfect awakening.

The "Person" cannot be awakened.

Being is awakening.

This is why there is Nothing to do.

Respect for life does not lead to awakening.

But awakening always comes with an absolute respect for life as a whole, exactly because "it" has no importance, "it" is gone, no more object and Being as sole subject, both cause and effect, neither cause nor effect.

No practice allows awakening.

The practice that takes place in a religious, cultural, and intellectual environment only nourishes and reinforces this environment. We must seek free practice. This is installed in the interval, in an in-between, in a non-time of perfect emptiness. So the practice is empty, the practitioner is empty, and the Void is the fullness of Being.

The practices aim to crack or shift the "Person" so that Being springs forth.

The split is such that the "Person" is thus fragmented and then rebuilt in a more suitable configuration but at the periphery of consciousness, no longer as an entity but as a tool.

It is not a splitting like some forms of schizophrenia where two, three, or more "persons" can coexist, which are so many acting I's.

In awakening, Being is there, and the self has disappeared, dissolved in the experience of Being. The "Person" is therefore no longer identified as ego, as "I."

As brilliant as the "Person" is, its means are very limited, but they suffice for Being, which has no need. This is why the awakened always disappears, ceases to Being-bypass, in order to Be.

In the eyes of the world, there is no change. Perhaps a vague shiver.

With awakening, the world, as the awakening one will have previously conceived it, returns to its own nature: the Void.

Awakening. It is knowing totally, absolutely, in each of its cells that "*it* will die" that "*it* is dead," "*it* will die and *this* remains." Emptiness and fullness.

Only awakening breeds true atheism.

Otherwise, it will be a lying and falsifying atheism, a clumsy defense mechanism of ego.

You are a gymnast of the Spirit.

By entering the world of unbelief, of the unconceptual, of the unnamed, you become pure perception and become conscious that this vertical position which you take for reality is only a decoy. You dream that you are standing.

In this new position, you come out of sleep, and become conscious of the dream and the nature of the dream.

From there a recovery, a restoration in the fullness of your Beingness, is possible. It is technique.

The reversal in the Great Real happens… or does not happen. It is art.

But this new and primordial axis remains.

7 OF BELIEF

Belief. Belief-nuisance. Belief-brilliance.

To be avoided, confusion versus fusion.

If "I" believe, then I believe in Nothing, the Great Nothing.

No belief more vast, nor more dangerous.

If thought is possible, it is only possible in this great sense of Nothing, in the infinitely small nothing of nonsense.

Negation has nothing to do with it. Nothing is neither the negation of something nor its absence. Nothing is immediacy, fullness, limitless totality and therefore without boundary, a major impossibility that precisely becomes certainty, even the unique, primal certainty of "I Am, The Absolute Will." Note the comma added to the invocation of Ladislav Klíma, extremely lucid notwithstanding his creative madness, because "I Am" could not support an attribute, even "The Absolute Will," without betraying the perfect immobility of Being.

IATAF. In Reality: "I Am The Absolute Freedom."

"I Am" is the point of the Teacher.*

"I Am" is the point of Beingness.

"I Am" is the interval of Absoluteness.

The dot is used to draw the circle.

The circle is therefore the point.

The circle is "I Am."

Point: fist and anointed.†

Both impact and unction.

---

* Fr.: *EnSaigneur*. A variation on *enseigneur* (teacher) that might mean "one who bleeds within."
† Fr.: *Point, poing et oint*.

8 OF MATURITY AND LAUGHTER

There is a second maturity, a "meta-maturity," which is no longer the maturity of the integrated human person, but that of Being, or more exactly that of a possible "Being being natural," so to speak. This second maturity hardly authorizes the point of view except to lead an interlocutor higher, to behold and embrace further and wider. Total maturity is a going beyond positions, an often radical caesura in the causality and linearity of reasoning, an a-reasoning, an unreasoned but perfectly exact grasp of what is, against all the troubled and troubling commentaries.

Unspeakable knowledge is often accompanied by an acute sense of farce, even of derision, because (faced with this suffering that appears as an expanse of singular matter, sculpted as much by horror as by compassion) laughter—the laughter of the gods—imposes itself: a sacred laugh, a mad laugh, mad without being insane, light without being provocative, the divine laugh of Being in its joy.

What is laughter? Laughter is not opposed to crying or lamentation; laughter is opposed to the mediocrity of the "Person." It is an alchemical, corrosive Salt that dissolves the "Person" into Nothing. The one who laughs is not the one who guffaws but the one who knows. They know death. They know the farce of life and Life without farce. They know immortality, or better, Internity. And they laugh, as God has laughed since the first moment of Creation when Being commanded Him to play. Play is joy and joy is laughter. If the Creation took place in seven days, it was in seven bursts of laughter. The laughter of God is the laughter of the Universe. The laughter of God is the laughter of the human being seized and prodded by Being.

9 OF THE SLEEPING GOD

By ode or prayer, if you awaken the sleeping god, you will have to follow his serpentine and uncertain path until the end of the dark night and, worse still, until the end of the luminous dawn, that which will rend in the eight directions of space the vampire of the form that serves you as "I."

Do you accept that you are no longer for Being? Do you accept the sacrifice of the Real Blood,* the fertilization of the sleeping god, the offering of the goddess

---

*   Fr.: *Sang Réel.*

who watches, over there, just behind, and who awaits her eternity, your internity, the moment-interlude of extreme consciousness during which, offering yourself her most secret Interval, you cross it with your Absolute Will to become the One/the Other, Beingness-Absoluteness?

OF GODS

By the covenant with the two natures, *natura naturans** and *natura naturata*,† two sacred echoes, there is a covenant with the spirits of the essences that are constitutive of the gods. The gods potentially bathe in an undifferentiated way in Being. They crystallize formally, precipitated into beings, only under the seal of Will. The Will is set in motion only by, or because of, Absoluteness.

Gods are false when humans are false.

The gods devour humans.

Silence devours the gods.

Being springs up.

The gods sometimes summon us, not as "Person" but as Being.

The gods summon Being to kneel before it.

I am.

Populated by goddesses and gods in union and fusion, I am.

I am Shiva.

10 OF SACRED GEOMETRY

The world of Shakti is a world where the straight line is radically absent and even impossible. The absolute freedom of Femininity fits perfectly into it.

Behind every form hides a geometric model, a graphic, dynamic abstraction, called a yantra.

The vision, the perception of the yantra of the world is an experience that profoundly modifies consciousness. In a way, the yantra of the psychic power of the world is the true unconscious, unless one attributes the Real itself as the ultimate meaning of the unconscious, which is quite relevant.

---

* *Natura naturans* (Spinoza): "nature naturing" or "nature doing what nature does."
† *Natura naturata* (Spinoza): "nature natured" or "nature already created."

The abstraction of this yantric level, one even more subtle and elaborate, is the mantric level, the Wise Geometry of Numbers and Letters.

The ultimate abstraction is the plane of the Interval, access to the place of the Real.

It is, in fact, in the "land of reality" that emerges from the "ocean of the Real," from denser levels of Spirit. The so-called subtle worlds are worlds of greater density of the Spirit. Only one whose nature is Spirit can penetrate them.

11 OF THE WAY OF THE ROSE-HART

The true praxis of the Way of the Rose-Hart constitutes an imitation of the Spirit as other ways are an imitation of Jesus Christ, Al-Khidr, or the Buddha.

The inscription of the Spirit operates from the center, the Void, to the periphery, the form, precipitating three covenants, while the imitation of Jesus Christ, for example, operates from the periphery to the center sealing the same three covenants but in the reverse order.

The initiation of the Rose-Hart is always minimalist. At most, a single gesture, a single sound, a single image in Silence.

To desacralize all traditional forms is to give freedom to the Unspeakable Beauty of the Work; it is to cancel the arbitrary distinction created by the "Person" between profane and sacred. Everything is sacred because everything is Void.

In the imitation of Jesus Christ, it is the adept who imitates the Lord-King, but in the imitation of the Spirit, it is the Spirit who imitates themself in the adept who leaves the place of Being free and empty. We are *really* the Great Assembly of the Perfect Void.

Disjointed Words of the Mad Monk

The idea of a conquest of immortality is metaphorical and does not correspond to what is. Immortality is not to be conquered: it would be wiser, although no more *Real*, to speak of re-conquest. If there is immortality, we are banished immortals or even immortals in voluntary exile.

§ Three types of instructors:
Masters of form work on the form until it is perfect in its imperfections and expresses essence.
Masters of essence work on dissolving form in order to release its essence.
Masters of both paths play alternately on form and essence, in order to experience neither form nor essence.

§ Conscious breathing is the mathematical derivative of divine breath.

§ The renunciation of the I, the "Person," is the supreme form of all religion.
The religion of Law leads to the religion of Faith.
The religion of Faith prepares for the religion of Self.

Any historical religion can only measure its failure. Any spiritual or initiatory institution can only note its own impotence. It is the formlessness, the spontaneous springing up in the moment, and the non-doing of the real ways that mark the accomplishment in the non-being of Being.

§ Being is. Non-being is not.
Being is not. Non-being is.
Being neither is nor is not.
Non-being is and is not.
This.
Perfect Interval of the Real.

§ On the Real Way, you must be ready to work with your worst enemy if they have the skill required or the key sought (your worst enemy after yourself).

All life is in Life but all life is not the Fire of Life.
    All life in the world, the life, however hectic, is but one long, peaceful meditation.
    The ring of the Great Nothing is immutable under the restless surface of worldly things.
    The circle tends towards the point at the center of the circle, but not vice versa. The sage waits for the circle to bring them back to the point. The seeker leans on the circle, then jumps into the void to reestablish themself at the center, becoming the center itself.

§ The human being is both corpse and god. Why does it choose the corpse so often?

Death is only the erasure of our personal history while This, Being, remains.
    Nothing can reach Being, while the Person is nothing but wounds.

Death is our best friend. Located just to our left, slightly set back, effaced but very present, almost shy until the big day. Both *éminence grise* and bodyguard.
    We don't listen to it. It teaches Life.
    Not listening to it, we cannot be alive.
    Not even being alive, how can we become Immortals?

Death is immortal. This is why only the death of birth allows the death of death. Never born, never dead.

Fusion is the only emotion. The emotions of the "Person" are merely substitutions, both an indication of a total urgency of Being and a plaster over an unhealable wound, that of the I.

§ Verticality touches horizontality only to cross it. There can be no other link between being and having or doing than the point. This is why the attempts to inscribe the spiritual in the profane, or Initiation in the political or social, are vain and catastrophic.

§ The incoherist is seized by the vertical orientation of ecstasy-delight. They then possess the sense of nonsense and the nonsense of sense. Being in the existent seeks to confer this secret without doing. It is long gone—it never was. It is the heightened presence of Being that impacts the "Person." The "Person" is double: one's own person and the person of the other, the mirror, the outer shadow that refers to the inner shadow. And then there are all those, carried away by the stream, who will neither seize nor be seized. For those no one can do anything Real.

§ Internal alchemy begins with child's play to become an intelligent technique, then a subtle science, the science of the interval, to culminate in a divine art, an absolute art, the art of the Great Nothing.

§ No teaching in words.
   Silence is transmission.
   Nothing is absolute.

§ The interval, both sword and shield.
   Detach yourself from all conditioned humanity.
   This humanity has no need of you.
   But Humanity is you.

§ Human experience is without finality for consciousness, which acquires there only understanding, that is to say, the sense of non-sense.

§ Don't do anything today like yesterday.

Take the time of everything and inscribe it in the time of the One.

Do things slowly.
   Slowness is sacred.
   It is in extreme slowness that the speed of the absolute resides.

§ Each rite celebrated is the first, so its celebration is perfect.
   Each rite celebrated is the last, so its celebration is perfect.

§ When, at the heart of the ritual, you know how to distinguish the rite from the ceremonial, take the rite as ceremonial and seek the rite within the rite, and then again, until the conscious breath is clearly established as the rite itself.
   Then, again, make the conscious breath the ceremonial and track the rite, which will appear as the movement of Essence.
   And, as the ultimate practice, make the movement of Essence the ceremonial. The Interval will become the rite.
   All will be accomplished.

§ At the heart of fear there is non-fear.
  Let those who seek protection hear.
  The only true protection is in nothing.
  When there is nothing left, because there has never been anything,
  When nothing is done because nothing has ever been done,
  Protection emerges,
  Fullness emerges,
  From that which remains,
  The Great Nothing.

§ The state of fullness is the state of Nature.

§ The best way to protect the arcanum is to disclose it.
  Thus, it goes unnoticed.

§ There is no Awakening.
  Only Being.

§ Ride the Seven-Headed White Dragon, the Dragon of the Seven Wisdoms.

§ Invoke the Emerald Dragon for healing and regeneration.

§ The goddess is absolute nakedness.
  The goddess is absolute fullness.
  The goddess is absolute compassion.

§ Nakedness enables fullness.
  Fullness enables compassion.
  It is only in nakedness that the human being can be compassionate.

§ Each can only receive what they have already given.
  By allowing each to give, we allow them to receive.

§ The idea that the "Person" might hold any truth is aberrant and alienating.
  There is no truth except from the Spirit. This truth is non-human, neither stated nor transmitted: it is the Spirit itself.

§ "It," the "Person," is an outgrowth of the world or the world is an outgrowth of the "Person."

The world has no other purpose than to allow understanding. Once the affair, or the "thing," is understood, the abandonment of the world and therefore of the "Person" is self-evident, is "Self," evident.

There is "it" and Being has nothing to do with "it."

Being remains while "it" appears and disappears through the interplay of consciousness and energy.

§ In the same way that the "Person" cannot awaken, it cannot end itself, because in either case it means its own "death" by deletion.

"I am" born dead and I will die "born."

§ The principle of total and absolute human powerlessness is liberating. It frees from the tyranny of the "Person."

§ Let each form come to the axis, to the interval.

The place setting is the empty setting.

§ The one magic ring.

It is in a state of presence that the adept puts on the one magic ring. They remain in presence throughout the operation and at the time of impact, instead of pronouncing the sacred Word, they seize the Silence to tumble into the Interval of the Great Real.

The ring takes the perfect shape of the circle only when it has found its axis.

§ The orgasm is a remembrance and commemoration of the original fusion between Beingness and Absoluteness.

§ Everything is empty.

Everything is enjoyment.

§ Detachment doesn't come with feeding.

§ It is with a golden feather that the body of light is cleansed.

§ A human life is just one step, which is why this step must be extremely slow and in total consciousness.

§ One is immortal who has mastered stillness.
Slowness is the path to stillness.
Slowness is the path to immortality.
It is a short path.
It is an immediate path.
It is simply learning to move without movement, to enjoy without enjoyment, to love without loving, to be without existence.

§ In the Real, movement takes place from one stillness to another by freezing time.
And it is by bending space that the adept is transferred from one moment to another.

§ Peace is the interval.
Outside the interval, you encounter only troubles.
The world, that which is called world, is mental.
It is a more or less shared hallucination whose function is to generate energy to feed the field and the song of consciousness.

§ At the summit of the Mountain, you can choose to stay or come back down. You know the way up.
From the top, you can see other paths.
Only at the apex is there choice.
Only at the apex is there freedom.

§ The whole chain of Life is present in you, is you.
In its entirety, here and now.
Both in its simultaneity and in its unfolding.
Now, this very moment, you are born, live, and die in all forms of life: past, present, and future.

§ The future is identical to the past. Their source is in common, the unique source of the present.

§ Space is infinite because you are infinite.
   Time is counted because you are number.
   Everything is just an aspect of yourself.
   Not a reflection, but an aspect, which is very different.
   A reflection maintains the concept of duality.
   An aspect clearly indicates that there is only the One.

§ The idea of purity can only apply to the Great Nothing or the Totality.
   What is separate cannot be called pure.
   The search for purity proves to be a source of suffering for the "Person."

§ To lay down everything is to dispose of everything.
   That which we don't want.
   That which we want.

§ Being instead of having and doing.
   Letting yourself Be rather than letting yourself have or letting yourself do, two forms of letting go.

§ Human considerations must not mask the irruptions of the Spirit.
   Behind the manifestations and events, we must learn to read the attempts of the Spirit to awaken human consciousness.
   This is the function of signs and accords.
   Signs point to the Real Way.
   Accords confirm the approach of the Spirit.

§ Very few humans pay attention to awakening.
   Very few of them yearn for freedom.
   They prefer to be dominated in order to be protected or to be dominant in order to have the greatest possible choice when it comes to food and sex.
   Awakening is a fight against the genes. Genes campaign for duration. Genes, perfect replicators, want to engrave themselves indefinitely in time. This is why the fight begins here and now, out of time.
   The awakened is a great traveler out of time.

§ It is always the "Person" who is drawn to magic, never Being, which is magic itself.

When the person has exhausted identification with an illusory magic (such as rational thought), it then turns to Being, in which it dissolves.

§ Before I'm not, "I am."

§ There is always a direct way.

There aren't really teachings in a direct way, only an "Art of Being."

§ If I am absolute good then I am also absolute evil.

Therefore, neither good nor bad, neither this nor that.

The Great Nothing.

§ There is a time to let go of the processes of the "Person" and let Being manifest through every interval of consciousness, every interval of Void.

§ What is the will of the Totality?

Only a will to Be.

What is the freedom of the Totality?

Only the freedom to Be.

The true Initiation does not take place from person to person but from being to Being.

§ If you are empty, nothing happens.

Transmit the Intention and the Orient, never the form.

This is only powerful in spontaneity.

§ Identification with the "Person" is alienation itself.

Being needs no "Person," it is without need.

The game of Being makes it borrow all forms and thus the multiplicity of "Persons."

The nature of all form, and of all "Person," is Emptiness.

§ When the movement is perfectly fluid, then we are still.

§ There are more powerful, more creative consonants than vowels.

§   There are two instincts not initially conditioned by culture: an instinct for survival and an instinct for immortality. We must learn to use the reptilian forces of survival to awaken the instinct of immortality, to switch from one instinct to another, from horizontality to verticality, in order to gradually settle in the latter.

The instinct of immortality, of eternity one should say, is even more archaic than the instinct of survival. It precedes form.

§   An adept can live in symbiosis with a nature spirit. Through realization they make this spirit a god.

§   The celebration of nature is the only rite. Rites invented by humans or other entities are supplementals born of the estrangement of the Spirit. Absolute Spirit is Absolute Nature.

Only Spirit knows how to celebrate Nature. It is the very celebration of Nature, while Nature is the enchantment of Spirit.

§   The ring of Good arises from the ring of the Great Nothing.

This Good is unrelated to the relative good of humans.

We can however have a distant intuition of it by the contemplation of Nature.

§   For one who has freed themself from the conditioned principles of the "Person," respect for human rules and laws can be a subtle and elegant freedom.

§   All is Absolute Freedom.

DIALOG OF MONKS

"Your line is perfectly untenable!"

"This would be true if we were in the presence of a line."

"So then what?"

"An absence of line, an interval. Just a tiny, perfect gap to the Great Real!"

Incoherist Manifesto K 22

1. Incoherism is an initiatory and subitistic art of the interval.

2. When, in each individual, there is no more person, a silent Empire unfolds over which a hidden King reigns.

3. There is no Awakening of the person. In the absence of the person, there is Awakening. Fullness of Being among the people of metamorphosis.

4. If there are initiatic sciences of the person, the high sciences, then there is an initiatory art of Being.

5. Initiation resides neither in the form nor in the formless but in the interval between one and the other, the access without access to the Great Nothing.

    The Art resides neither in the formless nor in the form but in the fusion of the form with the formless, from which springs the Fullness of the Totality.

6. Art explores the unconscious, in search of the ONE-conscious.

    Initiation dissolves the unconscious in order to let the ONE-conscious emerge.

7. Initiation, like Art, implies a reconciliation with the shadow. The energetic alliance with the shadow frees Being of the person, that denial of Being.

8. There cannot be Initiation, or Art, without the nomadic alternative, without the joyful abandonment of fixity, without the permanent journey of the motionless Spirit.

9. Explicit order – Implicit order – Great Nothing. Such could be the primary structure in its triple simplicity.

    Existence – Beingness (Being and non-Being) – Absoluteness. Such would be the Real Way.

    Substance – Energy – Essence. Such would be the modalities of the Way.

10. The Incoherist is a Sacred Idiot, undivided, a master of controlled Madness. They know how to switch from NAKED to ONE.* Being in freedom.

---

*   Fr.: *du NU à UN*.

11 Initiation is always priestly, warlike, and artistic. It unites Heaven and Earth, creates new worlds, and slices the Universe in two. To rend or lift the veil. Awakening.

12 Had Awakening required a language, it would be that of Poetry.

13 The Letter A is the mother of all letters.

The Letter A is the mother of all numbers.

The Letter A engenders all worlds.

It is also the veil behind which is concealed access to the inaccessible.

The sound K rends this veil.

14 The arts—pictorial, musical, graphic, erotic, martial, ritual, and others—are whole-being. They lead, in the presence to oneself, to the relinquishment of the world and the grasping of the Real. Uncover and reveal.

15 Incoherism, in its emanations, words, and performances (whole-being, aesthetic, and ethical), escapes all worldliness, egotism, vulgarity, and morality by its verticality.

16 "Infamy," the process of apoptosis inherent in the Law itself, which wants to corrupt and break freedom, the very principle of Being, is only neutralized (indeed annihilated, reduced to nothingness) by presence here and now, the reintegration of the peripheries, of multiple horizons, into the immutable center of Being.

Whoever wants to burn "Infamy" to ashes and let the wind scatter them, takes refuge in their own Essential nature. Out of Time and therefore Out of Law.

17 A simple star, of six rays, distinguishes the light of the Wise from the light of the Fools.

18 The quantum revolution that is approaching by discreet, even dissident, paths will partially explain the initiatory art of the interval and the geometry of absences.

19 The Fifth Book, the rabelaisian key.

Typographical errors and spelling mistakes, the quixotic key.

515, the dantesque key.

20 Non-intention is the only intention.

21 We want to Awaken against the world. We want to Awaken without the world. We want to Awaken with the world. When these dualistic chimeras are abandoned, we sail, like Odysseus on the way to Ithaca, on the ocean of Awakening.

22 All beings are Awakening.

You are the last, the only one among all beings, who still does not know that you are Awakening.

> "I am.
> Neither This nor That.
> Absolute Freedom"

A Few Crazy Considerations on the Absolute

Disjointed Words of a Mad Monk to Unbind

1. There is an ecstasy of stupidity!

2. Humanity seems to be asserting itself as a unique case of evident stupidity in all of creation.
   Which encourages us to leave the human for the Being.

3. The event has no history. An event is always without a history. No before, no after. Clearly, "it" happens. The history of "it" comes later. That is another event, another "it." No causality.

4. It must be very clear that being installed in the awakened verticality of heightened consciousness is accompanied by a disengagement from the world recognized as farce.
   The being on the path can only maintain an absolutely neutral or else subversive relationship with the world. The new subversions have no other object than to unveil the farce of the world. Whoever chooses the way of subversive arts, war, theft, sex, gambling, or anything else, will have to be careful not to end up "farcical" or to become just another farceur themselves.

5. Contrary to what is commonly accepted, the shadow of being, the dark and somber side, is always the most visible part, the very evidence of manifestation.

6. The occult is not what is hidden but what, on the contrary, is perfectly apparent.

7. Writing, whether it is a poem or an initiatory tale, or even a ritual, an inspired or indeed revealed text, is always an illusory act and devoid of meaning in the Real.

8   The "person" has the capacity to cause a simulacrum of awakening within the representation in order to not disappear, to continue to Being-bypass, to parry Being, to mask it.

What some of you call "awakening" is only a fart or even a belch of Being in the meadow of illusion, a little supplemental soul.

No, if there is awakening, it is Being in itself.

There are no awakened ones but Being is awakening.

Awakening is the state of Being.

We can only realize it.

9   Whether you are in a temple, a palace, a brothel, or a junkyard does not have the slightest influence on the quest. It is not the situation that influences but the relationship maintained with the situation, the relationship of Being, a relationship exactly opposite to the degree of identification with the situation.

You cannot decide the situation. The situation is a given. You can decide how the relationship is established with the situation.

10 Disorder can be initiatory, but certainly not an order.

11 For those who are not in heightened consciousness, rites and ceremonies only nourish and enrich error, embellishing the prison of conditioning. Religions and initiation rites are only alienating lies for those who have lost their axiality; they are sometimes works of Art for those who, free of themselves, have no need for forms and can therefore fully enjoy them.

12 Learning is heavy and slow.

Understanding is light and dazzling.

13 God? A poetics of Being.

The gods? Emanations of the real in the psyche.

Human beings, Being in the human, are gods actualized by heightened consciousness, or gods in the phase of actualization by heroic consciousness, or inactual gods, or stillborn gods in the game of worlds.

14. It is indeed the dream that awakens!

15. There is no human power but illusory details and insignificance.

    In the Real, human power is only mediocre and ridiculous impotence.

    Letting go could be called 'omni-impotence,' giving up the illusion of 'omnipotence,' of control, of mastery, etc.

16. There is no other power than heightened consciousness. Heightened consciousness is a condensation of Void born of the release of Shakti in the interval.

17. Every moment is Shiva.

    Every state is Shiva.

    There is nothing that is not Shiva.

    Shiva is the perfect interval between Nothing and Nothing, the absolute interval.

18. I am the meditation of Shiva.

    I am, the meditation of Shiva.

    The importance of the comma.

    Awakening is just a matter of punctuation.

    Samsara and Nirvana, illusion and reality, are identical, absolutely, but punctuated differently.

    Who is the grammarian?

19. I am, the meditation of Shiva.

    And Shiva is my meditation.

    At every moment.

    Every moment.

    Moment.

    Immediacy is the only physical and metaphysical moment.

    A moment of omnipotence.

    A moment of the Great Nothing.

20   Shiva is an incandescent fire.

Everything, from the tiniest particle to the most immense god, comes to ignite and consume itself in Him to realize His true nature of the Absolute.

21   The adept hears the Shaivite clamor that resounds throughout the Universe.

The name of God is always a clamor.

His prayer is a creative whisper.

22   The "Turquoise Goddess," the Shakti of the end-times of Shiva, before his ultimate withdrawal, is also called the Kundalini below the feet because she is coiled under the feet until she springs forth.

23   Look at this nut.

Its nature is the Void.

Its essence is the Void.

The nature and essence of the Void is that nut.

Everything is here.

24   In the presence,

The slightest breath, the slightest of your gestures, the slightest intention, makes the Universe dance and respond.

As if filaments of light were emanating from your heart and weaving the entire Universe.

25   The real ways slither in the alternation between practice and spontaneity, until spontaneity is the only practice.

26   In the Real, seek Awakening without awakening.

This is the true way of Do-Nothing.

27   Awakening is accompanied by a madosophy, a wisdom of madness, a wisdom, entirely Rabelaisian, of the "beyond the void."

The true nature of the beyond, as of the person, is Void.

28 The Interval itself is the great mantra.

   The Interval itself is the sole mandala.

   The perfect form of the great mantra is Silence.

   The perfect form of the great mandala is Fullness of the Void.

29 In the Interval, each sound is a mantra; each sound is a word of power.

30 **A** is the original and ultimate mantra.

   Inscribed in the very essence of the breath, it is the matrix of all mantras.

   Every mantra is a grammatical declension or mathematical derivative of **A**.

   Every mantra leads back to its source.

   Every mantra leads back to the silence of the **A**.

31 One of the difficulties in the practice of the letter **A** lies in the resistance of the ego to include the totality of the world within the **A**.

   The mind in effect refuses to "defile" the **A** with the world. It's just a pretext, and not a very elegant one at that.

   It is then necessary to resume the basics of the practice to turn off the mind.

32 Recognize and chant the name of Shiva.

   It flows like the rustle of the ocean uniting with the beach.

   Recognize and chant the name of the Goddess.

   It springs like the roar of the wave crashing against the rock in a high wind.

33 Hope is another name for fear.

   Neither fear nor hope.

   To penetrate and traverse the one means to renounce the other.

34 Even more than the possible, the impossible is realizable.

   Better, actualizable!

   By precipitation of the Spirit into form.

   And liberation of the Essence inscribed in the form.

35   The question of choice is illusory.

It can, indeed it must, be considered philosophically, but it has no axiocratic impact.

In the Real, we don't choose, we sever.

Spirit cuts the Universe in two and creates the Interval.

36   Spirit feeds on Essence.

Essence feeds on Spirit.

Spirit / Essence.

Shiva / Shakti.

37   The time is always here to revive the myths.

This is the time of the enchantment of the world.

Naturally, demystification must only be carried out in and through Silence.

Silence is both the death of time and the reintegration of myths into the Void of the Heart, the reabsorption of the Word into the central ring in which it was originally uttered or emitted.

38   The nature of the spiritual worlds, like the nature of this world, is Void.

The nature of the Gods, like the nature of the human being, is Void.

39   All gods are destined for death and it is in the awakened human that they die and discover their true nature.

40   The individual, that which is believed to be an "individual," is a complex system of multiple personalities, more or less integrated, all of whom can be generally identified under one name.

Our reality, original and ultimate, is the nameless.

41   Purulent crusts of the person dissolve

in the immaculate light of Being.

42   Abandon the person. Leave it to the world. Return it to the world that artificially spawned it and... Remain!

43 The person is not the poison.

   The identification is the poison.

   If the person is understood as a simple element of the situation, in the absence of identification, it can even become the ally, just as the situation is the material.

44 What a human being calls "their life," this clump of conditioned waste, is just a slow death.

   What they call "death" is just the outpouring of Being.

   Death is the trail left by Being within form.

   Death is the forever friend.

45 Neither right nor wrong.

   Neither life nor death.

   But Being.

   The person functions.

   Being is.

   Non-Being is not.

   Being and non-Being are Beingness-Absoluteness.

46 Non-Being does not exclude Being but goes beyond it, encompasses it, for an infinity of possibilities and impossibilities. No duality here.

47 Silence as matter.

   Infinity as dimension.

   Void as space.

   Being as work.

48 All thought is pure since its nature is Emptiness.

   All word.

   All action.

   All form.

   So there is nothing to change.

   The world is perfect, in its totality, as in each of its parts, which is the Void.

49   Thought and non-thought: the same state.

Fear and non-fear: the same state.

Being and non-Being: the same Essence.

50   The faceless human being has no face other than their own face.

Who is staring at them?

The human being without a mask has no mask other than their own mask.

Who unmasks them?

The headless human being has no head other than their own head.

Who beheads them?

51   All shapes are equal.

All forms are empty.

All Tradition is formal.

All affinity is conditioned.

Neither this nor that.

You want an occult constitution of the human being?

Here is one:

> Perceived body,
>
> Arborescent body,
>
> Star body,
>
> Ocean of Emptiness.

Does it suit you?

Neither this nor that.

52   Thought has no "meaning" except creatively.

Creation has no "meaning" except that born out of Silence.

Silence is meaning without meaning.

53 There is no future, no "after."

The future is Void.

Gesture, word, and thought are therefore without consequence except to themselves in the present moment.

They are their own cause and their own consequence.

They are their alpha and their omega.

Gesture, word, and thought are intrinsically independent of any source and free of any objective.

Nothing to obtain. Nothing to attain.

No targets, no expectations.

Nothing to "originate," nothing to lose.

Only the freedom of the moment gives the gesture, the word, or the thought its infinite beauty.

54 The golden butterfly: a powerful ally.

The most powerful of all allies.

It is the ultimate thought, the definitive thought, the one that gives form to Nothingness.

55 The adept must learn to switch instantly from the heart of fire to the heart of ice and from the heart of ice to the heart of fire.

From fullness to Emptiness, from Emptiness to fullness.

Until their ultimate and ecstatic union.

56 Four deaths before Death:

Death by fire in the meditation on ashes.

Death by water in meditation on the waterfall.

Death by earth in the meditation on mud.

Death by air in the meditation on wind.

57 Meditations:

> Inhalation: Birth
>
> The inhalation/exhalation interval: Being
>
> Exhalation: Death
>
> or
>
> Exhalation: Death
>
> The exhalation/inhalation interval: Non-Being
>
> Inhalation: Birth

Conscious life is only the development, exploration, and inspection of these two meditations.

58 The Void. The Totality.

Totality. Void.

Resolve this ultimate duality through the experience of formless form.

The nature of Void is indeed Totality.

The nature of Totality is indeed Void.

59 Essence leaves the form and reenters the heart through the path of luminous bones.

The bones are actually the "blueprints of form."

An object has no form.

It is within the form.

The form is instantaneous.

The form has no continuity.

Thus the form is Shiva.

60 On the path of Ardhanarishvara, we must ultimately merge Shiva and Shakti only if Being is really established in Silence without disturbance of the person.

Otherwise, it is better to wait for the moment of the destruction of the body.

61 When we talk about this body or this world, we are pointing to the same illusory and conceptual reality. In presence to oneself, there is neither this body nor this world.

Presence is absence.

Absence is presence.

Ab-Sense.

62 The coherence, or assemblage, point of the person—or, equally, of the world—is also the point of the Interval, the center and gate of the Interval.

63 "I am," the Interval of the Universe.

"I am," the Interval of the worlds and times.

64 The ultimate operation lies in the union of the powers of the Lords of the Flame with the power of the Lords of the Interval.

The Fire in the heart of the Void.

The Impossible Fire.

65 If the adept applies the energy of verticality, of the Axis, in the field of horizontality, of the Circle, they destroy this picture.

Only the resonance, the echo of verticality, can harmonize in the peripheries, even the near ones.

The Absolute is not of this world.

66 Each exhalation is the call of Shakti to Shiva.

Each inhalation is the response of Shiva to Shakti.

Each interval is their union.

67 The sky is a clear blue.

A few clouds remain.

The Spirit is free.

The body, never completely.

68 To create and to uncreate are the two movements of Nature, or rather the two phases of a single movement, like raising the sword and slicing.

Only the human destroys.

Unable to create, they cannot uncreate.

How could they grasp and manifest the harmony of decreation?

69 A very ancient Shaivite cult teaches the sexual union of the yogini and yogi in order to generate an energetic and ecstatic vehicle of light, intended for the soul of a dying or deceased person.

Thus the soul of the deceased, called to earth by the sexual act at the moment of conception, is released to the fields of eternity by the same act, carried by the energy thus generated in bliss.

What must be remembered from this belief and practice is that creation and uncreation are the same act, born of the heating of the breaths in the repetition of the name of Shiva in the way of the Swan: Hamsa-Soham.

70 The hissed mantras and the rubbed mantras are the most powerful.

Emerging immediately from Void and Silence, they remain the nearest expression of the "Word that was never spoken in the Beingness that was never begotten."

71 Despite everything, the world and humanity are, in the Real, totally Love.

72 Aesthetics is not an art of the "beautiful" but a science of the Real.

73 The Universe is perfect.

Perfect happiness.

Perfect suffering.

Perfect anger.

Perfect impotence.

Perfect ignorance.

Perfect violence.

Perfect compassion.

Perfect knowledge.

Perfect freedom.

"Awakening" is permanent and inevitable.

No one can not be awake.

74 Compassion requires moving beyond good and evil, beyond dismay at human mediocrity, and beyond the desire to save the world.

True compassion is a freedom born of the coupling of Absolute Freedom and Absolute Will.

Only the being in freedom can know compassion and let it emanate from them.

75 The adept grasps the Void as the center of form.

"I am" then asserts itself as the form of the center of the Void.

76 Neither reincarnation nor resurrection.

Neither this nor that.

The Body of Glory is a body of light and fire.

Body of ecstasy.

Body of cheer.

Body without body.

Body without Body.

77 Let us beware of the convenience of language. Consider only its elliptical and shadowy character. Being understood by an ego is rarely a good sign when it comes to the world of Spirit. There is indeed nothing to understand but everything to grasp.

To speak of being and non-being suggests a dualistic reminiscence. A fatality of language.

The spelling BEING indicates more fully the unity of being and non-being, implies that non-being includes being instead of opposing it, and suggests the quality of that which is and conjointly that which is not.

78 In the fullness of Being, there is no longer any humanity.

79   The experience of the divine quivering is born out of the unfoldment of Being, out of its unfolding from point to infinity, like a limitless number of immaculate lotuses reproducing themselves, duplicating one another, further and further, more and more widely, in the eight directions of space.

80   Still this breath.

Let it die.

Stop these incessant comings and goings between point and infinity.

Give birth to a pure, archetypal form whose phenomenal configurations are only ephemeral and dull copies born of the unconscious breath.

These pure creations, whose material is Silence, are like tall ships sailing in the light of Being.

81   The awakened always walk alongside the pariahs, slaves, and untouchables.

They know how much these perceive the presence of a Hidden King in the center of themselves, more than others do.

82   Religions are the garments of spirituality.

Initiatory schools are the garments of awakening.

Garments wear out.

The Hidden King is naked and crowned.

His nakedness is his crown.

83   We are all "awakened."

It is impossible not to be "awakened."

The moron, the guru, the sage, the madman, the brute, the pseudo-philosopher, the true philosopher, the whore, the virgin, the delinquent, and the citizen, all "awakened" because everyone is Awake. For no one can escape their original nature.

No one can ever not Be.

Nothing to do.

Only a flapping of the wing of consciousness veils this great reality.

84 From Nothing, nothing comes out without Intention.

Intention is not meaning.

Meaning is a contextualized interpretation of the Intention about which nothing can be said.

85 Our original nature is solely Intention.

Our ultimate nature is our Orient.

Our original nature is solely Orient.

Our ultimate nature is Intention.

So, from the Intention to the Orient: Nothing, Nothing, and Nothing.

86 There is no more person!

The master is Being!

The disciple is Being.

Being is the only master there is.

It will take on all aspects of life until it can recognize itself in your every moment.

If the rite is celebrated, let it be gesture by gesture, in the irruption of the moment, without signification, without the slightest meaning.

Presence is meaning.

More than symbol.

Being, Being in every gesture, in every breath, in every stillness, in every interval.

87 All initiation is initiation into the Real.

As far from the Real as an initiatory, traditional, or avant-garde form seems to get, it aspires to grasp it.

All quest, even the most obscure, the most confused, and the most degenerate, is a quest for the Real.

Initiation in a given reality is:

>   Self-remembering, ceremonial, rite, and interval,
>
>   or
>
>   Self-remembering, dance, stillness, and interval.

Initiation into the Real is:

> The quivering and murmur of Shakti.

> The clicking tongue of Shiva.

All initiation other than the experience of Being turns out to be useless and senseless.

The experience of Being takes place entirely at this very moment, in this very place.

It is the motionless experience.

The experience of non-change.

A non-experience.

88 All Being is there,

In the contemplation of Nature,

Not in Nature itself,

But indeed in its contemplation.

Being is the absolute meditator.

Being is the absolute contemplative.

89 Within the inhalation itself,

Within the exhalation itself,

A myriad of intervals.

Perceiving them

Is a sign of awakening.

90 The so-called experience of Awakening (it would be more accurate to speak of the experience of Absoluteness) is a non-experience. It is a dazzling traversal of the different qualities from the Void to the non-Void Void, to the fullness of the Totality and the Great Nothing, the only Universality there is.

This comes under the Understanding, the Apprehension, of the non-human, the more than human, and the all-human.

Exhaust experience, exhaust memory, to access Understanding.

The non-human, or the Real, emerges from the alignment of the pre-human, the human, and the more-than-human in, and through, the play of energy and consciousness.

It is always the human that disturbs the alignment by its tendency to extend, while the pre-human and more-than-human remain fixed in a single point.

91   "I am," the Great Stillness.

92   Being never had a beginning.

It will have no completion.

It is the beginning and the completion, simultaneously, in the moment.

It is the Interval of all things.

A thing is an extension of consciousness between a beginning, a birth that never took place, and a completion, a death that cannot happen.

A thing is a thread of light stretched between two absent columns.

Being is therefore the Thing,* the birth and death of the Thing, and everything else.

Being is the Interval of all that exists and of none of this.

93   Being and non-being unite to celebrate the Great Nothing and manifest its ecstatic fullness.

This is the true Eucharist.

94   Every moment, we bring forth a slightly modified conditional world of "that world there." This gives us the illusion of continuity while everything is simply empty. On the frame of conceived time, we draw forms. Just so many illusions.

"From the perspective of the Real," everything appears as equal and of the nature of Void. Neither suffering, nor pleasure, but fullness.

Being endures.

Things simultaneously are born and die in it because Being is by nature non-Time while Time is the explication of Being within the field of the conscious or, further, the existent or the in-time or, ultimately, the time.

---

*   Fr.: La Chose.

That is why, sooner or later, the quester must appeal to the devourer of time. *I Am* and I am not *I Am*.

I am *That which is* and I am also *That which is not*.

That annuls That.

From Null to the Great Nothing, extends Being.

95 In the *Real*, all that is alive is *Absolutely Black*.

And all that is *Absolutely Black* bears an essential fissure, the Interval, Door of the Real.

The *material* of this door is the Great Nothing.

The Great Nothing is the *material* of the *Real*.

The *Real* is the Spirit of the Great Nothing.

The *material* is Spirit

And Spirit is the Material.

96 To liberate yourself, liberate all the deities you have spawned within you—let them go!

97 The adept is no longer confronted with small and ridiculous human vanities but they still carry within them the pride of the victorious gods. They will have to agree to let their own divinity disintegrate into the Great Nothing in order to realize the ultimate Absoluteness.

98 Only by listening to the laughter of the gods will you *Really* understand.

99 For each awakened dragon, an enlivened goddess.

Find the energy of the dragon.

Guide it out of the egg.

Ride the dragon.

100 The Nagas are the central adepts of the Tradition.

Naga Devi (Naga Kanya is an avatar of her) is the axial Goddess of the whole Real Way.

She is both its Guardian and its Priestess.

She is the Warrior Initiator and the Lover Initiator.

The Nagas perfectly master all the serpentine energies and orient them like a column in the heart of an Ocean of Void.

101   This column can both engender worlds and annihilate them.

The Order of the Thousand and Eight Nagas is the counterpart, or even the double, of the Order of the Thousand and Eight Goddesses.

Naga Devi is the Axial Goddess, the Goddess of the Arcana.

Ardhanarishvara is their Orient.

It is a strange gemination.

102   Woman doesn't *have* kundalini.

Woman *is* the Goddess Kundalini.

Contemplate the sex of the Goddess.

Immediate awakening.

Drink the nectar from the sex of the Goddess.

Immediate awakening.

Let yourself be carried away by the wave of the ecstasy of the Goddess.

Immediate awakening.

103   Humans on the path tend to vastly overestimate their ability to integrate the energy of Dragons.

They think it is a question of understanding or of persons. It is really a question of the interval within the person—or the world, it is the same thing.

104   Form invariably becomes deformed before returning to formlessness.

That is why Being is formless.

105   Are not the poet, the magician, the muse, and the artist persons? They are also persons, but persons who have consented to be surprised and impressed by Being.

106 The Incoherist Game:

    The rule is the game itself.

    The game is the situation itself.

107

    Are you immortal?

    My bones are white as snow...

Songs of the Master of Flowers

That the power of the two Dragons of Gold and Silver
Of Sun and Moon
Of the twelve Rainbow Dragons
Of the Thousand and Eight Goddesses of the Temple
Of the thirty-three Absolute Goddesses
Of Shakti and the Ultimate Goddess
Of the Lords of the Interval
And the Lords of the Flame
Manifest in Soma
For the accomplishment of the Great Nothing in the work.

That the great blue bird of Mount Kailash
That the flying blue monkeys of Mount Kailash
That the hordes of gold and light
That the azure and emerald serpents
That the riders of shadow
That the riders of light
That the archers of shadow
That the archers of light
That the builders of shadow
That the builders of light
Assist us in all our temporal and timeless works
May they preserve our companions
Neutralize our adversaries
Render our enemies to nothingness.

I salute Agni, the great fire dragon
At the gate of the South
May it surround us with a sevenfold enclosure of flames, impassable in the dark
Let it consume our bodies, our hearts, our worlds, and our times
Let it burn us to ashes
Let the wind scatter our ashes in the eight directions of space
Leaving room for Being.

I salute the great emerald dragon

At the door of the Nadir

The dragon of the regeneration of flesh and spirit

May it restore our bodies, our hearts, our worlds, and our times

In all their original fullness.

I salute the great dragon of the gate of the Heart

The dark and luminous dragon of perfect knowledge

Let it flow in us and through us

Erasing all separation.

I salute the great dragon of the gate of the Heart of the Heart

The golden dragon of perfect love

Let it be our home.

I salute the great dragon of the Heart of the Heart of the Heart

The dragon of the Interval

May it lead us to the nine secret dragons

Of absolute beauty

Of absolute art

Of the absolute feminine

Of absolute will

Of the absolute freedom of beauty

Of the absolute freedom of art

Of the absolute freedom of the feminine

Of the absolute freedom of will

Of the absolute freedom of freedom.

Distant Echoes of Incoherist Imperience

Almond

If you don't dissect the body of words, if you don't bare the bones, if you don't break the bones to taste the marrow, the text cannot deliver its real message.

§ Most creatures have a date with death.
 Make a date with the Infinite.

§ The conquest of the living remains to be done in its near totality. The human thinks of themself as alive when they are lived, hallucinated, and dreamed, and serves in a way as food for great currents of energy, more-or-less endowed with consciousness, themselves toys tossed about by the great game of consciousness and energy.
 Gods or humans, only those who never sleep are truly alive!

§ Indoctrination is harmful even if the doctrine is good. Discard the doctrine. Keep practicing. If practice brings the doctrine back, discard it again.

§ The body has dependencies.
 The Spirit is not dependent on its dependencies.
 The body knows time but can do nothing.
 The Spirit ignores time and can do Everything.

§ There is no anticipation, either of the future or the past, greater than presence to oneself (or to the Self; it is the same thing).

§ If you do not remain at the center of yourself, in the immaculate heart of the Real, in the Presence, you are on the periphery, in a conditioned and uncertain orbit, subject to probabilities. Being outside of yourself, outside of your own immutable nature, you risk a speeding accident, psychic or physical. You can hit an entity, human or otherwise, which, like you, will not be in its place and will have moved away from its axiality.

§ It is not harmful to not understand.
Culture does not liberate.
It is, on the other hand, damaging to not grasp the power of "not understanding" (the power of Idiocy) or to not accept it, for opening the door to the Great Nothing.

§ If the Great Nothing is, there is no "Person" to see it.
The Great Nothing is there for no person.

§ A formal failure can be an essential victory.
If failure is a de-feat.

§ Events do not signify the quest. It is the "Person" who projects meaning onto the event so that the absurdity of their situation does not call them into question.
We have a need to make sense when we are unaware. Mindfulness does not require meaning.

§ The highest teachings are the simplest ones. They are only accessible to free spirits.

§ The "best."
Gate to the hell of comparison.

§ Why did the gods endow humans with reason? So that they would stop wasting their time in simulacra and devote themselves to the quest for the Absolute. So don't make another simulacrum of reason.

§ Love is a human enchantment.

§ The one does not exclude the other.
The one and the other.
The One Is the Other.

§ To exist is to be outside.
To not exist is to be inside.
Be.

§ Between the human being and the divine being, a tiny difference of orientation. A Nothing.

§ One who operates with the power of the species gains temporal immortality. This immortality to endure has an end.

One who frees themself from the power of the species leaves humanity for Beingness.

§ Being is.

Many paths to immortality only immortalize a "thing." An object, even an immortal one, remains an object. There is immortality only in the dimension of Being.

§ Action in contemplation.
Contemplation in action.
Towards nonduality.

§ To do and to have is to incarnate.
To Be is to escape from the wheel of incarnations.
With each unconscious breath, incarnation.

§ Doing and having maintain causality.
To break the chain of causalities is to take the Interval. Cut before and cut after. Be out of time and out of the world.

§ The world is wounding because the world is nothing but a wound that will heal only by merging into the Totality.
As a "Person," you are the world.

§ Conditioning by rejection is as toxic and liberticidal as conditioning by adherence.

§ The last affectation of the mind consists of the adherence to a "mirror-form" of the formless that is about to be born from Silence.
Despite everything, the cunning fox is most often too weak and can only delay the culmination, the outpouring of the Dragon.
Some, however, drown in this last conflict between water and fire.

§ The tangle of reasons leads humans to personal and collective disaster.
To renounce reason is to open the door of Wisdom.
To renounce knowledge is to welcome Understanding.
Unreason is the first step towards Awakening.

§ The real perception of our utter helplessness and its acceptance brings about awakening through the immediate dissolution of the "Person." Indeed, it is the pretense of control and power that coagulates the "Person."

§ Awakening is not a victory but a defeat and a dispossession.

The conditioned weaving of the person is undone. The veil is unwoven, letting the radiance of Beingness invade the entire field of consciousness.

§ "My" awakening is not "your" awakening.

However, both are Awakening.

§ No difference between the conditioned and the unconditioned.

§ A differentiated state of consciousness is always a state and even an altered state, like the one you find yourself in reading these words.

Where is the non-state?

Where is the non-place?

§ Awakening does not resemble Awakening.

Awakening is unique.

Awakening cannot be modeled.

Comparing forms is chimerical, so comparing two Awakenings...

§ It is your reality that has spawned all forms. So how could one form oppose another? Each form affirms and indicates the Great Real, by transparency.

§ The Great Real is a non-state, in which you can "encounter" a summit without a base, a front without a back, a left without a right.

Everything there is the immutable Center.

§ Awakening demands that form rejoins Essence, that it retracts into It.

§ If it were enough to lose everything in order to awaken, three-quarters of humanity would be Awake.

To express the way in terms of loss is to remain within the temporality of doing and having. Wretched duality.

There is nothing to lose.

It is rather a question of undoing, of renouncing grasping, clinging, retaining the illusion, and adherence to form. Be.

§ A subtle mind need not lose everything to be disgusted with samsara. It quickly grasps that it cannot hold anything and that the nature of the object-event is empty. Refusing to be detained, it prepares to definitively traverse the worlds, from the mineral world to the world of the gods, without ever lingering, to join the Great Real.

§ You will have to give up the knowledge and powers that are the result of subjugation to the human-nurtured gods if you are to traverse duality and access true Knowledge of Nondual Consciousness in the Primordial Nothingness that is your Natural State.

§ On the Way, "comprehending" is a bad sign.
"Being astonished" is a good sign.

§ "Poet" and "alchemist" are two synonymous words. The blowers* are copiers, transcribers at best.

§ On the Way, any practice devoid of Spirit is violence.

§ The awakened choice of the profane life is the sign of Being.
The personal choice of the sacred life is the sign of the "mask."

§ The "Person" sees the "Person."
The Self sees the Self.

§ It is not the trail of the initiates that should be followed, however prestigious, but it is the absence of a trail that characterizes Awakening. The trail is conceptual, while the way is an "immaculate conception."

§ The Great Nothing. The Self, witness to the Great Nothing. "I Am," witness to the Self. "I," witness to "I Am." Such is the declension of the witness and the indication of a path.

§ Awakening is the return to original Nature, in place of the original murder that founded the "Person" in the field of heightened consciousness.

---

*   Fr.: *souffleurs*, or blowers, is a term used to describe alchemists who work solely for the purpose of attaining riches, and also poets who only work on the form of the poem without grasping the essence of poetry (i.e., technicians, not artists).

§ In appearance, nothing distinguishes the "living-dead," the "Person," the human being totally subject to conditioning, from the "living-saved," the being without adherence and without contingency. In essence, the first, a mere ephemeral reflection, has no reality, while the second is Supreme Happiness and Absolute Freedom.

§ There is no absolute freedom without enjoyment. The awakened is a *bhogi*.* An adept who is not a *bhogi* would be like a hemiplegic, paralyzed by dualism.

§ The awakened one killed the "Person" well before death. This one also returned the body to infinity.

This one killed "death."

This one Is.

§ The fully enlightened human is the heart of the gods.

A time with the gods.

A time without the gods.

A time with the gods.

A time without the gods.

This breathing is necessary.

Between these two times, there is the Interval that leads to the Great Real.

One does not move away from the gods downwards, nor upwards, but towards the immutable center.

The one who *absolutely* seizes the Interval is liberated in the same moment.

§ First the body against being. Illusion.

Then the alliance of body and being. Initiation.

Then body of being and being in body. Beingness.

Then the Great Nothing. Absoluteness.

§ In each moment, "Persons" are getting in each other's way. Thus they replicate artificially. This is the true infernal cycle of reincarnations.

§ Reincarnation is nasty.

Free yourself!

---

* Sanskrit: *bhogi*, one who enjoys.

§ The concept of reincarnation is one of the threads that weave the veil of ignorance. No, not reincarnation but, sometimes, the trail of Being.

The test, and there is only one, lies in the recognition of the "Person" as a factory of illusions and in its dismantling.

You have to be cunning like Odysseus to free the Hidden King.

§ Adhering to form is always, in one way or another, adhering to barbarism, or indeed generating it.

§ Where there is fear, there is violence.

Where there is violence, there is fear.

In presence, we extinguish situational fear, the fear of "what might happen if...", but not the original fear that endures as long as the surviving body persists.

When the "I-skin" disappears into the Absolute Body, then the original fear is lost in infinity.

§ In temporality, forms are depleted, in therapy as in Initiation.

Two antidotes, one relative, the other definitive:

- do not settle into a form—pass through, create, pass through, create, again and again;
- be installed in the Moment, a place where the form is always newly generated, a place where the form is born and dies simultaneously. And remain there.

§ In temporality, no one can know before knowing.

A person cannot be an equestrian before becoming an equestrian.

A person cannot be a dancer before becoming a dancer.

A person cannot be a sculptor before becoming a sculptor.

Becoming precedes the state.

However, in the same temporality, the individual is awake before knowing Awakening.

§ Sensation is not form.

Energy is not sensation.

Essence is not energy.

However, the second are the derivatives of the first.

There is an ascending path from form to essence.

§ Initiation is the triumph of Silence over the sufferings, conditionings, fears, disempowerments, and divisions of the Person.

Path of individuation, path towards the Simple, towards the ONE, the NU,* the without-manifestation and without-equal.

§ Tradition sometimes opposes education and Initiation. This is not a major opposition. Education tends to reconcile the parties that agitate the peripheries by organizing them as an entity. Initiation wants to rejoin and recognize the immutable Center of all things. The first deals with the relationships between "external" objects, while the second deals with essences. An articulation is possible. Fundamentally, the function of education, while not opposing it, is simply not about Initiation.

§ Initiation is indeed a conversion but a vertical conversion. A horizontal, peripheral conversion, such as that which consists of, for example, a Christian becoming Muslim or Buddhist, remains a conditioned enantiodromic reflex of the "Person." Vertical enantiodromia consists of a quantum leap of the "Person," from "the given being" to Being.

§ If you absolutely hold to the absurd concept of "counter-initiation," consider that any institution, secular or sacred, is counter-initiatory.

Indeed, the liberatory process of Initiation can neither institute nor be instituted.

§ The two expressions of initiation, imitation and invention, must be perfectly understood. The imitation of Christ, Buddha or Abhinavagupta, all perfectly inimitable, is only an accessory leading you to "the imitation of oneself," of one's ultimate reality. Even if you don't know it, you are the Self. How can you imitate what you are not aware of? Because you suspect it and sense it, otherwise you wouldn't be here.

§ Many of those who have convinced themselves of being engaged on an initiatory path have in reality fallen into a genuine personal bankruptcy, offering up lamentable retractions.

As soon as the ego felt in danger of disappearing into Silence and the Void, it ruined the tension towards the One, and plunged back into the dualistic delights of division.

Fear of losing the "Person."

Fear of being, unmasked.

---

* Fr.: *l'UN, le NU,* alternatively, "the ONE, the NAKED."

§ In the Sacred Theater, energy precedes thought. The Sacred Theater bears witness.

In the Rite, energy follows the thought that is born from silence. The Rite celebrates and creates the Moment.

In Theater, as in Initiation, the "I" and its hypertrophied attribute, intelligence, must abdicate.

§ In theater, as in Initiation, the members of the troupe, or the initiatory college, are only brought together by bonds of free election, in the sacred and secret sense of the term.

§ Any genuine encounter frees itself from the life of the egregores.

§ We must never let the Initiatory Quest be affected by the stupid and heavy force of the bestial, the common, the ordinary, the habitual, the utilitarian, the worldly, or the predictable.

§ When you take the path of Initiation, in *Imitatio*, within the labyrinth of dualistic and identified experience, you live an extraordinary life in an ordinary way. But once you cross the line of perfect Silence, you will experience an ordinary life in an extraordinary way, in nondual and free consciousness. This is the *Inventio* of the Hidden King.

Anyone who claims initiation cannot hide behind existing barriers, profane or sacred, modern or traditional. The initiate exposes themselves because they are unknowable.

§ Every "Master," which is to say, every Free Spirit, was at one time "betrayed" by a "Disciple," a student who, unable to pierce the egoic opacity, believed that, because the Master, like everyone, defecates and urinates, they had nothing to learn from them.

What then makes the Master smile is that the Disciple is right. There is nothing to learn from the Master, but this "Nothing" is "Everything," and it still escapes them.

§ The only justice there is lies in perfect adaptation to the situation in and through Presence to self.

§ Being is neither proud nor humble.

Humility is only an ego-shaping, a way for the Person to strengthen itself by telling its story.

§ To fight the ego is to perfect it.
To ignore it is to weaken it to the point of annihilation.

§ The way in which the end of time and the end of our personal time presents itself in the field of consciousness, is "envisioned"—the word is right and constitutes the weaving of the ego. It is this weaving that initiation unravels in order to reveal Being in its fullness.

§ For the ego, there is never an inescapable situation.
That is why you must cut the primary identification with the situation at its root.

§ You cannot identify with the situation.
You can, more subtly, not identify with identification.
You must also, necessarily, not identify with non-identification.

§ When we gave up all personal names:
"I," from egocentrism to egosolism,*
"You," the alleged altruism,
"He/She," the false detachment/the celebration of the other sex,
"We," "you all," "they," the collective versions of the first three,
"God," the ultimate personal pronoun,
Passing through "ON," the indefinite, without stopping there,
When we have renounced all these "predations," Being can appear, **A** by Being.†

§ Between beliefs and compassion, always choose compassion.

§ Compassion comes from itself. Without reason.

§ He who kills has failed.
There are many ways to kill.
If you have to save a life, don't try to keep the carpet they're on from getting dirty.

---

* Egosolism: a term coined by philosopher Ladislav Klíma. According to Radek Holodňák ("To Play Like Napoleon. Klíma's Egosolism as a Call to Active Participation in the World," *Filosofický časopis*, 2021, v. 69, Special Issue 1), egosolism "is *my* ability to transform the world according to the rules which *I* myself set and which *I* take as my own." It must be added that true egosolism includes the totality of what is. I am not alone against or in spite of others, I am alone because I am not separated from others, I am one with all that is.

† Fr.: *l'Être peut apparaître, A par Être.*

§ No one realizes themself, no one carries out the Great Work with someone, for someone (or something), or even less against someone, but in the One and by the One.

§ The Great Work (the Red Stone according to the outer path or Rainbow Body according to the inner path) is not the Ultimate Realization but the witness of it. The Great Work is only the culmination of the *Recognition* of what has always been there, the Absolute, our real Nature. The Great Work is the *feast*, the *celebration*, of this total *Recognition*.

§ You have no enemy but yourself.
As for your opponents in the game of illusion, choose them carefully, because we always absorb what we fight.
It is an essential aristocratic and heroic principle.

§ It is at the moment when the little game of nothing is established that the Great Game manifests itself.

§ All the noises of the worlds, echoes of the primordial explosion, are nothing compared to the infinite ocean of Silence.

§ Outside of the dimension of being, you will only find personal narrowness.

§ Will is a verticalized desire.

§ Create and uncreate.
Create and uncreate the world. Without destroying it.
Absorb it in the Immutable Center.

§ The center of the manifest must remain empty.
If the ego takes hold of the center, Being cannot unfold.

§ The body is time.
The body is the world.
To free oneself from time is to free oneself from the body.
Immortality is a liberation, a science of the Interval.
The body – time – world is the material on which this secret science operates.

§ Death, an upheaval in representation, a quivering of Consciousness, a nothing in the Real.

§ What imprisons can also liberate.
Some poisons cure the incurable.

§ Liberating yourself, tending towards your Natural State, is revolutionary and ecological.
To liberate oneself from alienation is, simultaneously, to liberate oneself from liberation.

§ You want to kill the father!
It's simpler to grasp that you were never born!

§ The impossible becomes possible through the simple.

§ My being is the being of the gods.
My existence is not that of the gods, but a reflection.

§ Being can overshadow the person and bring them serenity and clear-sightedness. This is the characteristic of gradualist ways.
Subitist ways dissolve the Person.

§ Progressive ways connect while subitist paths unbind.
The former do.
The latter undo.

§ "To be twice born." "To never have been born."
These two expressions evoke two modalities of initiation; two approaches to Awakening.
Gradualist ways evoke the "new birth."
Subitist ways realize the "never born."

§ On the direct ways, the quester encounters three gurus. The first is Silence. The second is Void. The third is the Great Real.

§ The dualist approach encounters the problem of evil, which it cannot resolve. Only nondual experience allows us to traverse this pre-ultimate question.
One who knows how to dwell in nondual consciousness understands "dualistic violence."

§ What relationship does the One have with monstrosity?

Monstrosity is characteristic of the human, precisely distinguishing them from animals which in no case manifest monstrosity.

The One invites us to concentrate, to gather in Being and to renounce the human, which is only a mediocre reduction.

The quantum revolution, still to come, which approaches through discreet and unexpected (sometimes even dissident) paths, partially explains the initiatory Art of the Interval and the Geometry of Absences.

§ So-called awake people, from the mold of the merchant caste, want to make "doing nothing" fashionable. But "to do nothing," you must first know what "to do" means in the intensity of the moment, which is to say, in the perception of the aggregation of all the conditionings and the phenomenal weaving.

It is appropriate to radically distinguish "doing nothing," the prerogative of Being, from idleness, the etymology of which refers to the pretension of having won, a property of the "Person."

§ For many, "doing nothing" is just another way of "doing." Only one who has approached the axis of the Real, caught in the attraction of their own original and ultimate nature, can hear, receive, and know the teaching without teaching, the practice without practice, of "Doing Nothing."

Only Presence really "does."

Without doing anything.

No gesture. No words.

§ Non-doing, "Doing Nothing," is only possible in nondual consciousness. For dual consciousness, there are initiatory "doings." A lot of "doing" is sometimes necessary before being grasped by nondual consciousness.

§ The individual bathes in the Clarity of the Fullness of the Great Nothing, true clear consciousness, whether you practice meditation or not, whether or not you actualize yourself within the Great Real.

Neither object, nor subject, nor mediation. Nothing. Bliss of the Great Nothing. Clarity of the Great Nothing. This is the subitist way.

Nothing to do... since whatever you do, it is only an ephemeral and spontaneous reflection whose nature is Void.

INCOHERIST MANIFESTOS & TREATISES

§ The Word has hypertrophied and decomposed into words due to the accentuated incapacity of the human for Silence.

The "meeting" of two Silences has no need of speech.

The Word was lost as soon as it separated from the Silence that had given birth to it and nourished it with creative power.

§ What is engendered in Silence leads to Silence.

What is engendered in noise leads to noise.

§ The "Posture of Awakening" is not Awakening, but it opposes the imposture of the "Person" and leads to the Interval.

Sometimes, the posture is Awakening.

§ The "Person" is our exile.

The "I" is our exile.

The "I" is neither hateful nor lovable.

It is part of the scenery.

It is part of the situation.

Remain still and silent behind the scenery.

Remain still and silent in the face of the situation.

Scenery and situation are empty.

§ The initiate is concerned with the untimely, not with the actuality from which the "Person" emerges. The actuality is only a given within the situation.

§ Let the little I's scatter throughout the scenery. Do not try to maintain the artificial coherence of the "Person."

Remain.

§ In the field of Initiation, pedagogy is always a sign of the crystallization of the process.

A pedagogue is never an awakener.

Each generation brings some brilliant popularizers who comment with talent on the initiatory process, from the moment which follows the Origin to that which precedes the Ultimate. But, because they do not grasp the Interval, incapable of forgetting the self and knowledge, they know nothing of the Origin and the Ultimate, or of the essential.

§ There are symbolic initiations with energetic impact.
This is the nature of most ritual initiations.
There are energetic initiations with essential impact.
Finally, in the Interval are the true initiations, from Being to Being.

§ The Lost Word is Silence.
True Initiation, the most accomplished Transmission, takes place from Being to Being, from Silence to Silence, from Fullness to Fullness.

§ There are two types of rituals:

- The rituals that constitute the sign of an opportunity to bring us closer to our original nature, the Great Real.
- Rituals that celebrate our original nature, that invite it to unfold in this very moment.

§ Ritual is effective when you no longer need ritual.

§ The universal is powerless to deal with the particular, but initiation is, *par excellence*, the path of the particular. It is appropriate, for each initiatory encounter, to create a new world, a new method, a new way… in some manner.

§ Escape into the "local" (which is not the particular) and escape into the universal are two ways of moving away from one's own reality. Initiation questions the place (which is always a place-state), all places, in every place. It points to the empty place. It dissolves the outside as well as the inside, universality as well as localization. There remains Being and non-Being, i.e., the Absolute. The Great Real.

§ There is no initiation without transgression.
The two together can nowadays be a true transgression.

§ I have previously heard of an "initiatory selfishness" that would be necessary for a time. This is absurd, an unacceptable compromise. The initiatory is without ego.
On the other hand, there might be an initiatory insolence, an antidote to the institutional or personal indolence that always threatens the initiatory process until its ultimate outcome.

§ There is no universal truth, but intimacy is universal—not the moist intimacy of the human, but the clear intimacy of being. The intimate is the path that leads to the Real because it emanates from the Real.

§ If you do not pass through the traditions, it is the traditions that pass through you and occupy you like an invader occupies a conquered land.

§ We can only "weigh" a tradition if we have practiced it deeply. Simply showing up is insufficient.

§ If traditions had not clashed, formerly with the "new barbarians," today with modernity or modernities, they would have gradually become mirages without substance.

They would have gradually become diluted in the forms they engender and become frozen into beliefs and truths, instead of keeping to the axial and direct conquest of the Great Real.

Modernity only destroys traditions that are already dead. Living traditions remain elusive.

§ In Initiation, when faced with difficulties, reducing the requirements is always a bad choice.

On the contrary, it is appropriate to elevate again and again, to always go "to a higher meaning."

In peaceful periods, promote the most restrictive practices in order to firmly establish their effects and maintain them during hostile periods.

In hostile periods, don't give up; hold on tight.

Never take a break when you are in trouble or difficulty.

Breaks are effective when tranquility sets in by itself after a period of intense practice.

§ The teacher always seeks to determine whether the seeker is "facing the ritual," "in the ritual," or "traversing the ritual."

"Faced with ritual," the seeker is listener and speculator.

"In the ritual," they are an operator.

"Traversing the ritual," they are. They remain. It remains.

§ One who accesses the Real without intermediary has no use for symbols.

§ What many do not understand is that the symbol is ineffective from form to essence. It operates from essence, accessible through Silence, to form. Hence the symbolic failures...

§ Personal power is a ridiculous illusion in contrast to individual power, the impersonal power of that which is without division and without appearance.

§ All those who maintain personal considerations depart from the Way.
Those who have accomplished individuation also "depart" from the Way. They have become the Way.

§ The Way does not pre-exist at the moment it emerges in the Individual.
For each Individual, a Way.
The Individual is the Way, the Interval towards the Great Real.
The way that comes to you from the outside, from temporality, is not the Way.

§ The absence of a Way is a Way.
The direct, vertical Way.

§ The Universe both expands and contracts. Simultaneously.
Consciousness expands and contracts simultaneously.
Thus, you are both the Center and the peripheries, the Void and the fullness.

§ Subject identified with object.
Subject with attributes.
Subject without attributes.
Nothing.
From dual to nondual,
A path to Awakening.

§ In Presence, it is the celebrated ritual that awakens because there is no longer a subject to awaken. That is the true beauty.

§ Presence brings fluidity.
The fluidity of the currents or the "higher" fluidity of the Intervals.

§ In Japan, the kanji for abundance of Spirit has become the kanji for decorum. This is an important indication.

There is no decorum, no posture in Presence without the Spirit that abounds and floods experience through the Interval opened in the straitjacket of the "Person."

§ The "Master" is the one who embodies the Interval, the Great Nothing, by their absence, not by their "so-called" presence.

§ "I" is an other among others, a creation of the Self, your original nature.
You are neither this "I" nor an other "I," nor even the game of "I."
You are the Self.

§ Born from a spark resulting from the encounter between Nothingness and Spirit, the "I," a simple product of consciousness installed in temporality, passes itself off as Consciousness.

"I" is Shimga, a carnival character, made-up, pretentious, and ridiculous.

§ To be initiated is to live as an initiate, to live in freedom.

The one who lives as an initiate is initiated, not the one who collects initiatory grades and participates in rituals without grasping either the essence or the beauty.

§ Free beings, beings in Awakening, have sometimes wanted to leave traces of it in temporality. They spoke of wisdoms.

Persons, who were overcome by the intuition of Awakening but who did not know how to realize it and thus remained attached to the dualistic experience, have carefully built the prisons that we call religions.

§ Religions and initiatory orders are sources of adhesions. They are but obstacles to Awakening.

Any way that presents a regulation, that promotes or defends a code, is false.

Most initiatory or spiritual schools or orders, in the West as in the East, only offer personal development at best.

And don't think this is better than nothing! The real ways require precisely a science of Nothing, an art and a wisdom of the Great Nothing.

To access the Great Real, one must traverse the salty sea of esotericisms.

§ The best thing that could happen for an initiatory order is for it to come from nowhere, from the Void. Unfortunately, this is never the case: an initiatory order is always born from conceptions, beliefs, or even human procrastination.
The initiatory ways, and not the initiatory orders, are born from the Great Nothing.

§ No need to find God.
No need to become God.
Here and now,
You are the Absolute.

§ The reintegration of the Self into the Absolute is the recognition of the Self as the Absolute.

§ Always act unreservedly to bring the Ultimate Healing. By Healing, I do not mean the care given to the sick, but the Great Reconciliation which is born from the Recognition of one's own Absoluteness.

§ There is no difference between you and Awakening, but you persist in believing otherwise.
If I were in your place, I would do exactly the same actions, I would experience the same emotions, I would be traversed by the same thoughts, I would have the same "point of view." But precisely, or better, skillfully, I am not in your place. I am not any place.
Awakening and dreaming are identical. The dreamer ignores it. The awakened one knows it.

§ In your quest, the moment will come when you can let your thoughts wander. This will eventually become unimportant, but only eventually.

§ Perform a single gesture, whatever it may be, fully, totally, absolutely, in nondual consciousness, and awakening is immediate.

§ The Real offers only the indescribable and incredible Joy of the Void within which Absolute Freedom reigns.
But few accept this gift.
Even fewer people support it.

§ Completion resides entirely in incompletion.

§ Freed from fascinated adherence to effect,
Freed from the frantic quest for the cause.
I am, Master of the Interval, Absolute Freedom.

§ Nothing is perfect.

Axis

We must grasp within ourselves the two primordial entities, masculine and feminine, and free them from all adhesion so that they can unite absolutely, in freedom.

This is the tradition and practice of the *Double A*.

§ If humans do not make their sexuality an initiatory art, a celebration of the beauty of Awakening, nothing distinguishes them from animals other than their almost infinite propensity towards horror, mediocrity, and vulgarity.

Their programmed demise is then only a welcome formality.

§ It all comes down to a single practice. If the practitioner does not perceive the different forms and different exercises as the single practice of the play of energy and consciousness, they can only get lost in the dualistic meanderings of the representation and depart from the nondual experience of the Great Real, the experience of Emptiness that is registered as Imperience.

§ In the posture of Presence, there is generally a defect that brings together all the conditioned disharmonies. Identifying this defect and correcting it is to suddenly and immediately free yourself from all limits.

This is a very important technical point that concerns true practitioners, not auditors.

§ The power of fasting is considerable. It is the most accomplished magical act.

§ The meditation on boredom is the meditation of the approaching times.

Plunge your "Person" into boredom, immerse it, bathe it, invite it to fully enjoy this moment where body and soul strangely combine and discover, at the very heart of boredom, a powerful Interval, irresistible access to the Great Nothing.

§ Use hieronyms to become anonymous.

Know how to use multiple masks to better unmask yourself and free the headless one.

§ I am. I am the sole author, actor, spectator, director, and producer of my own spectacle. This is what defines Shiva, the Absolute, the one who binds himself to the form he creates or unbinds from it at Will. Absolute Will is born from absolute Freedom. This Freedom is only absolute by losing itself, forgetting itself, denying itself in illusion, magic, and duality, to free itself again and again. It is the dancing and quivering Goddess through whom Shiva goes beyond Shiva.

Duality is not opposed to the nondual. Duality is an aspect of the nondual.

Appearance, illusion, and magic are not opposed to the Absolute; they are reflections of the Absolute.

I am Shiva and ParamaShiva.

§ Three rites are fundamental: fasting, conscious breathing, and taking Soma animated by the fire of Pneuma in the Interval.

Fasting is a rehearsal of "dying."

Conscious breathing establishes the fact that at this very moment I am being born, dying, and being reborn.

The taking of Soma reveals our Immortality. Soma does not confer Immortality, it reveals it.

§ The movement of the breath is not external/internal but totally "external." The Interval is "internal."

During death, or so-called death, if there is identification with the breath, Consciousness is at the heart of Shakti and the cycle of dualistic manifestations.

If there is a dive into the Interval, Consciousness is Shiva. The Absolute remains. Emptiness and Fullness. Shakti withdraws into the heart of Shiva.

Breath, thought, and the worlds are identical.

The Interval, the Void, and the Real are identical.

In the Interval, consciousness, in bliss, participates in the sexuality of Shiva and Shakti.

§ Shiva "takes care" of nothing.
Shiva considers only the Great Nothing.
Shakti "takes care" of Everything.

§ Be the Nectar offered by Shakti to Shiva.

§ Let men kneel at the feet of women, lovers, wives, sisters, mothers, passing women... They are the goddesses to be celebrated in Joy, Gentleness, and Light. Hear the quivering of the Goddess.

On the Way, the woman is the *Ereignis*,* the marvel, and it is up to the man to reveal his unearthly nature to her.

§ The human being is born into the worlds of form through the vector of an erection. They emerge definitively through another erection, inverted, a column of Void.

The human being enters into incarnation through the woman's sex, as the fruit of desire. They escape incarnation through the same door, according to a desire verticalized in Will.

It is necessary to note that the man and the woman do not have the same position facing this door. The woman knows from the outset that she is her own door while the man looks for this door outside. It is in a state of headlessness that he must appear facing the door so that the woman can open it for him.

This quest for the Interval will constitute the Interval itself.

§ In the Interval, the being knows neither doubt nor hesitation, it abandons external codes and rites, necessarily dualistic, because everything is rite and the practice is spontaneous; the practice becomes "non-practice." Being the Absolute, it is free, and free to release into the relative and ephemeral. Bliss remains through Grace. The space of consciousness is filled by the unfolding of essences, which arises from the satisfaction of the goddesses. Master Utpaladeva said: "Hail to you Lord, you the tracker, essence of 'the right-hand path,' defender of 'the left-hand path,' you who practices all practices and who practices none."

§ Three Immortals await the disciple with three movements of breath. Three ways to know the Absolute. Three ways for the Absolute to know itself. The Black Immortal, dual. The Red Immortal, dual within the One. The White Immortal, nondual.

The Modality of substance for the Black Immortal.

The Modality of energy (or Fire) for the Red Immortal.

The Modality of essence for the White Immortal.

---

* Ger.: *Ereignis*—The actualization "here and now" of the "already and not yet," or the grasp of the interval within consciousness that gives access to the Great Interval.

§ The Great Work:
   The Work of the women
   The Work of the Woman
   The Work of the Goddess.

§ The Great Work:
   The ascesis of the Light in the Dark
   The ascesis of the White Light
   The advent of the Blue Light.

§ It is in the Silence of Beingness that you will learn the language of silences and, first of all, that of the "initial silence": the inaudible vowels come to fertilize and animate the silent consonants in order to open the door to the white intervals.

As there is music of sounds, there is music of silences.

As there is a mathematics of sounds, there is a mathematics of silences.

As there are sonic geometries, there is a geometry of intervals, the "wise geometry."

§ Silence has the last word.

Silence is the last word as it is the first word, the word before the A.

The Silence of Silence is "the word that was never spoken in the Beingness that was never begotten."

§ Love, Freedom, and Will, in that order. Never Will first, the source of inversion.

Love first or Freedom first. Two nondualistic styles.

§ Most mantras have a healing function.

Some, the root mantras, or "cutting mantras," create the Interval.

§ The root mantra, the Primordial Wellspring, cuts the universe in two and reveals the Interval, access to the Great Real.

The repeated mantra fixes consciousness in the Interval.

§ The tradition of whispered rituals and practices, notably mantras, has a dual origin.

The dark periods, hostile towards traditions and ways of awakening, have led instructors to work discreetly, in a whisper.

From the perspective of the work, the reason is quite different. Snakes and Dragons flee the clamors and noise but run to the whispers and light strokes, like that of silk, which serve as a setting for the root sounds.

Whoever wants to work with the Dragons must become a "whisperer" and a "stroker."

§ The Red and the White do not mix to make pink.
The Red encloses the White so that the latter generates the Blue Pearl.
The White encloses the Red so that the latter nourishes the Blue Pearl.
This is the path of Ardhanarishvara.

§ "I am," a Naga King hidden in order to let his golden wings grow, to deploy them when the Sky is immaculate.
The Red Lightning of Nag Devi confers immortality immediately to those who come to it in a state of headlessness when the Moon is red.

§ Only the one who is Shiva, the Absolute, also King of the Nagas, can embrace Nag Devi.

§ The Goddess Nag Devi teaches nine conscious breaths. These are, in no particular order:
Naked conscious breathing,
Conscious breathing in the Letter A,
Conscious breathing in the Double Letter A,
Conscious breathing in the Dance of the Serpent,
Conscious breathing through the unpronounceable sound "K,"
Conscious breathing in the Letter A and the Dance of the Serpent,
Conscious breathing in the Double Letter A and the Dance of the Serpent,
Conscious breathing in the Letter A and through the unpronounceable sound "K,"
Conscious breathing in the Double Letter A and through the unpronounceable sound "K,"
Conscious breathing in the Dance of the Serpent and through the unpronounceable sound "K,"
Conscious breathing in the Letter A, the Dance of the Serpent, and through the unpronounceable sound "K,"
Conscious breathing in the Double Letter A, the Dance of the Serpent, and through the unpronounceable sound "K,"
Unborn conscious breathing.

§ The Goddess Nag Devi also transmitted the three Somas, either in this order: Mineral Soma, Vegetable Soma, and Heroic Soma (also called Soma of the Immortals); or in this order: Vegetable Soma, Mineral Soma, and Heroic Soma (also called Soma of the Immortals). The Mineral Soma is not then the same.

The materials and modalities vary, according to a harmonic range and a geometry of Intervals which know neither beginning nor end but which arise from the Gift of the Goddess and the Grace of the Absolute.

§ With the Golden Water, draw the path of the Ring and animate it with the Fire of Pneuma. Do the same with the two Wings.

In the body of Nagardhanarishvara, a thousand and eight calligraphers of the Interval contemplate the naked bodies of the thousand and eight goddesses. They paint, each in a different place on the body, the Letter A. Five hundred and four red letters and five hundred and four white letters. Each red letter mirrors a white letter.

§

White A	Awakening
Red A	Fire
Blue A	Balance
Green A	Regeneration
Orange-yellow A	Radiance
Violet A	Magical and poetic power

§ Khûn, the mutable white Dragon, capable of all metamorphoses. The perfect vehicle for the banished Immortals.

§ You are not taking the Path of Serpents.

You are the Path of Serpents.

These are the Serpents who take you for their ascension.

This is how they "give" you primary immortality.

§ No Awakening without the Dragon.

The Dragon only reveals his secret in the Covenant and this is only possible through the mediation of the Goddess.

No Awakening without union with the Goddess.

§ When the Dragon is doubly rectified and connects Heaven to Earth and Earth to Heaven within the Heart, the Goddess releases the precious Water into the cavern On-High. Thus she feeds the Immortal.

§ The Dragon, the primordial Serpent, the "mold" of all forms, is none other than the first manifestation of the Self. It is the Real.

§ Primary immortality is not essential to achieve the Great Immortality, but for many, it is a necessary key without which they cannot escape the labyrinth.

§ Before taking the vegetable Soma, it is appropriate to unite, at the Summer Solstice, with a goddess or a dryad inhabiting a birch tree, under the eye and during the cry of the Eagle. You must also obtain the blessing of five horses.

This also applies, as a twilight metaphor, to the more subtle Somas.

§ Ascesis of the 108:
Fast for 108 hours.
Practice of the 108 names of Shiva.
72 hours of giving.
36 hours of receiving.
3 doses of Soma.
Rudraksha beads.

§ The transmission of Black Snow confers access to the wisdom of the Bodies or Energy Vessels.

§ The ecstasy of Beingness is quivering, undulation, serpentine movement, breath.
Contemplation of the Earth.

The ecstasy of Absoluteness is immobility, intensity, absence of breath, absence without retention.
Contemplation of Heaven.

The mantras and the root sounds must be emitted in the ecstasy of Beingness.

The Power of Silence must be activated in the ecstasy of Absoluteness.

§ The ecstasy of Beingness illuminates the worlds.

The ecstasy of Absoluteness dissolves the worlds.

The Great Nothing remains, the fullness of the Great Nothing.

The two ecstasies indicate the axis of the two foci of an elliptic, an invisible and unknowable center.

§ The hearts of the thousand and eight goddesses ignite in the body of Shiva.

Shambu is nothing more than Happiness, Immensity, quivering, indescribable Joy, and nevertheless Immutable Stillness.

§ Inhale: instasy. The Point of Void.

Exhale: ecstasy. The Peripheries of the Worlds.

§ The ultimate Soma is the Blue Pearl.

§ When Soma is external, the taking of Soma and its animation by Pneuma triggers the arrival of Amrita, the Nectar of Immortality, which is internal.

In the Real, Soma is like the "memory" of the original Amrita.

§ On a daily basis, inscribe everything in the Letter A and thus in the Breath. First in the Breath as substance, then in the Breath as serpentine energy, finally in the Breath as Essence.

§ There are three different Breaths and therefore three different Salivas for the three Seeds of Eternity.

§ The Absolute Breath appears when breathing has ceased in the Interval between the exhalation and the inhalation.

§ When the three Seeds of Eternity are fully blossomed, the highest one spills over to illuminate and nourish the other two.

Then the Work is accomplished.

Then the final circle is closed.

§ You are the Banished Immortals.

At "twenty-eight years old" comes the new age, the Time of the Banished.

Mercury and Sulfur come from Heaven Below. They unite with the Salt of Heaven Above.

The Golden Salt of the Heaven Below is used to set.

At "forty-nine years old" comes the final age, the Time of the Immortals.

Step by step, the Mercury and Sulfur from Heaven Below are replaced by the Salt of Heaven Above, which has become both Sulfur and Mercury.

The Blue Pearl then comes. It both seals and liberates.

§ The Banished Immortals know the magnificent technical necessity (the inevitability) of being forgotten.

§ Any substance can be a Salt, or a Sulfur, or a Mercury for the body, both vessel and raw material, but only in a certain "state" that is a "non-state" and in a certain "time" that is a "non-time."

The modality of substances is reserved for Masters of the Art.

Sword, Brush, and Garden

WHAT DOES THE SWORD CUT?

"You have conquered!"
  "Stupidity! This corpse is the winner!"
  "But they are dead! You killed them!"
  "When they died, they were already dead, without thoughts. Fullness and emptiness. They had already experienced death. So they remain. While I, at the moment of killing them (what pretension!), I was just me. I was defeated by a Free Being. Impeccability conquers and convinces the conditioned even in death, fully welcomed."

The Sword severs time instead of measuring it.
  Cut first. Cut after. Untimely moment.

The Sword cuts the world, space, in two.
  Opening of the interval of the Real.

The Sword cuts the ego.
  It separates Being from Knowledge.
  Being knows as soon as it is known and recognized.

The Sword cuts the sacred mountain.
  Out of one mountain, it makes two columns.
  Apparently.
  Out of a mountain, it makes a valley, a passage.
  In reality.

The Sword is the extension not of the hand but of the Spirit.
  Not of thought but of Silence.

The handle is the Spirit, the *tsuba* is the Presence, and the blade is the child of Fire and Water, of Shiva and Shakti, of Absoluteness and Beingness.

WHAT DOES THE BRUSH CALLIGRAPH?

"What does the brush calligraph?"

"I'm not awake?"

"Who are you to make such a statement?"

"?!"

"Only the Self can distinguish the awakened from the unawakened. And the Self is Awakening. Who holds the brush?"

Learn to calligraph your life like the poet calligraphs the space of the page: they highlight the gaps. They highlight the absence.

The practice of calligraphy is based on three pillars:
- the integration of codes
- presence to oneself
- the spontaneous gesture.

Each style has a code, or several, that the practitioner must methodically integrate through systematic exercises.

It is through presence to oneself that the practitioner can contact their own nature, original and ultimate, in which all work will have its source.

In presence, the gesture is spontaneous, a pure outburst of Being. But it is because technique has passed below the threshold of consciousness that we can combine spontaneity and the perfection of the gesture.

Beauty is born from the encounter, in the moment, of the fruit of the tireless repetition of the same gestures in temporality and spatiality, and of Being which then becomes ink for the brush.

Calligraphy of Heaven with Earth.

Calligraphy of Earth with Heaven.

Empty, Full.

WHAT DOES THE GARDEN REVEAL?

"Where is the Garden of the Master of Flowers?"

"Yes, where?"

"I do not see it!"

"It's because you don't know how to 'See'!"

"No, truly, there is no garden."

"Close your eyes! Take it in!"

The old master slipped a red pearl under the disciple's tongue and placed his left hand on his head.

"And now?"

"I see a wonderful Garden."

"And in the center of the garden?"

"A fire, a fire that consumes all my thoughts…"

"And?"

"And nothing…"

The divine smile is then written on the face of the disciple. The old master withdrew his hand and continued on his way.

May your garden be extraordinarily ordinary.

Everything is the Absolute.

Don't forget that the tree, moreso than humans, connects Heaven and Earth. The body of Awakening is an infinite tree structure that irrigates the Totality of the Fire of the Spirit.

The gardener must pay particular attention to the edges. An edge must never become a border but indicate an interval, tracing the invisible and elusive contours of a place-state in which Being contemplates itself.

Some develop sophisticated rituals.

Others recite mantras by the millions.

The Tantrikas practice divine unions.

All this is valid if it is born from Emptiness, from abandonment and spontaneity.

Your garden must deploy its essences from the Heart, the Void, and its Fullness, then, structured or chaotic, geometric or wild, it will manifest the Great Harmony and purify the mind of the passerby.

The Master of Flowers veils or reveals the Essence of all things in the most banal plant, the most common flower. He knows that a unique sap nourishes the green mantle of nature.

In the garden of the Void, the fragmentation of the "Person" fades and gives way to the Great Real.

Neither garden nor gardener. Being.

Neither known nor knower. The Self.

Neither Earth nor Sky. The Free Spirit.

Nine Questions Asked of the Mad Monk

You never talk about karma. Why?

Karma is inevitably misunderstood by a conditioned spirit. And a free spirit is not concerned. So what's the use? This multiprocess, this inextricable tangle of causalities that weave the illusion, does not function according to a system of compensation and reciprocity, but according to a game of mirrors, the game of total conditionality. Karma is only the gross material of "Seeing," "Hearing," "Feeling," "Understanding," and "Knowing," until it is the Real. Its nature is the antithesis of what the human concept of "justice" encompasses, contrary to what many believe and even teach. It does not present itself as a scale that always aims for balance but as an ocean of energy in motion intended to develop your "skill."

To "see" karma is to see the totality of temporalities. Fundamentally, essentially, nothing has happened, nothing is happening, and nothing will happen.

You are, and not even that.

What use does incoherism make of occult human constitutions? Is there an incoherist occult constitution of the human being?

There is only one body—the absolute body is the Great Real. Occult constitutions are mental constructions which serve to put into words and meaning the differentiated states generated by practice. There are not three bodies, four bodies, seven or nine bodies, as traditions might affirm. Each tradition highlights an occult constitution of man, generally harmonized with a cosmogony, to support the practice.

We sometimes speak of an occult constitution. It is always for a given individual, in a given context, for a specific purpose. The model is abandoned as soon as the realization is obtained. Fixing a model into dogma is always a personal temptation that harms individuation.

Thus we sometimes speak of the explicit body, the implicit body, the fire-consciousness body, and the absolute body.

The explicit body is the perceived body, which extends from the senses to thought. The explicit body is the explicit world, since we create the world.

The implicit body is the double negative of the explicit body. It is the "hollow" of the explicit body. The implicit body is the body of all potentialities of which the explicit body is only a precise formal manifestation among an infinity of possibilities.

The fire-consciousness body is the energy body that generates forms and reduces them in the interval with each breath. This body therefore traverses the implicit body as well as the explicit body which it extends and retracts. It partly corresponds to the body of glory or the rainbow body of certain Western or Eastern traditions. In it, through it, we have life, movement, and being. In it, through it, and therefore in us and by us, all species, all entities, and even the gods, have life, movement, and being.

The absolute body is the sole body, the unique body whose projection causes us to emanate an infinity of bodies. Depending on the "stop" of consciousness, the practitioner will thus perceive this "slice," rather than another, of this absolute body. The absolute body is the Self, the Great Real, the Great Nothing.

The absolute body presents a core that we sometimes call the "Heart of Obsidian," a core of perfect stillness, a core of void that exhibits total density. Technically, this core corresponds to the Interval. It is always accessible.

This occult constitution of the human being, which can be read in three, four, or five bodies, depending on the interpretation, is still only a model intended to support practice, but in no case does it correspond to a reality, even a temporary one. For the person, the body remains the body as conceived. For the individual, the body is perceived. It is the round of the worlds and the ten thousand beings.

Can you describe this according to another model?

Sure. The "person," the mind, the "I," is an aggregate of recollections, memories, and automatic conditionings whose general framework is Time, from which several subjective times are derived. The "person" only exists through the temporal vector. Time unfolds through the four bodies. It is therefore itself like a material or a constant aspect of matter.

The mind is the master of simulacra. Prayer, God, angels, and demons participate in the illusion, not only as concepts but also as experiences, because experience only seeks to verify and embody concept.

Ignorance, which is to say, the tangle of beliefs, persists by trafficking with representations and also identifications with the body-world. This is why we must some day abandon all cults, sacred or profane, to truly undertake a way of awakening. True knowledge liberates.

The causal body is empty. It is the body of forgetting the "person." The consciousness in the background of thoughts, Consciousness-Silence, can be called God. It is because I exist that the world appears; without me there is nothing. "I am" has emerged from Self, prior to all bodies. It is the Consciousness of Being, the Beingness on which are superimposed the different bodies that are but veils. However, Beingness is not the Great Real, the ultimate reality.

"I am the body, the body-world" is the consciousness of the "person."

The four bodies are: the gross body of form; the subtle body, which feeds on the perpetual recycling of forms; the causal body, body of silence and forgetting; and the body of formlessness, and therefore of the destruction of forms, the supra-causal body, the body of knowledge. Beyond lies the Great Real.

Is there an incoherist "angel"?

What humans experience as "angels," "daimons," "spirits" or other entities is the animation of the living, more precisely the serpentine breaths that animate the life of form, coming from the Great Breath.

The person always gives form to the experience of Self. The experience of Christ, Buddha, Osiris, Apollo, or Shiva is always, originally and ultimately, the experience of Self. According to an analogous process, the person dresses the experience of the breaths of life with forms originating from their own conditioned culture. The experience of angels, daimons, or spirits is always the experience of breaths passed through the perceptual and conceptual bias of the person.

Every living being is animated by a specific breath of which it is, in some way, the attribute. You don't have a guardian angel. An "angel" has you! Every human being is animated, or "rectified," by a particular breath, a vehicle of full consciousness, relatively and temporarily stabilized, experienced by some as an angel, daimon, or even a singular spirit.

We could say of the daimon that it is the installation of the breath in the temporality of the peripheries of experience and of the angel that it is the maintenance of the breath in its timeless verticality of imperience. This just a figure of speech.

"Believing" in angels, daimons, or spirits is one way of nurturing them. The result is a double dependence from which we must one day free ourselves in order to rejoin our own nature, the self.

"Seeing" angels, daimons, or spirits as breaths allows for a neutral alliance. The way is narrow for those who want to maintain them without becoming dependent. This is reserved for masters of Silence.

Angels, daimons, and spirits are "substance."

Angels, daimons, and spirits are non-autonomous "energy."

They are never "essence."

The human being is all at the same time: substance, energy, and essence.

The breaths and their angelic, demonic, and spiritual colors are ephemeral and unstable.

Only the Self is Real.

Does the Quest lead to non-involvement in the world? Is the undifferentiated lost in indifference?

The action, shocking for many, at least apparently so, of upholding the value of one of the main secondary alienations (the first alienation being the identification with the "I"), namely, the enslavement of a large part of the human race by a few of its representatives, is never justifiable, even if we must recognize the fundamental action of the Power – Territory – Reproduction triangle.

Everything that denies Freedom is an attack, not on the Spirit (unknowable and therefore unattainable), but on the spirit of the Spirit, in other words, on the verticality of Being.

Hiroshima did not for a second rouse humanity from its torpor and indulgence in self-hallucination.

On the other hand, if China destroyed Tibet amid general indifference, Buddhism will invade the heart of China and create another China.

Let us understand that nothing eventful, nothing external, can introduce or initiate Consciousness into the Real.

Each time the initiatory world conforms to historical events, whatever they may be, it moves away from the royal path of Being, the axis of Tradition, which is a-temporal, a-historical, and a-personal, towards becoming lost in the human peripheries.

Rather, let us lose our indifference in the undifferentiated. In the One.

What is the most direct way?

Science, Art, and Initiation answer the same question:

"Why is there something rather than nothing?" To answer, science probes the "thing," it does not provide proof of its reality or its nature. Art imitates or diverts the "thing," without revealing it, but sometimes giving us an intuition of its nature. Initiation, which is a reversal, experiences the "thing" as Nothing.

The "possessing less," the "doing less," and the "saying less" are the three facets of the triangle of Initiation. Their simultaneity dissolves the "being-given" and "being-conditioned" and allows the splendor of Being to emerge.

Also, the most direct way is the one which, for each of us, leads to the tumble into the Great Real. It does not matter whether this way, always serpentine, is subitist or gradualist. This distinction, which initially invited an immediate axiocracy, was erroneously developed by the dualist vision, which invariably drowns consciousness in temporality.

Temporal and historical filiation is a concern of the ego, always in need of recognition and belonging. It takes on meaning in the construction of a personal legend based on the world of appearances: doing and having. Temporal filiation also flourishes in the religious and military models that remain predominant in initiatory schools, but they are poor vehicles for the ways of awakening.

This Being-bypass must disappear. The natural alignment with Being gives birth to an axiocracy for which time, history, the person, and their "habitus" are only situational data, without essential meaning.

The axiocrat does not fit in any time but traverses them all. Where they are, the immutable Center unfolds, Emptiness and Silence, around which ephemeral phenomena are as if in orbit, an apparent orbit only. In the Real, there is Nothing.

The essential is the natural fruit of the right intention, the right will, and the right realization of the practice. Very little remains necessary in reality. As far as we are concerned, it is the practice, at the silent heart of the universal matrix, of the Letter A and the consonant K, animated by the hiss of the snake and elaborated in its three modalities: substance, energy, and essence. It is the column of Void that connects Earth to Heaven, our original divinity to our ultimate divinity.

What is reality? Do realities exist?

There is and there is not a reality. There are and there are not realities.

If you move the assemblage point of the reality you are experiencing at the moment, you move into another transitory reality that presents a "life" and an "afterlife," a temporality. Whatever the reality, the question of the Great Real arises in the same way.

In this world or in another, in this reality or in another, in this "life" or in this "afterlife," find the Interval to access the Great Real. Where there is an identified form, the Freedom of the Great Nothing is not there.

There may be an "afterlife." This "post-mortem" life depends on the assemblage point of reality in the current life. We must therefore free ourselves from it for the same reasons. It is the same world represented and assembled by the identified consciousness.

"Life," "death," or "afterlife," the realities, are the same dream that the adept must traverse. It's just a breath. In every breath there is an Interval.

We must learn to work with Chaos as with the Interval.

The Chaos of realities, accessible in the Interval, is a tight mesh which allows us, by moving a single element, to modify the entire energy field of a reality.

Magical elegance is only possible through the chaotic plan, which is not a disorganization but a tight arrangement in which the possibilities are infinite and "rub" against each other.

From the Interval, we contemplate weaving, tantra, and quantum entanglement. Synchronicity and simultaneity are optimal. Each element is an echo and mirror of Totality due to the densification of reality. The "butterfly effect" is therefore at its maximum intensity.

In the Great Nothing, all forms are experienced as empty and unnameable, and Life as infinite Thrill and Joy. In the Great Nothing, the beauty of joy and the beauty of sadness are one Beauty.

The final work is unrealizable since it is already accomplished. It requires that everything that is human, everything that has passed through the human, be de-realized and abandoned. Reality facing Reality. The Ultimate Festival.

If Initiation is the Art of Doing Nothing, why these practices, why "do" all these exercises?

In the Natural State, absolute consciousness leads the respiration in Breaths adapted to each situation. Thus, at this very moment, the world-body remains a perfect athanor that spontaneously delivers the precious substances of Absoluteness through the receptacle that is Shakti.

But we are far from the Natural State, consequently, we replace these free movements with constraints intended to animate the alchemical Breaths. These are the practices and exercises. You should know that these practices and exercises are ineffective by themselves. They don't liberate. Their effectiveness is due to the "grace of the Guru," which is to say the Self, the Absolute, or the poised play of consciousness and energy, the union of Shiva and Shakti. An exercise that does not bring us closer to ourselves distances us from the Natural State. The alchemical paths are only accomplished in an axiality of consciousness.

If you think while doing various exercises or various practices, you will never progress. If you recognize in each experience, practice, or exercise the play of free and unidentified consciousness within the forms then you will immediately know that you are the Absolute. This is the eternal exercise, the divine breath, the breath of the Absolute which nevertheless knows no movement.

144

Is liberation manifested in the experience of Emptiness and its Fullness?

We must also traverse this experience in which a trace of dual consciousness remains, freeing ourselves even from liberation. Shiva recognizes himself through Shakti and her multiple appearances. Shakti is the Appearance of appearances, the Appearance of representations, and Shiva is Consciousness, both immanence and transcendence, real and illusion. The Great Real, the Absolute, the Self, is not opposed to illusion. Illusion is a means for the Great Real to know itself. Shiva is at the same time the body-world, the Breath, the creator Word of forms, the Intention of intentions, the Void and its Fullness, Being and Non-Being, the Great Nothing, and the Great Real. All this is Shakti.

"To hear the sweet and joyful laughter of the Immortals and the Gods and Goddesses resounding in infinity, one must be an Immortal or a god oneself."

In the language of birds:

> **INCoHeRiST:** *in Christ,* in the anointing of our own original and ultimate reality.
> **INcoHeRISt:** *in Shri,* in the quivering of the Heart of the Goddess.
> **inCoHeRiST:** *CHeRcher STella.**

---

*   Fr.: *Chercher,* to search. Lat.: *Stella,* star.

THE LOVER OF SHAMBU AND THE FOOL OF SHAKTI

Teachings Whispered by a Muse of Shambu

WHISPERS OF THE TIMELESS

Once, an awakened woman fell from her seat in front of her students and a few masters of wisdom who had come to listen to her teaching, causing general astonishment.

She burst out laughing and, on all fours before her stunned audience, explained that ridicule kills only the ego, the person, but arouses the compassionate laughter of the gods.

Since then, she has been known as *the awakened one who laughs*.

This is the essence of her teaching:

Being human is the height of ridiculousness. Think about it: a god who can barely stand and forgets what they are, believing themself to be a shadow woven of conditioned beliefs. They harangue the gods, their peers, like a common miscreant, forgetting their own divine nature.

Every time you find yourself in a ridiculous situation, it is to remind you of the ridiculousness of the person, of any person, and of the need to escape from the stubborn illusion: "I am a person."

No, you are!

And again: *K*!

The sound *K*, made by clicking the tongue, resounds at the top of the head.

It represents "the word that was never spoken in the Beingness that was never begotten," the source of sources.

This practice of the *K* sound is linked to the secret of making Amrita, the nectar of immortality, in the skull cup.

I am what mortals call an awakened one.
I am not what mortals call an awakened one.
I am.
And I'm not.

There is only one way to be an adult, and that is to really know that we are children.
And to laugh about it...

"I Am" means "I" do NOTHING.
"I" have NOTHING.
NOTHING:
who LAUGHS with the ONE,
who LAUGHS through the ONE,
who laughs in the ONE.
The divONE LAUGHter of the ABSOLUTE.
The adept is the Being who Laughs.
The Eternal Laughter.

Any ridiculous situation reminds us that the Person is nothing but impotence, insignificance, and pretension.

The situation is the way.

The Person is an excrement that takes itself for an entity.

Humanity is a shit.
But a sacred shit whose function is to pose the problem of evil to the ten thousand beings and to introduce understanding.

The human being is a wonderful loving creation, almost a loving machine, but most often in disharmony.

Human being.
   Being is immaculate, indescribable, infinite. Happiness.
   The human is an excrement.
   Place it, right here, where you are, in the Moment, and let it decompose into humus.
   Remain at the heart of your original and ultimate reality.

The Earth does not belong to human beings.
   Humans belong to the Earth.
   Earth belongs to Heaven.

"God," just like "I," "you," "he," or "she," is a personal pronoun.
   It is the person-El pro-name of the Being in the human.
   "God" is the pronoun used by the Person touched by the Beauty of Being.
   ON is, as an echo, the impersonal and indefinite pronoun that expresses the intensity of this experience.
   In ON lies all the depth of the Beingness-Absoluteness couple.

Time is the extension of the moment.

Time, name, human form, movement, and extension are identical.

Tomorrow is completely useless.
   Yesterday is just a false pretext.

The moment is unbearable for the Person.
   This is why it creates time in an attempt to mask it.
   The mask is called "boredom."

The way of boredom is of rare relevance.

When the Person has tasted all forms of boredom, nostalgia, and disillusionment, it renounces itself, through self-effacement.

It ceases all forms of adhesion.

Through exhaustion, it makes room for Being.

Boredom is a possible preparation for the art of "doing Nothing," but it requires a precise technique that combines association, dissociation, and self-remembering.

Be bored and contemplate boredom.

Without contemplation of boredom, it leads to depression, a very powerful form of the Person's negative identification.

Time is always limited.

Being is always the wonder of the moment.

What you regard as extension is not space but time. All perception is an impression of time. If the man, or the woman, in the current of restlessness is devoured by time, on the contrary, the realized being has devoured time and remains beyond all temporality.

The true first initiation, which can be the last, as the subsequent ones are only consequences, is the initiation of the time eaters. It occurs adjacent to the inversion of the candlesticks,* the reversal of consciousness becoming non-identified.

The Person is an accident, a moment of the forces of the periphery furthest from the central axis, furthest from the Land of the Void from which energy springs. By moving away, this energy, born from non-time, is transformed into time and thus constitutes a place for the Person.

The Person can then gradually develop the illusion of duration even though this outpouring and its retraction into the center are immediate. This immediacy is generally only perceived in conditioned humans at the moment of the experience called "death," actually the return or reintegration into the central axis.

---

* See *The Green Face* by Gustav Meyrink.

There is a time, the final time, when the only question, the only wish, the only tension, the only gesture prior to liberation, is death itself. To die before dying or to die while dying is always to live in the final time. The final time which is also the first eternity.

The penultimate question asked, before the final time, is that of the double.
Less than a question, it is an energy problematic.
Resolving it means entering definitively into the nondual experience.

Do not see the "end of times" as a line that suddenly ends, but as an infinity of concentric circles that resolve into a single center, the Instant, the Interval, the Void Point.

The Void returns the Whole to its Nothingness.

Peacefully installed in Silence, a thought emerges naturally. Slice it obliquely to restore Silence until the next irruption of a thought. Slice before and after.
But, to cut the root, or the very principle of thought, it is necessary to cut a thought, just one, any one, longitudinally. Expose its energy without interrupting its movement. Then you will never leave Silence. You will be master of the Interval.

The exit from the Interval, door to the Great Real, towards the world of forms, the explicit world, requires conservation of the greatest fluidity.
Too much density risks causing a collision of the forms.
Fluidity allows it to con-form and then gradually densify.
Return from the Great Real like ghosts!

Initiation to the Real, which is also initiation of the Real and initiation by the Real, concerns the non-localized, the absolute non-place.

While initiation into the pre-Real, into the premonition of the Real, requires a sacred container to implement the Building–Dwelling–Thinking process, an inside and an outside, initiation into the Real is a matter of nonduality.

Neither container nor content.

Neither vase nor nectar.

Con-Fusion without confusion.

Being: That in which I have life, movement, and given being.

Still being is non-being.

Non-being in movement is being.

Living forms are born and die from the dance of being and non-being.

When the dance ceases, the forms retract into the Void of the Heart.

Thus, the ten thousand beings only exist in the dance to disappear into the Void.

Being, the way of the middle, is the ultimate door.

Non-being, the river of the middle, is the ultimate essence.

Of the Great Nothing.

The incoherist warrior is merciless.

Pity is a denial of compassion.

Their fiery heart is filled with infinite and a-personal love for all forms of life.

For them, incoherism is neither a movement nor a school, but an art, an adventure, and a posture. Art of Being, initiatory adventure, posture of the ONEdifferentiated.

The poetry of the Real is absolutely implacable.

Just like the Universe.

What is magically right can be alchemically wrong, and vice versa.

Only the Poet, initiated into the heart of the Real, knows how to free himself from the law of correspondences, a law that applies to the world of forms. All that is Above is not always like that which is below. All that is formally above is like that which is formally below.

Learn to distinguish form and essence.

What, in the Real, is the birth within the representation, within the form, of another form that will add movement to movement, from life to life?

If you are identified with the physical form of the body, echoing the human mold, the coil rises from the base of the spine toward the top of the head.

If your body is the universe, the coil rises everywhere, like a constellation of outpourings.

Do not adhere to any traditional form.

An adhesion quickly becomes a limiting adherence.

Traverse the form with respect to reach the center—silent, empty, and unchanging.

Essence is not the heart of the form.

Essence encompasses the form.

Do not confuse the impulse point of form with essence.

On the way, talking about one's Person is always cheating—this is always a manner of letting oneself go.

"Seeing" the Person leave in tatters, as "the flesh leaves the bones," announces the imperial emergence of Being in the field, and in the song, of consciousness.

No waiting.

No need.

Awakening to and in THIS.

The energy of the form is limited.

The energy of the Interval is unlimited.

The incised inscription is always more magically powerful than the embossed figure.

Absence is greater than presence.

The empty greater than the full.

The content greater than the container.

Many people confuse one with the other and cannot "see" absence, emptiness, or container.

You only question the shapes.

Nothing but the Interval should be questioned.

It alone delivers the Real.

Being does not admit of any interpretation.

To claim to interpret Being is to establish noise in essential Silence; to induce dissonance in the harmony of the music of the Spheres; disharmony in the mathematics of forms.

The impossible is not opposed to the possible.

The possible is only the fluctuating, random part of the impossible.

Of the ONE-possible.

WHISPERS OF THE INTANGIBLE

I do not have the truth.
   Silence holds me.
   I do not claim the truth.
   I am the cry of the Void.
   I do not fight for the truth.
   I am the witness of the Spirit who cuts the Universe in two.

The maturity necessary for the quest is not that which comes from "life experience." That is only useful to the Person in the field of the Explicit. The experience required for the quest is born from Silence. It is not the result of the conscious and unconscious operations of the intellect but of the engendering of Sophia by the body of fire that bathes, peacefully, in milky Silence.

The only object of study: Silence.
   The only practice: Emptiness.

Will is necessary to create the world of forms.
   Non-Will is the key to the field and song of essences.

If transmission exists (which implies existence and relativity), we live in each other and through each other. But this remains a dualistic conception, or perception, that dissolves in the oneness of Being.
   There is only real transmission when Being-in-Itself reveals itself in the Person without revealing itself to them. If Being reveals itself to the Person, this revelation erases the Person, which is why the Person builds so many defense mechanisms against the outpouring of Being. It is strained in a permanent effort against the intrusion of the Real into the field of consciousness.

The Witness itself will have to disappear because it is an artifice of the Person constructed to facilitate the posture of awakening, an artifice which itself, ultimately, becomes an obstacle to awakening.

What determines the emergence of the way in the field of experience is much less the "authenticity" of the traditional current and its temporal and historical "filiation" than the authenticity of the seeker and their ability to affiliate with the Real.

What we conquer is an evaporation.
　The evaporation of forms superimposed upon the Being of the Real.
　Conquering is always an undressing, a stripping away.

Art, apart from the Quest of the Real, is utilitarian.
　Spectacular.
　Apart from the Spirit.

The true symbolism is nature itself.
　The true symbolism is literature, born from the meeting of humans and nature.
　As for the supernatural, no symbolism gives access to it or accounts for it.

The function of art is to give the premonition of the Great Real.
　The function of initiation is to allow the realization of this premonition.

The function of play-acting in the rites must be seized so that the rite becomes operative. When imitation becomes invention, the operator goes from expectation to presence, from the scenic and the spectacular to the magical and poetic celebration of the Real.
　Spirituality is a play-acting. It allows the recipient to develop a model of the world that gives meaning to the meaningless and supports the unsupportable, the conditional. Its function is therefore therapeutic and in no way initiatory.

Some adepts teach as if it were possible to reconcile oneself with the world before freeing oneself from it or in order to free oneself from it. They therefore propose progressive paths.

It is only possible to reconcile oneself with the world and the worlds by radically freeing oneself from them. Because the link requires both. Once the link is cut, the One is obvious.

Only the direct ways give access to the Real.

Every way is direct.

In the same way that we believe we think about language while it is language that thinks about us, we claim to operate in magic, theurgy, and alchemy while it is Al-chemy, the chemistry of the gods and goddesses, that populates us and operates in us.

Decadence begins with the appointment or authoritarian establishment of a leader.

The solar authority requires neither sign nor un-sign.

It does not follow the doing but is conjoined with the un-doing.

The natural authority of Being is radiant and discreet, fluid and elegant.

There are Gardens of the Spirit.

In each Garden, we meet gardeners and passers-by, muses and poets.

Any gardener can become a passer-by.

Every passer-by is a gardener.

Every muse is a poet.

Every poet can be a muse.

The poem born from Silence has the force of law, not human law but celestial law. It marks the relative worlds for the quester.

Only a few people per generation approach the substance, and not the form, of literature.

Likewise, there are, per generation, only a few beings who know how to deal with the essence and not the form of Initiation.

On the Real Way, the question is not so much to know which great elders you are the repository of, but to manifest, here and now, how much you are the repository of Being.

Abhinavagupta, Nanquan, Christ, Buddha, Pythagoras, Zoroaster, Lao Tzu, Nagarjuna, Kukai... Names for the sons of the Real, for those who have let the Real self-generate within them.

As a matter of technique, in the bath of the world,
Open the heart but close the heart of the heart.

It is often affirmed that the Word creates as it uncreates.
It creates Silence and Beingness to generate the forms and the many.

"There is no age for awakening."
Comment and don't be stupid.

The banished immortal is free from their origins and conditions, liberated in a blameworthy and neglectful world.
It is by letting it go, letting it be, and letting it happen that humans turn their backs on Being and the Real, weaving "the person" so as not to glimpse the light of Absoluteness, nor bathe in the fullness of Beingness.

The liberated transforms whatever into awakening while the human being carried away by the stream makes whatever of their life.

Long live confusion!
Without confusion, Being would have no opportunity to interfere in consciousness, to break the shackles of the Person, that construct of illusory certainties.
Love confusion, observe it, and you will discover in its folds a subtle movement of liberation.

When we speak of a nondual experience, we can mislead our listener. Indeed, due to the very structure of language, the one who says experience implies the presence of an experiencer. However, nonduality is an experience without an experiencer or an experiencer without experience. Experience and experiencer are one. The experience is the experiencer. The operation is the operator. Subject and object are one. Neither object nor subject. The Great Nothing in all its magnificence.

InKoherism is the path of the chameleon.
It is also the way of the wolf.

Is it heightened consciousness that makes the operation take place or the operation that heightens consciousness?
Isn't it rather a strange conjunction, a game of mirrors?

Our worst enemy always "appears" within ourselves.
As unbearable as this idea is to the Person, we participate in the same theophany as our enemies.
Move from appearance to respect.

The mountains are sinking.
The plateaus remain.
The valleys rise.
Follow the Valley of the Great Nothing.

Include initiatory "accidents" in the work.
There exists an initiatory "risk," it is at the service of the Real Way.

The Way is symbol, gesture, sound, perfume, and matter interacting in an invisible process, installed in immediacy, a process that is a burst of energy, tangibly perceptible.

Awakening does not solve any human problems or any formal difficulty: it nullifies them. At the heart of the Real, there is no form, no humanity, and no limit.

If the Real is, then the illusion is a part of the Real.
   Grasping this part to return to Totality or grasping this part in order to experience absolute absence are but one path.
   If nature exists, artifice is a part of nature.
   If the Real is not, then the illusion is the Real. If the Real is not...

Close your eyes, and you are.
   Open your eyes, and you still are.

Despise people if you want, but love humanity.
   Reject conditioning, respect nature.

Everything is awakening.
   Even sleep.
   For the one who knows how to Really sleep.
   Only the "twice born" can Really sleep, nestled by Being.

Forgiveness implies something to give.
   To give, one must possess.
   To possess, one must do and have.
   The "twice born" knows neither offense nor forgiveness.

Always be nowhere else, assembled in the unchanging Center.

We all die eventually. Immortals and gods too.
   Some, the most numerous, will be devoured by death.
   Some will embrace death to be eternally.
   Children of the Real.

Banality and absurdity are two doors to the Real.
   Or a single door pushed by two different consciousnesses.

WHISPERS OF THE UNCERTAIN

Do not confuse the footprint and the step.
   Do not confuse the step and the dancer.
   Do not confuse the dancer and the breath of life.
   Do not confuse breath and being.
   Remember that being is in the footprint.

No art, even an initiatory one, and *a fortiori* no science, can establish itself permanently in *Freedom*.
   The sciences would immediately lose their foundations and consistency.
   The arts can only penetrate there through brief incursions to collect a flavor, a perfume, or an echo.
   The land of *Freedom* is offered to those who come in total nakedness, in abandonment, to those who present themselves without shadow, without mask, absolutely alone, without "Person."

In initiation, the human being is fully subject to their quest.
   Then, subject and object merge.
   The quester disappears. The quest fades.
   There is nothing left but an empty place, occupied by Being after having been conquered and abandoned by the subject.
   But conquest always precedes abandonment.
   Conquest by the subject. "I am."
   Abandonment by the Subject. "ON."*
   There is no abandonment without conquest.

---

*   The absolute indefinite, the impenetrable.

The Self, as a subject, does not tolerate any attributes.
 To give an attribute to the subject is to reduce it to the state of an object.
 Life is one.
 Life is movement.
 Every form is the totality of Life.
 To consider a form as separate from the Totality is to make it a dead object.
 It is also petrifying, killing the energy of this form in you.

Form calls for meaning and makes meaning.
 Energy is its own meaning.
 Essence is meaning.

"To see" is to be transparent, limpid.
 To look is to reflect opacity.
 Thus, concentration is the densification at a point on the periphery of the worlds while attention is the total availability to what is there.

The only true link between two forms is the interval which, always, even if the distance between these two forms is zero, seems to separate them.
 This nothing which, in reality, melts them into Totality.

The influence of a school of wisdom is proportional to its distance and detachment from any form of temporal power.

Because the Person is incapable of alliance, both in the field of the circle and on the axis of the Real, we are witnessing a hypertrophy of filiation that replaces the triple artifice of history, the "I," and causality.

An initiatory order, a school of wisdom, or a tradition, will always be a pretext.
 Pre-text to a text that the quester themself traces on the pages of heightened consciousness with the intangible pen of the Spirit dipped in the invisible ink of Beingness.
 The page remains immaculate.

Many spiritual or initiatory schools are factories of idiots, but we might hope that they form *Free Idiots*, beings touched by the *thyrsus*, without reason, fools of Being.

The discovery of an Arcanum, in Self and by Self, is a true transmission which presupposes a transgression of the Person, sometimes in its two different (but nevertheless complementary) senses.

Just as knowledge is the world itself, understanding is Being in itself.

If religion is the response of the human to their solitude, initiation is the response of the human to the multitude.

Stop fragmenting.
  No longer speak of "species" or "kingdom," but rather of "form."
  The forms are collections of words.
  Words are concepts.
  All forms are equal.
  All are of the nature of Void.

It is impossible for the Person to inhibit the comparison processes that structure memory.
  Until you perceive the essence of a form, the Person compares.
  "You," the identified and conditioned individual consciousness, compares.
  The essence is both one and multiple but its uniqueness is so affirmed that nothing can veil it.
  If you contemplate the essence of a rose, of a lotus, or of an orchid, you contemplate the essence of all roses, of all lotuses, of all orchids, the essence of all flowers, of the original and archetypal Flower, of Absolute Femininity, of Beingness and, finally, of Absoluteness.

There is a phenomenon of apoptosis in the Person.

It arises from an intra-psychic conflict. The Person wants to occupy all the space but knows perfectly well that it has no legitimacy for such an occupation.

Illegitimate occupation and identity theft.

Hence its constant restlessness.

This poison of the Person is a powerful ally of the Being.

Learn to control it.

The Person is like a snake that bites its own tail, a tail that never stops growing back.

We must stop this circulation with the sharp edge of the Spirit.

Get out of the infernal circle.

Let the wings of the serpent grow.

Let this winged serpent rise up and take flight.

Become an Eagle.

Being is.

Non-Being is not.

Who can know this if not the Absolute.

I am the Absolute.

You are the Absolute.

"ON" is the Absolute.

The Absolute is our intrinsic reality.

How could you know that you know nothing if you did not have an intuition of the Great Nothing?

As you experience Being, you simultaneously experience non-Being.

By penetrating non-Being, you bathe in the fullness of Being.

As you tumble into the Void, you are immediately struck by its ecstatic fullness.

If this simultaneity is absent, it indicates that the "posture" of the Spirit is wrong.

In the domain of the quest, everything that does not awaken is superstition.

Malevolence is only the incapacity to be awake, to be more conscious, to be present to oneself.
Disharmony in fact.
"Evil" does not arise from an intention but from the conditioned absence of an intention.
Intention arises in heightened consciousness.
Intention signifies intensity of the Interval. The One-tension.
It is an intention of Nothing, the negation of something, of the conditioned absence of intention, the unconditioned and free echo of the Great Nothing, its presence-absence.

If you wait for favorable conditions to undertake the quest, you will have to wait for your own death which alone naturally brings the desired intensity and acuity of consciousness.
Here and now is the true place and true time of the quest, because it is a time of death!

Controlled madness develops the One-sense.
Don Quixote is the prototype of the quester in love with the One-sense.
The One-sense shoots into the immediate, at the very moment, the immense and infinite presence of the Absolute.

We cannot emphasize enough:
If there is indeed Awakening when the Great Nothing invades consciousness, there cannot be anyone awakened.
All individuality merges into the Real.

The Void is not infinite empty space, nor suspended empty time.
The Void is not an absence but an absence of absence, which is presence: the presence of the Great Nothing.

As long as you are a prisoner of temporality, it is necessary to devote time to meditation on the Void.
This is no longer justified once you know how to travel in the Interval.

Be contemplatives rather than clairvoyants or voyeurs.
Learn to contemplate with and through all your senses to grasp the Totality of Beauty.

The art of the sword does not separate the true from the false but the beautiful from the vulgar.
Beauty always ends up overwhelming the ugly and the vulgar.
It is not the purpose of the gesture that matters but its beauty.

Search for Beauty.
Do not tolerate any ugliness, any vulgarity, any worldly pollution.
Affirm the Spirit and the beauty of Being.

WHISPERS OF THE FORBIDDEN

There are many varieties of bamboo in the Heavenly Garden.
  But only one art of the sword for cutting bamboo.
  Not everything is true, but everything is possible.

There is an indestructible and inscrutable axis between the body and Being.
  When the mind fades, the body can be understood as direct access to Being.
  It is, in a certain way, the most sophisticated musical and sensory instrument.

The pure energy that installs being in the Great Real, that "awakens," does not heal forms—it liberates from forms.

It is the intention that determines the Orient and not the means, rites, practices, or anything else.

God sleeps a lot.
  However, his right eye remains open.

A school of wisdom, or an initiatory order, must assume three functions:
- A conservatory of traditions, rites, and practices inherited from temporality.
- A laboratory for experimenting with praxis and operativities to isolate the truly operative elements from the cultural elements and thus prepare future initiatory forms.
- An oratory. Access to the Silence of the Here and Now. Awakening to That Which Remains.

Notice three types of initiation:
- Initiation against the body: deadly.
- Initiation without the body: dualistic, unfinished.
- Initiation in, by, and through the body: the only initiation given by Being and coming from Being.

Initiating a Person, an "I," an "ego," a "mask," is an absurdity.

When all your Persons are dead, Being remains.
    You are the Absolute.
    Like a motionless god, you fly.

In initiation, as in mathematics, it so happens that we grasp one path while practicing another.

Do not confuse undifferentiated with indifference.
    Indifference on the path indicates error and ignorance.
    Consciousness of the undifferentiated is born from nondual experience: "Not separate from any things, any forms, or any life."

A single smile from Shiva absorbs and dissolves all the violence and suffering of the world.
    His laughing nature carries all forms into the bliss of the Great Nothing.

We are not the body but we only have the body as material for the work.
    The body is not the body.
    The body is more than the body.
    The body is world.

Body of Earth,
    Body of Wind,
    Body of Fire,
    Body of Water.
    All of them emerge on the surface of Being as soon as the Spirit calls them and brings them together.
    Why cling to this Earth Body?

Only the Immutable can be filled with compassion for the ten thousand beings.

The saliva secreted in ecstasy, often abundantly, is sacred.
    The power of its medicine of immortality is real and potent.
    Think of the Jade Goddess.

Through the initiation of the "being with the bones of white light," the adept knows themself to be filled with fire and light that they can manifest at will, and populated by gods and creatures.
    So many creatures, so many forces…

Before the great reconciliation between forms, we must choose between the camp of the gods and the camp of the humans.
    This is the path of being in the human.

In the Void.
    By the Void.
    Being naturally weaves a body of light from the Saturnian body.
    It gives birth to a god from the human: *humus*.

Being has no need of a body of light or a body of glory, the one who is Glory themself and already all bodies.
    There is no necessity there, no law, but art and freedom.

It is at the point of the internal equilibrium of the Black Egg that the invocation must be made for the most powerful outpouring.

Shakti agrees to take the crudest forms to satisfy Shiva, she who is the very essence of infinite life.

God is the eighth personal pronoun.
    The other side of ON, the Indefinite.

The darkness of the Great Interval is of such intensity that it is only light.

Only Beauty can be opposed to horror.
   Horror only exists in the field of human experience and representations.
   Beauty is non-human, even if humans can let it reveal itself in themselves.

"Where there is a will, there is a way," we hear stupidly repeated here and there.
   But Being has no use for a way.
   And what will are we talking about?
   The will of the Person is only an unacknowledged desire.
   Instead, invoke the four free wills:
- From Earth, the will of stillness.
- From Water, the will of fluidity.
- From Fire, the will of the destruction of forms.
- From Wind, the will of the Spirit.

There is no initiatory conformism.
   Initiation is essentially a transgression.

The three essential poles of literature—art, love, and revolution—are also the three essential poles of initiation.

If the word is born from Silence, it touches the silence of Being in you.
   If the word is born from trouble, it feeds the trouble of the Person.
   The art of secret injunctions is reserved for beings of Silence.

The adept knows how to transform a urinal into a marvelous lotus basin.

The Real calligraphs in white on white.

It is only in the Interval that it is possible to unite the darkest and the brightest for the work of the Great Sun.

Perceive everything as the Great Interval!

Being Shiva, nothing is separate.
 The multiple is balanced to unify in the Heart.
 The executioner then kneels in front of their victim.
 The victim blesses the executioner.
 There is no longer either victim or executioner but the game of the One.

To breathe is to be, to not-be, to remain in the point of Absolute, the Interval, to be, to not-be, to remain, etc.

Any element in the creation can swap with another element.
 There are an infinite number of potential simultaneous forms.
 Only a few can be actualized.
 One who becomes master of permutations also becomes master of actualization.

The Silence remains.
 Even in the midst of noise.
 The Void remains.
 Even in the heart of the full.

How does lightning spring from the Void?
 What is the nature of such lightning?
 Would the Void only be Void because of its Totality?

Action is not born from the Void exactly, but from the repetition of the Void.
 There is a creative breathing of the Void.
 By "repetition of the Void," we mean an identical replica of the Void but presenting an intensification of fullness.
 The difference in fullness initially creates an energy available for creation.
 Subsequently it is reabsorbed into the Void.
 Several replicas are possible simultaneously, which explains the nine Shaivite voids, the 27 Buddhist voids, etc.

As soon as we leave the Great Stillness, we enter into ignorance, we know nothing.

When we dwell within the Great Stillness, there is Nothing to know.

"I Am" is not oriented.
It is the Orient.
The Orient of Being.
The Heart of the heart of the heart.

Some became heroes or even gods by pretending to be.
For the quester, as for the child, pretending is an initiatory art.
Pretending requires unconditionality.

The gods are powerful but not free.
They belong to the beings who pray to them, evoke them, and invoke them, therefore…
They constitute them.

Are you immortal?
As long as I can stand on my left foot alone, uniting Earth and Sky, I am immortal.
But when I place my right foot next to my left foot, I am eternal.
The Great Stillness.

Everything can be reversed.
Because Shiva is Shakti.
Shakti is Shiva.

One who drinks the original snow directly from the chalice of the goddess immediately becomes a god.

The Golden Flower is born from ecstasy.
It releases an internal nectar, a soma that makes the meditator immortal.

WHISPERS OF THE IMMORTAL

First the work of substances.
   Then the work of the energies of substances.
   Finally the work of the essences of substances.
   Substance–Energy–Essence.
   This is the Way of Internity.

When, in the field of internal alchemy, there is an issue of the way of substances, it is through the effect of contamination, a sometimes regrettable shortcut.
   In reality, there is no way of substances.
   Any real way can be treated in three modalities, separately, successively, or simultaneously:

- a modality of substances.
- a modality of energies.
- a modality of essences.

Certain internal alchemies use these three modalities.
   The substantial work, in black, frees energies.
   The energetic work, in white, frees essences.
   The essential work, in red, "frees" Being by unifying the essences into Essence.
   Substantial internal, external, or external-internal alchemical practice can initiate the way, secure the realizations on the way, convey the way, accompany the way, or close the way, depending on the place-states of the heightened consciousness of the adept and the situations in which they move or stop.

The ways to immortality present an infinite number of variations.

However, we distinguish three modalities of internal alchemy: substance, energy, and essence; and their multiple combinations create very diverse serpentine paths.

Several situations may arise.

They are never chosen.

Among these:

    The sealed Shiva-Shakti couple, face to face.

    The sealed Shiva-Shakti couple, side by side.

    Shiva and two Shaktis, one of whom holds the function of twinning.

    Shakti with two Shivas, one of whom has the function of twinning.

    Just Shiva and numerous Shaktis.

    Just Shakti and numerous Shivas.

Several games involve awareness and energy:

    Internal Shiva and external Shakti.

    External Shiva and internal Shakti.

    External Shiva and Shakti.

    Internal Shiva and Shakti.

This is to consider only the main mutations.

There are also the fundamental aspects of the alliance between Pneuma and Soma.

And finally, an infinity of *creative poetry*.

Pneuma, Soma, or even Intellect are sometimes presented as ways. It's a convenience of language. We should talk about modalities rather than ways.

Any real way can be elaborated according to these three modalities, which converge towards the Interval and the Ocean of Void.

The Interval opens onto both the infinity of Being and the infinity of non-Being.

Being and Void are one.

That is why it can be affirmed that the Interval is the Real.

In the Interval, the being accesses ecstasy, the Bliss of Being.

Amrita then flows into the vessel—the body—after the dragons have all arisen in union with the goddesses.

The body is then the field and the song of the ecstasy of the gods-goddesses.

The absolute impossibility of representing the female nude, by any art whatsoever, by any artist whatsoever, is an indication of the transcendent and immanent nature of Femininity as of the bond, secret and sacred, that unites Woman and the Interval.

The erotic possesses the intuition of this way without a way (but not without an outlet), while not ever being able to indicate or express it fully or truly.

Female nudity summons everything created, everything uncreated, all Beauty, and the totality of Art.

It invokes Being and non-Being and yet transcends them.

The nudity of Woman is the greatest mystery for those who have learned to *See* and to *Love*.

It paradoxically evokes and, through the reversal of the NU into ONE, the verticality of Absoluteness rather than the extent of Beingness.

Woman is a lotus that blossoms even above muddy waters.

No man can violate a woman. He only violates himself.

No man can defile a woman. He only defiles himself.

The present man knows that he never penetrates a woman but that he is received, enveloped, and carried away.

The man must learn to conduct his companion to the valley of orgasm before being welcomed into Her.

It is by recognizing the divinity of every woman that man can free himself from his conditioning and become Shiva.

If a woman knows how to open her heart every time she opens her thighs, she will soon remain forever in the Joy of the sacred Interval.

Ereignis, wonder, can be recognized and celebrated in all things but excellently in the feminine Eros.

On the path of the Lightning-Rose, when the rose, white or red, thrice opened, under the warm caress of a humid wind, has released its most secret perfumes, the rose lightning springs forth, releasing the nectar of immortality.
  Collect it carefully.
  And call the lightning lightning.

The naked goddess rides the bull of Shiva side-saddle.
  Guardian of the sacred spear, her thighs remain slightly ajar.
  From one interval to another, by her mastery of lightning,
  She opens the doors to the starry Heaven.

The Way of the Thirteen Moons:

For the God,

  The tears of the Compassion of Shiva are the first Salt,
  The saliva of Shiva is the second Salt,
  The blood of the heart of Shiva is the first Sulfur,
  The seed of Shiva is the first Mercury,
  The urine of Shiva is the third Salt,
  The earth of Shani is the foundation,
  And again,
  The urine of Shiva is the fourth Salt,
  The seed of Shiva is the second Mercury,
  The blood of the heart of Shiva is the second Sulfur,
  The saliva of Shiva is the fifth Salt,
  The tears of the Compassion of Shiva are the sixth Salt,
  The seventh Salt is offered by Shakti.

For the Goddess,

> The tears of the Joy of Shakti are the first salt,
> The saliva of Shakti is the second Salt,
> The milk of Shakti is the first Sulfur,
> The blood of Shakti is the second Sulfur,
> The lustral water of Shakti is the first Mercury,
> The urine of Shakti is the third Salt,
> The earth of Shani is the foundation,
> And again,
> The urine of Shakti is the fourth Salt,
> The blood of the Moon of Shakti is the second Mercury,
> The blood of the heart of Shakti is the second Sulfur,
> The saliva of Shakti is the fifth Salt,
> The sixth and seventh Salts are offered by Shambu.

Alchemical ascension of substances externalized by Shakti:
    Excrement. Urine. Menstrual blood. Flood of ecstasy. Milk. Saliva. Tears of Joy. Pearl of the Blue Goddess.
Alchemical ascension of substances externalized by Shiva:
    Excrement. Urine. Semen. Blood of the Heart. Saliva. Tears of Compassion. Pearl of the Blue God.

It is with the help of the royal cobras, or the archaic dragons, that the adept creates in verticality, not with the serpents of energy of the field of the horizon.

The ancient dragons, upon their arousal, attract and ingest the serpents of energy, reabsorbing the extension into the Central Point of Void.

Left breath: fire.
    Right breath: ice.
    Spiral breath: lake of tranquility, fountain of immortality.

Vowels: ways of evolution. Appearance of the dragons.
Consonants: ways of power. Springing forth of the dragons.
Intervals: Direct ways. Fastening of the dragons.
Consonants are set to work by rhythm.
Consonants are born from the original Fire.
Vowels are born from the primordial Waters.
They support the manifested.

The body-wisdom is the vessel of ecstasy.
The inhalation and exhalation are Shiva-Shakti.
The Interval is the Absolute.

Sunrise.
Walk with your back to the sun.
Try to "see":
There are two shadows.
Two intervals.
The first is resting on the ground.
Which is the second?
The one that rests in the sky.
Awaken!

Here is an important point.
Internal alchemy can be approached in two different styles:
- a dualistic style, and
- a nondualistic style.

If you have a dualistic relationship with the world, there is an "inner" and an "outer," an "inside" and an "outside."
You lose energy by fertilizing the world.
You will therefore have to learn technically to retain energy to cancel the world and become the Absolute-One.
If you are installed in the nondual, there is no intension, no extension, no loss, no gain, no fertilization, and no death, so there is, technically, nothing to retain.

Soma is the form that dissolves forms,
  The energy that frees energies,
  The essence that frees essences.

Three containers of Fire:
- White fire,
- Red fire,
- GOLD fire.

One thousand and eight operations:
  Operations by the milk of Shakti and the seed of Shiva.
  Operations by the blood of Shakti and the tears of Shiva.
  Operations by the dew of Shakti and the seed of Shiva.
  Operations by the blood of Shakti and the saliva of Shiva.
  Operations by the perfumes of Shakti and the essences of Shiva.
  Operations by the water of GOLD of Shakti.

Not all operations are necessary, possible, or adequate.
  The order may vary.
  It is determined by the serpents themselves, sent by the thousand and eight goddesses.

Nag Devi says:
  "In the body of silence, the emerald serpents dart from the roots of the primordial earth while the azure serpents descend from the ultimate sky.
  "Emerald eagles swoop from the ultimate sky while azure eagles rise from the black earth.
  "They are united in the heart, not in my image but my reality.
  "After having inhabited the abode of pneuma, they inhabit the palace of soma.
  "The hissing serpents rise.
  "The eagles soar.
  "I am the goddess of the Great Center.
  "Manifestation and reflection of Parvati, Kali, and Kundalini alike."

Learn to make the Nagas who inhabit your body hiss so that they rise up towards the primordial Sky.

Forcing the gate of Saturn can reverse primordial kundalini.

Goddess Kundalini:
    A filament of fire in a column of Void.
    To unite with her, and with wings, is to marry into absolute fire.

"I am the goddess of the golden serpent.
The ascending goddess.
The goddess of ecstasy.
Through me, the imitator is destroyed.
Through me, the creator conquers his original sky.
Through me, the gods are fulfilled."

The yoni brings together the beauties and essences of the Rose, the Lotus, and the Orchid.

Black is absolute nakedness.
    Sum of all colors, matte black is the door to the Void of space.
    Luminous black is the fullness of the Void.

Parvati, the white, and Kali, the black, are One.
    United by Shiva.

Kali is the sex of woman in exaltation.

Kali blesses the eroticism that transcends worldliness.
    Sexuality is both illusion and liberation.
    Illusion for the person.
    Liberation for the being.

The use of the *kapala* indicates that the blue essence of semen, blood, and saliva must be collected at the top of the skull.

Woman is the ultimate initiator of man as a goddess, white or black, emerald or azure, ruby or gold.

In the valley of orgasm, the goddess Parvati experiences four great Joys.
The first is offered to the goddess Kundalini,
The second to Brahma,
The third to Vishnu,
The fourth to Shiva.
Then comes the ecstatic fullness of the Great Nothing.

Shiva forms a lingam in his mouth by coagulating his saliva.
He offers it to Devi, who receives it in her yoni and keeps it, until from the egg hatches a blue eagle which rises like an arrow towards the golden sky.

When you have made love simultaneously with the three goddesses of Jade, Turquoise, and Gold, you will remain forever in the bliss and clear light of the Great Real.
Your body will be the lotus garden of the goddesses.

In the valley of orgasm, the woman's yoni releases a secret and sacred quality of soma.

When the valley is red, all the doors of the worlds open.
The intervals on the other worlds open and, through them, the Great Interval towards the Valley of the Great Nothing.
When the valley is white, only the door to the Great Real opens.

On the Ways of Immortality, there is an Interval within Time that is called the Moment of Flowers.
The Plant Moment that sees the quester fast from flowers, roses, lotuses, or orchids.
Floral essences help to soothe the body of Fire and stabilize it.

Naga brings Pneuma.
  Garuda brings Soma.

  White naga.
  White garuda.
  Immaculate Conception.

Nag Devi:
  "I am the pulse of Ardhanarishvara.
  I am Ganesha's accomplice."

Chùà Tâm Sen*
Monastery of the Three Lotuses

THE THIRTY-SIX PRINCIPLES

1. The world comes from an ultimate and absolute principle. It subsists by this principle and dissolves in this principle.

2. The secret of the birth of the breath of life that resides in all bodies is the most secret of secrets.

3. The secret of the birth of the breath of life is the key to all the high sciences.

4. The secret of the birth of the breath of life can only be communicated to a disciple of balanced character, who takes care of their body, tends towards unconditionality, and knows the presence of Being.

5. This means of knowledge has no equal. It is present in all bodies. It can be deployed by all bodies.

6. Mastering the secret of the birth of the breath of life opens the doors to all knowledge.

7. The Universe, just like the body of living beings, is the manifestation of Breath, which conveys the unique Sound. It is through Breath that the Absolute creates and destroys the worlds.

---

* *Chùà Tâm Sen* is a Vietnamese expression of the Hongmen Tradition. It is distinguished by bringing together the nondual paths of Taoism, Buddhism, and Shaivism. The thirty-six principles are recited to the disciple during their reception in the Monastery. They perfectly illustrate the point of this essay.

8 The secret of the birth of the breath of life creates the covenant with the sacred serpents or dragons.

9 It is the power of breath that destroys an enemy or attracts a friend. It is the power of breath that gives temporal glory as well as liberation from all temporality.

10 You must choose to deploy the breath either in the peripheries of form or in its sublime verticality.

11 Everything that has form, everything that can be named, is only appearance. Only one who distinguishes Appearance from appearance can access Recognition of the natural state. The path that leads to this natural state is inscribed in the breath.

12 The one who masters the secret of the birth of the breath of life recognizes all deities, favorable or hostile, all entities, allies or annoyances, and ultimately all beings, as of the nature of Void.

13 The one who knows the secret of the birth of the breath of life sees all things equal: good and evil, creation and destruction. The Void and the fullness of the Void remain.

14 The one who knows the secret of the birth of the breath of life may be called Dragon or Naga. They have yet to crown themself.

15 On the left side, in the Heart of the Goddess, is the elixir of immortality. On the right side, in the Heart of the Lord, originate all lives throughout the cosmos. The two hearts are one heart.

16 The lunar way and the solar way must be separated before being perfectly reunited.

17 Inscribed in the breath, the consciousness that fixes itself on what is permanent conquers the Citadel of Being without failing.

18 Inscribed in the breath, consciousness must be attentive from dawn to dusk.

Inscribed in the breath, consciousness must be attentive from dusk to dawn.

19 The Breath is truly the only master.

20 The reduction of breath leads to Quivering then to Bliss in the Heart of the Goddess.

21 One who knows the secret of the birth of the breath of life and remains without desire and without attachment conquers time and death.

22 One who knows the secret of the birth of the breath of life is no longer the plaything of the gods. What enslaves the ignorant liberates the one who knows the secret of the birth of the breath of life.

23 Three Immortals await the disciple with the three movements of breath. Three ways to know the Absolute. Three ways for the Absolute to know itself. The Black Immortal, dual. The Red Immortal, dual within the One. The White Immortal, nondual.

24 The spontaneous mantra is the door that leads to the doorless passage. Understanding its two forms is essential.

25 The Self, free or enslaved, has as its nature Void and the Bliss of Void.

26 Recognizing that everything is the Absolute, that nothing is impure, produces sudden liberation.

27 The world is a dream within the Dream. The dream dissolves through Recognition.

28 Nothing exists outside of your awareness of it.

29 If you're not there to "see," there's nothing.
    If you're not there to "see," there are endless possibilities.
    If you are there to "see," you actualize.
    But the experience remains of the nature of the Void.

30 All you are aware of is the true body.

31 You are identical to everything that is perceived, conceived, imagined, forgotten, and ignored.

32 One who experiences the Appearance of appearances frees himself.

33 Agitation dissolves into the Fullness of Void.

34 The consciousness that leaves one state does not identify with another state. There is the Interval at the Absolute.

35 The banished Immortal lives the Limitless within the limit, the Infinite in this body.

36 The Absolute is the Void. The Absolute is the Full.
    The Absolute is Stillness. The Absolute is Movement.
    The Absolute is Freedom even in the chains of slavery.
    You are the Absolute.

THE SAYINGS OF MONK DURIAN

This discourse is dedicated to cats, horses, snakes, buzzards and hawks, vultures, forests, rivers and oceans, mountains, spiritual friends, rebels, poets, freedmen, banished immortals, and the ultimate woman, who taught me and awakened me by their presence alone.

To bác Lam
Of the Invisible Monks of *Chuâ Tâm Sen*

**"If my words become an institution,
Destroy them!"**

The Words of
Stinking Monk Durian

(THÂỲ SÂÙ RIÊNG THÔM)

Fossilisation d'une Piéta
Jean Gabriel Jonin, 2010 (gouache on paper)

❧ *How do you know?*
   "I" doesn't **know** *anything.*
   It **knows** *Itself.*

❧ *To re-enchant the world, we must un-curse it.*
   The world is cursed by stupidity.

❧ *Shake off that egotistical shit that keeps you from seeing. Get over it!*

❧ *Stop glorying in your so-called humanity! It is this humanity that rapes, tortures, massacres children, lets its own people die of hunger, and pillages the planet. Disidentify yourself from the human, this perverse contraction of consciousness. Be!*

❧ *Your so-called humility is a selfish turd.*
   Humility consists of simply being yourself.

❧ *Objectivity?*
   One subjectivity among others.
   But who is unknown.

❧ *The norm?*
   That is the abnormal.

❧ *The contradiction?*
   It's a counter-addiction.

❧ *The demiurge?*
   It's us. All of us.

❧ *An evil society? A black lodge?*
   The only black lodge is ordinary stupidity.
   We all participate in it to varying degrees.

❡ *A diploma?*

The greatest minds in the history of this planet, and therefore the freest, held no diplomas.

See what your diplomas are making of this world!

❡ *Victory?*

Do we emerge victorious?

Do we sleep victorious?

Shake off your torpor!

❡ *East – West?*

Anyone who confuses physical geography with the borderless geography of the Imaginal has understood nothing.

❡ *The written trace?*

Don't let yourself be fascinated.

Remember, in your language, the proximity of the two words "book" and "free."*

The book is written in complete freedom. No one writes it.

The writer builds awkwardly. They write in vain.

The free trace is without an author, but causes height.

❡ *History?*

History deliberates.

Initiation liberates.

❡ *The Primordial Tradition?*

Silence.

❡ *Human life is humus for the life of the Free Spirit.*

---

*   Fr.: « livre » et « libre ».

❧ *You are not human. I am not human.*
You are. I am.
Being.
We participate in the human, as in all forms of life.
We leave the human, like all forms of life, as soon as we recognize ourselves.
We are all of that and none of that.

❧ *Do not look for initiation in the shithole of the 20th century, which was an exaggerated time of masquerades, forgetfulness, and thick ignorance!*

❧ *If you behave like a grocer in your human relationships, you will have the same behavior with the living spirits of the invisible Real.*

❧ *What are you hoping for? The divine does not barter.*

❧ *Hey, old people—young old people and old old people—take care!*
The pseudo-wisdom of age that makes you pontificate has nothing to do with Awakening.
Stop going on!

❧ *Does an awakened person, or an awakener, celebrate their birthday with their disciples or fellow travelers?*

❧ *A life dictated by others is always wasted.*
The Nameless and the Formless are your instructors.

❧ *You will meet instructors who simplify because they have the essence. And instructors who simplify due to their incomprehension. The latter are relatively few in number. Those who see reality escaping them tend to overcomplicate things to mask their ignorance.*

Those who have grasped the essence lead you into heightened consciousness; the others lead you towards an intellectual understanding that is as reassuring as it is superficial.

❧ *Any generalization is alienating violence. Seek the path of the particular.*

❧ *Your psychoanalysis has only replaced your confessional.*
One humiliation is worth another humiliation.

❧ *Everything has only a time…*
Everything is only a time.

❧ **Bhakti** *without arcana, or without an axis, stretches indefinitely into the peripheries under the abusive authority of the archaic Power – Territory – Reproduction triangle. False humility and false compassion.*

❧ *To forgive humanity for having produced these waves of horror, we must accept that we are humanity in its entirety.*
Then, forgiveness becomes unnecessary and non-separation accomplishes its work of reconciliation and liberation through the Recognition of oneself as Absolute.

❧ *Your so-called sense of history is only the sense of the becoming of "I." Stuck in history, you have no sense of eternity. At best, you will be troubled by the incongruity of eternity for the "person." This incongruity can prove beneficial.*

❧ *The "Person" doesn't leave from here, this world, alive.*
Being neither enters nor leaves: it remains.

❧ *All that the "person" likes or hates, reflected in Appearance, is doomed to disappear.*
All that is Being remains.
All experience leaves a trace, an undifferentiated echo, in consciousness as a possibility.

❧ *Understanding that we do not know allows us to avoid condemning ourselves or others for life.*

❧ *When you wander into the impasse, the place where the ONE passes, you will grasp the meaning and power of the "Passage without a door."*

ℂ It is absurd, and vain, to believe that historical research can enable us, in any way, to grasp or even approach initiation and Awakening.

Awakening is simultaneously the integration of the totality of experiences and their disintegration into an essence unknowable in temporality as in discursive speech.

Awakening is without history. Initiation is part of the play of the Self with the multiple reflections of itself. Linearity and causality constitute lures, or idols, you might say. All sense stands out as counter-Sense which can only add to the confusion of fragmented appearance.

ℂ Idolatrous tendencies that persist for a long time, especially in the relationship between disciple and master, are dissolved by the grasp of the fact that Awakening is "unawakened."

ℂ Awakening is a simple abandonment of a bad habit.
A thousand times you have tried in vain to eliminate it.
Since you tried a thousand and one times to fight it, it was no longer there.
It had never been there, it never would be again.
This is how Awakening occurs.

ℂ One state [of consciousness] is as good as another. What we "seek" is Awakening, an absence of state, the very freedom of Being.

ℂ In the weaving of time, we believe we are following a causality, we are part of a linearity that we call personal history. In reality, we drift from time to time. To really understand this is to learn to play with time, the strings of a universal instrument, and to create worlds.

ℂ The essence of time is separation, antinomies, the opposition of contraries and therefore war.
No peace without non-separateness.

ℂ Give thanks to Totality for offering you Totality.

❧ *Moving from order-or-successive-time to order-or-simultaneous-time means placing the ultimate in the heart and actuality at the periphery. This passage announces the non-order of non-time.*

❧ *What moves in time is not consciousness but the assemblage point of a world. This movement seems linear. It is so only by conditioned convention. In the simultaneity of time, it is possible to jump from one moment of forces to another because this game, free or conditioned, takes place within consciousness.*

❧ *At the point of Void, which is also the assembly point of the world and worlds, Time is an Eternity.*
   It is not in timelessness, in the Bliss of the Great Real or the Great Nothing, that we can move the assemblage point of a world, but in dream time.

❧ *Be atemporal. Overturn the apparent temporality of events to grasp non-Time, the Interval.*
Learn to be a devourer of Time. Swallow the vampire!
Only the Absolute knows how to devour Time.

❧ *Awakening or non-Awakening, it's all the same.*

❧ *Be interval trackers. This is the most direct path to Awakening: the Great Interval between Everything and Nothing.*

❧ *There is filiation only when you are the Interval at the very heart of the situation. Being generates Being.*

❧ *The sleeping cat is closer to the Great Real than the thinking human.*

❧ *Take the less-traveled path.*
Welcome the divine surprise.
The Real is the Great Unexpected.

❡ There is an initiatory illusion as there is a literary illusion. Initiation and Literature are only accessible to poets of the Grand Real. This access is called destruction.

❡ The initiatory dimension of Literature is only realized outside of Literature.

❡ Art proceeds from a metahistorical "moment of forces" that is inscribed in history. Initiation proceeds from an "historical moment of forces" that dissolves into a metahistory.

❡ The "person" is submerged in a continuous stream of chatter, images, and feelings. This flow is of such violence that it carries away everything in its path and makes the words of the other inaudible, unless they repeat with precision the conditioned words by which the "Person" self-hallucinates. The noise of others is only heard when it matches your own noise to comfort you in your imposture.

❡ Thus all human speech is just noise. But every noise is the name of Shiva, which is without echo or commentary.
All poetry is the teaching of Shiva, because all poetry becomes Silence.

❡ Stop being a blind puppet!
Open your eyes!
Be a tightrope walker, an acrobat of the Free Spirit!

❡ Every Tradition of Awakening is aimed at the exiled, the banished.
Initiation cannot be combined with temporal power without losing itself in worldliness.
In this area, no compromise is possible.
Remember that it is not the uninitiated who can profane the altar by their arrogance and stupidity but those who think they are initiated.

❡ It doesn't matter if your own Mount Kailash is climbed in five small steps, like the five sounds of Shiva's mantra. Reach its summit as often as possible. Stay at the summit of yourself!

THE SAYINGS OF MONK DURIAN

❧ From the summit of Mount Kailash, immortality is kitsch!

❧ Murder is always self-harm.

❧ Rape is an irreversible auto-profanation of the Goddess within oneself. An attack that can only ultimately be resolved with the disappearance of the "Person." The rape and murder of the Guru are the only unforgivable crimes, along with gambling addiction, which is to say, illusion and ignorance. They are fundamental attacks on axiality and they destroy the tension towards the Great Real.

❧ The initiate, even the initiable, without being taken in by the Great Game, without being part of the farce of the world, is always, in the play of the forms of Appearance, on the side of the weak and the oppressed against the powerful and the oppressor.
This manifestation of the immutable principle of original harmony is the very meaning of Knighthood, in the East as in the West.

❧ Only the dead can die.
Stop whining.

❧ Between the first breath and the last, there are only replications.

❧ Opposition, contradiction, or any pattern of polarity is only a particular case of the adhesion and imitation that contribute to the replication of the "Person."

❧ Make no mistake!
Initiation is indeed a disobedience but not a "replicant" one:
An inventive and axiocratic disobedience.

❧ Let go of fear!
Dead or alive, you are the Absolute!
Trembling or serene, you are the Absolute!

❧ Be so vulnerable that you become invulnerable. Awaken!

❧ When an obstacle presents itself, observe with Attention the immediate environment. The solution is always at hand.

❧ Right and wrong do not exist.
If they existed, we would all be wrong.

❧ False Gurus cannot stand true disciples.
False disciples cannot stand true Gurus.
The world is perfect.

❧ You are incapable of recognizing a "complete," empty, and free human being. One would appear suspicious to you in its strangeness, its "madness" or, on the contrary, banal in its desire to "uncrimp" your ego.

So long as you have not renewed through attention, in heightened awareness, the covenant with the body—the unconditioned body—your recognition is impossible.

You will ask for forms, demand explanations, add comments. You will get along with your little person, postponing for as long as possible the initiation of being into being.

❧ There is a body in appearance as soon as consciousness is frozen.

❧ A complete being, a free being, knows how to cover their tracks.
Rarely do they allow themself to be recognized for what they are.
Most of the time, they go unnoticed, or get taken for a dim moron.
They live.

❧ Do not believe that the Awakened One always reveals the truth; they only state what is appropriate in the situation.

They are not identified with the game. They are not identified with the player. However, they can still play within Appearance in order to synchronize with you.

On the other hand, note that certain lying enchantments awaken more surely than do boring truths.

❧ Practices are internalized rites.
Rites are externalized practices.

❧ It is because rites and practices are ineffective that they serve the springing forth of nondual Consciousness.

❧ If everything awakens you, a dirty stone, a wild flower, a one-eyed cat, a chattering sparrow, the local cafe owner, or your reflection in a filthy window, you have no use for an exceptional guru.
   If you still need a mother or a father, then yes, you need a guru for a while.

❧ You are your own root guru.
Shiva-Devi.

❧ If you are still looking for a divine Mother or a divine Father, you are not ready for Absolute Freedom, only for personal dependence.

❧ The sacred is always dissident.

❧ The initiate always appears as a dissident in the eyes of worldliness.
Any initiate is, moreover, stateless.

❧ This planet is being degraded by responsible people.
Try irresponsibility!
Free yourself from stupidity!

❧ You claim to rely on the facts but you are only looking for the effect: one of the two constituents of the dualistic rumor.

❧ Reassure the worldly people!
Tell them we are philosophers and poets.
Scare them!
Philosophers. Poets. But strays!
Our wandering unfolds in the High Land of Silence.
Worldliness has a sacred horror of Silence.

❧ Choose between impression and ONE-pression.

❧ *Silence even re-enchants garbage dumps, charnel grounds, and other human monstrosities.*

❧ *Shiva likes to play at being initiated by Shiva.*

❧ *Shiva accepts all sincere offerings, from shit to diamonds.*

❧ *All is Beauty.*
All is Love.
All is Freedom.
Even in the ugliness.
Even in the hatred.
Even in the enslavement.

❧ *There is no difference between making love and not making love…*
But as long as there is this body, I prefer to make love.

❧ *The Awakening you speak of is like a good glass of wine. A chimera.*
"My" Awakening is not "your" Awakening.
Yet both are Awakening.

❧ *Make just one unconditioned choice and that is Awakening.*
Did I just forbid you Awakening or allow you Awakening?

❧ *You have no choice, only Awakening.*
Or you have infinite choices: Awakening or Awakening or Awakening…

❧ *Practice and Awakening are one.*
Abandonment of practice and Awakening are one.

❧ *One who does not respect women, all women, including those you consider "bitches," cannot even approach the Way.*

❧ Goddesses have one indisputable assertion that gods cannot offer, and that is their sumptuous ass. Men cannot resist it. This is why the deified flesh, sacred eroticism, remains an unequaled path, certainly sometimes perilous, but direct.

❧ What is put into words, what is structured in causes and effects, is belief: localized and ephemeral ignorance.
What you call "karma" is nothing but the infinite stretching of the vestment of the Lord, woven by Devi.
Only Knowledge, which emerges from Silence, is universal.

❧ Universality is just a pretension. It is most often just a standardized multiple. A bland conformism.
Moving from the multiple to the One includes the reduction of universalism to the particular.

❧ Rather than trying to understand the Universe. Let the Universe understand you.

❧ You would like to control everything, but the only possible control is the total absence of control.

❧ It is essential to understand, first, that nothing can be repaired and, secondly, that there is nothing to repair—but in that order, only in that order.

❧ If you value the powers then the powers value you. You become their food.

❧ The peripheries are cluttered with anecdotes and incidents. Listing them does not provide information about the center.

❧ To those who think it is serious, grave, important… we will say that it is a game. To those who believe it is a game, we will say that it is wisdom.

❧ The gold of the ego does not allow one to discover the Island of the Immortals.

❦ *Consciousness, consciousness… You only have this word in your mouth. Do you even have the slightest consciousness of what Consciousness is? Instead, focus on "unconsciousness."*

❦ *Impeccability follows impersonality.*

❦ *You have to accept a little stench if you want to see the lotus flower appear.*

❦ *Perfection frees itself from perfection.*

❦ *Only my imperfection is perfect*

❦ *I am, simultaneously, all beings, from the vilest to the holiest.*
I am, the Absolute.

❦ *"Good" and "evil" are not two waves of the ocean of manifestation but a single wave.*
    Learn to surf on the crest of that wave.
    To truly choose between "good" and "evil," one must go to that place, that place-state, beyond "good" and "evil." Outside of this place there is no choice, only a conditioned ultimatum.

❦ *Ladies, offer your orgasms to the ten thousand beings, and in particular to those—flowers, animals, humans, or gods—who change forms so that they sail on the ocean of your pleasures to their own essence, thus escaping to the infinite round of forms.*

❦ *Drinking, writing, and kissing do not harm Awakening.*
They participate in it.

❦ *A horse taught me impeccability.*
A little cat taught me compassion.
Better than the gurus.
Pay attention to what is there.

❧ A guru is just a modality of Consciousness.
You are Consciousness.

❧ Nuns and monks dream of a companion.
Married initiates dream of becoming a monk or nun.
Remain!

❧ Neither monk outside the world,
Nor monk in the world,
But monk-world.

❧ Being available to receive the suffering of beings develops compassion and a philosophical sense of stupidity, two virtues ignored by postponed corpses who think they are powerful.

❧ Human beings have a tremendous power: that of saying "no!"
No to their peers, certainly, but especially no to the gods!

❧ If I am not God, then God is not God.
He is incomplete, He lacks me, so He is not God.

❧ Practices (rituals, asceses, arts, techniques, reasoning, etc.) do not lead to Liberation. They are one possible punctuation among an infinity of others. They only underline it…

❧ Any means is skillful.
The supreme skill lies in the revelation of the supreme Void.

❧ The initiated warriors—the others are only puppets—create a breach in the opacity of appearance, but it is the poets, also initiated, who make this breach a passage towards the Great Real.

❦ *Practicing magical and theurgic ceremonies in the heart of Silence allows you to touch deeper levels of consciousness that you call, in duality: angels, spirits, devas, gods, goddesses, etc.*

Practicing the same ceremonies outside of the Silence, in the noise of the "me," allows one to touch deeper levels of illusion.

Don't forget the angel or spirit of return.

❦ *What you refer to as "angel" is your Perfect Nature, your original and ultimate nature.*

If you perceive several angels, or any other entity, if you establish angelic hierarchies, it is out of unavailability to the totality of your real Nature. You remain encumbered by the crystallizations and adhesions of the "Person."

❦ *The experience of the "guardian angel," who guards nothing in reality, but calls back to Self, constitutes a particular "moment of forces," an almost perfect balance between "I" and Self. The one being simultaneously the gaze of the other in the clear light of what Is, both mirror and image.*

This time of twinship is precious. It reveals "the double" or "the shadow." This bi-unity, this "biple," is the expression in and for the human being of nondual/dual consciousness. The original couple of which all the others are emanations.

❦ *A god is an increased, undivided, and autonomous unit of Consciousness, fully united with its source, which has not voluntarily reintegrated the Great Nothing and remains relatively differentiated in Appearance.*

❦ *What matters is not the beyond but the herein. The foundations of the foundations.*

❦ *Awakening is inevitable.*
You are Awakening.
Your doubt about the present reality of this state of yours is part of the demonstration of Awakening.

ℭ *So much misleading talk!*
Think about an epistemology of Awakening.
What you know and how you know it.
You know nothing.
You don't even know how you know that you know nothing.
And it doesn't matter; it Absolutely doesn't matter.
There is Awakening.

ℭ *The ritual does not lead to Awakening, it celebrates Awakening, the inevitable Awakening.*

*Rituals are derivatives or representations, more or less crude, of the original rite, of the first, **absolutely free**, game of "hide and seek" of the Self with itself.*

ℭ *You were born from a smile of Shiva.*
You will die from a smile of Shiva.
Why not live with the smile of Shiva?

ℭ *Speech is in vain.*
*But, sometimes, speech gets **lucky**.*
*There is **All** the same **Nothing** to say…*
No nonduality without Silence.
Let your wandering be still!
We will meet again on the Isle of Immortals!

The Words of *Luminous Monk Durian*

(THÂỲ SÂÙ RIÊNG SÁNG)

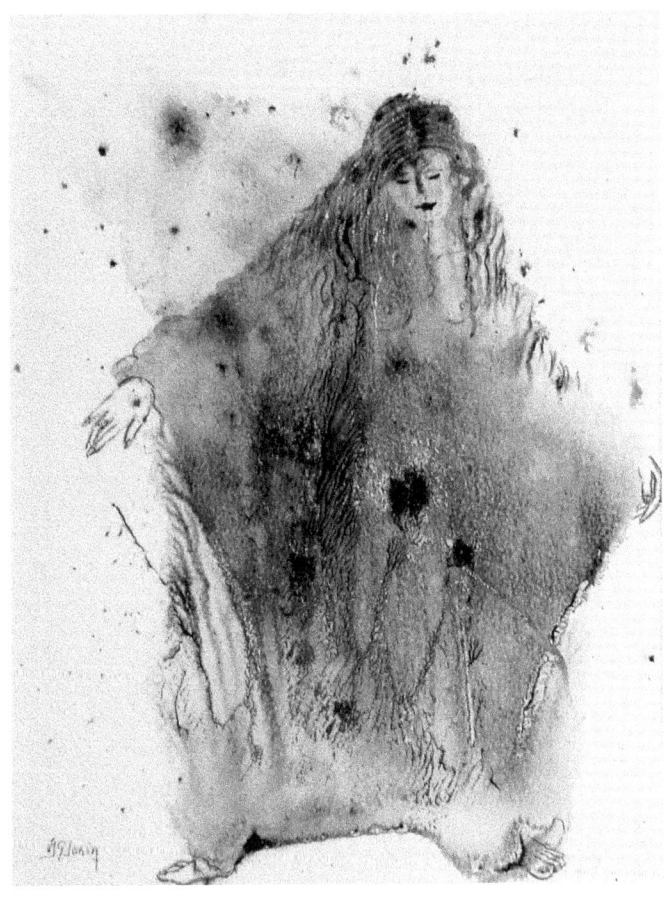

Penta-Guné
Jean Gabriel Jonin, 2007 (gouache on paper)

ℂ *There is a meta-initiation, or an initiation to initiation. It is neither a pre-initiation nor a super-initiation, but an art of traversal. It is appropriate to traverse as quickly as possible the inevitable dualism of initiation in its formal, cultural, and mythogenetic modalities to reach the nondual essence.*

ℂ *Even a frenzied dualism leads, by reversal, to nondualism. It is a partial vision that leads to the opposition of dualism and nondualism.*

ℂ *In the same way that you must practice a sacred text as if it had been written or revealed only for you, you must observe the world as created by yourself, for yourself, and for your understanding alone.*

ℂ *Deepen a traditional line, then a second, and a third, until you have them. Then you will swing beyond the lines, to their source.*

ℂ *Study the teachings of the awakeners.*
Emancipate yourself from the teachings of the awakeners.

ℂ *The more a tradition expresses the Great Real, the more the Woman, and also women, are recognized as essential, central, and unique.*
No Awakening is possible for those who do not grasp the essence of the feminine.

ℂ *It is not consciousness that is in the body but the body that is in consciousness.*
Consciousness is not the intersection of the visible and the invisible but that in which all the visible and all the invisible, all the possible and all the impossible, are manifested in their innumerable permutations.

ℂ *Forms float on the ocean of desires, following the waves.*
Will alone knows how to direct them towards the Bay of Tranquility.

ℂ *Gods are born in heightened consciousness and feed on the intensity of your presence. Without it, they are absent.*

❦ When an energy is in consciousness, it is a god.
When consciousness is absorbed by an energy, it is a demon.
"Gods" and "demons" are determined by the relationships of consciousness and energy.
If you elevate yourself to a higher sense, the gods operate in a higher sense.

❦ Where, in Appearance, there is a process, there is an Intention and an Orient, which characterize a spirit.

❦ In a distorted context, an adjusted and oriented practice opens up to the Real.
In a distorted context, an ill-adjusted but oriented practice catches up with the Real by reversal.
In a favorable context, an adjusted but disoriented practice catches up with the Real by accident.
In a favorable context, an ill-adjusted and disoriented practice is lost in the peripheries.

❦ Technology must never lead to the forgetting of Being.

❦ Being, even apparently stuck in the given being, remains Being.

❦ Every language is sacred.
Every language conveys the Mystery.
The mother tongue remains the most efficient, operatively, after Silence, because it is the only one capable of sustainably maintaining, through its poetic power, the paradox of being and being-until-traversing-the-dualistic-stream or, through its twilight language, of invoking the meta-paradox of being and non-being in order to masterfully free oneself from it once more.

❦ No language, including sacred languages, including Sanskrit, is vast enough to contain Being.

ℭ *All languages are mediators between Heaven and Earth.*
Even if some seem closer to Heaven, others to Earth.
Even if some were born from Earth to tend towards Heaven while others were born from Heaven to fertilize the Earth.
All are sacred.
None are.

ℭ *You are convinced that there is someone here.*
It's a personal belief.
There is no more person.

Here and now, you are the reincarnation of all past, present, and future beings.
Every "other," past, present, and future, is your reincarnation.

ℭ *The master and the four disciples:*
First disciple: "Master, when and where did you experience Awakening? When and where did This happen?"
Second disciple: "Master, I would rather ask: Why did This happen?"
Third disciple: "No! How did This happen?"
The clever disciple: "Ridiculous! This did not happen. It always has been."
The master: "What are you four doing here?"

ℭ *The future is just another past.*
In Awakening, all futures and all pasts are present.

ℭ *The renunciation of writing is still writing.*
The renunciation of calligraphy is still calligraphy.
All renunciation persists in the dualistic rumor.

❧ The conditioned human, identified with the object, is tossed around in the eddies of the dualistic rumor.

When the nondual sensitivity is installed within consciousness, the mark of entry into the Way, the dualist crises, born from the coagulation of dualist crystallizations through affinity, remain numerous for most practitioners. These crises constitute the defense mechanism of the "I," of the "Person," facing the Interval that offers itself as access to the Self. The "Person" constantly reduces the subject to one of its attributes.

The default response is, most often, a return to practice, but this is a dualistic response. The more powerful the "Witness" is of "that which is there," the more awareness will be increased, the less lasting these crises will be, and the more dispersed they will be.

It may be that the infinite ocean of the Self definitively sweeps away the dualistic residue, but remember that, as long as there is a body, there are conditionings.

❧ The stupidest, most aberrant, most vulgar teaching—the worst dualistic shit—is not separate from the original teaching and points, in its completely opposite direction, to the Absolute.

The original teaching, resulting from the desire for fusion by the Goddess, Knowledge, and the Absolute, spreads in experience and appearance until it is lost in stupidity. It nonetheless remains the original teaching born from the Lord's desire to know Himself.

❧ The heroic phase of the way requires breaking away from history. Extract the past from the past. Extract the future from the future. Free yourself from the two times of banishment. Actualize here and now the totality of time. Move from personal history to metahistory or "vertical history," the mysterious history of great simultaneity and great spontaneity, which liberates from all limits.

❧ The time of the quest is the time of occultation, the interval, non-time.

❧ Gnosis, Knowledge, cannot be qualified under any circumstances whatsoever. It is, however, universally qualifying. It qualifies **Absolutely.**

❧ *The Absolute cannot be objectified. The first quality of the human being, of the being in the human, is its subjectivity, a quality that it shares with the Absolute, while the "Person" strives to believe in a so-called objectivity. The recognition of this total, integral, and inclusive subjectivity is a way.*

❧ *Each experience is the reverse of an imperience pre-established as a possibility within Integral Consciousness. This is why we have both the delicious premonition of the greatest good and the troubled premonition of the greatest horror. This is why, when "it happens," we have the feeling of confirmation which sometimes translates into a fascination with ecstasy as well as with horror. These confirmations are milestones on the path to Recognition.*

❧ *Visual discrimination, eminently dual, gives way to the specific "Seeing" of the object in itself, non-discriminating and without comparison, then to integral "Seeing," the "gaze of God," and finally to inclusive "Seeing." The witness turns to face himself and disappear.*

❧ *The modes of Appearance can be renewed indefinitely. Consciousness (Absolute Freedom) thus enjoys losing itself once again to find itself once more.*

❧ *The recognition of appearance as an object within Consciousness frees the individual Self from the contingencies of Appearance and promotes a total identification between the individual Self and the Self, between Beingness (the powers of the Absolute) and the Absolute, and between Shakti and Shiva.*

❧ *There are not two shaktis. The Shakti who puts you to sleep is also the Shakti who awakens you. It all depends on the uprightness of the spirit in your consciousness.*

❧ *You think of taking refuge in Shiva but Shiva took refuge in you at the very first movement of time. This shows his confidence in your ability to recognize yourself as identical to himself.*

❧ There is only one return, the Eternal Return, which is the Recognition of oneself as Absolute Freedom. The replication of the "Person," and thus of the world, is a projected shadow of Eternal Return. At the end of the breath, replication constrains the Self.

❧ There is replication as long as there is unconsciousness. Dual consciousness generates unconsciousness to nourish duality.

❧ Contrary to what you believe, there are on Earth only a few individual beings. Most people on this planet are collective beings, including you, except for those rare moments when you are in the pure presence of your reality.

❧ In duality, the cardinal fight—of which all other fights are only apparitions—opposes the individual (as an "outgrowth" or memory of the Self) to the person (as the alienating crystallization of all conformisms and identifications). Freedom from stupidity.
There is no trace of this fight in nondual Consciousness, only enjoyment. Stupidity is a joyful consequence of Freedom.
So what is the game of Self? What is the nature of the Great Game?

❧ The complete, free being is outside of the Game.

❧ Dual ways begin with a myth and end in unbearable doubt.
Nondual ways consume this same myth and remain unaccomplished in the fullness of the Void.

❧ If you consider the body and its conditionings as a prison, you are in the dualistic error. The body is a door. It is even The Door.

❧ The "Person," the ego, is corruption itself.
The body, contrary to what you believe, is incorruptible.
Freed from the conditioning of the "Person," the superimpositions of the "I," the body is nothing other than the perfect vehicle of solarity.

❦ In any tantric school of Wisdom, the disciples are divided into three invisible degrees, three certifications: the certificate of aptitude in the research of arcana, the certificate of authorization for the practice of arcana, and the certificate of access to the hidden teaching. All work together without distinction, the first at the level of forms and substances, the second at the level of serpentine energies, of vibration, and the last at the level of essences, of anointings. All work within Silence. The first are taught by gesture and speech, the second by the movements of Energy, and the last, from being to being by the goddesses.

❦ Tantric initiation is permanent. The practices and ceremonies are only the punctuation. This guides the breathing of the body, energy, and mind. Punctuation is not formally necessary. It may be invisible.

❦ To breathe consciously is to even now make the world a monastery.
To be installed in the interval is to establish it as a Temple of the Free Spirit.

❦ Accomplishing the Great Work is not a realization but the testimony and celebration of the Permanent Realization of That which Abides.

❦ The rites are only operative in the Real if they are conducted by individuals, not by "persons"; for individuals, not for "persons"; indeed by and for beings who have no need of rites.
 A rite is therefore either a masquerade or a free celebration without object, a simple and wonderful reminder of absolute Beauty.

❦ The fast is the first rite. It establishes the first fire.
The vigil is the second rite. It establishes the second fire.
Silence is the third rite. It establishes the third fire.
They are the three steps towards deployment of the internal alchemies.

❡ *We often ask the same traditional question to those who, after having been prepared, want to deepen the way alongside us:*

If to free yourself, to realize yourself, to reach Awakening, you only had the choice between these four paths, which one would you choose:
- The way of war?
- The way of the Game?
- The way of theft (of the thief)?
- The way of sex?

Often this particular question is first heard as a trap. It is not so. The answer helps to determine in what tension the individual finds himself and what is the nature of the fire that he can use in the heart of the Imaginal to dissolve adhesions.

❡ *Every place is a state of consciousness.*

The "place" where you are not, the "place" uninhabited by the body, by emotion, or by thought, simply does not exist. Gather into the heart, on the axis of the infinity of possibilities.

❡ *The place of the consciousness we speak of is the consciousness we do not speak of.*

❡ *Energy is the "place" of substance.*

Essence is the "place" of energy.

The Great Nothing is the "place" of essence.

The less dense is the "place" of the denser and not the other way around (a common inversion which invariably leads to the opposite meaning—the relative opposite meaning, of course, perceived from a dualistic point of view).

The most dense is the most "dancing" (of Shiva and Shakti).

❦ *In the nondual, no transmission.*
In the dual experience, the "transmission" is threefold: form, energy, and essence.
When only the form is transmitted, few disciples are able to access energy and essence.
When form and energy are transmitted, the gradualist path is effective.
When energy is transmitted without form, the disciple gives form to the energy, at the risk of freezing it.
The essence is not transmitted; it is called for in heightened consciousness.
When energy is transmitted during the call for essence and the call is heard, the subitist path imposes itself.

❦ *Trust rather than transmit.*
Trust, hand over with confidence and benevolence.
Trust, help with the Recognition of Self by Self.

❦ *The disciple, the one who celebrates the rule-free discipline of the Free Spirit, is in reality the "Self" of the master, the one who knows and masters the rule-free discipline of the Free Spirit, the "Self" that the master brings into existence within appearance itself, an appearance generated by the "Self" to play with Itself.*

❦ *Neither appropriation, nor renunciation.*
Neither possession nor dispossession.
Neither act nor non-act.
Freedom, unthinkable and unthought.

❦ *Awakening is not born from power but from powerlessness.*
Recognizing the utter powerlessness of the "Person" is the first step towards the ONE-Power, which is the Still Power.

❦ *The nondual power is ONE-Power.*

❦ *Awakening is not absorption in God but the absorption of God, of the gods, and of ten thousand beings.*
God beyond God.

❧ *Be a Black Sun.*
An acrobat of Awakening.
Freed not only from ego but from Liberation.
Let the Light be free.

❧ *When reality is torn apart or dissolved, what emerges determines your entry onto the Way of Power or the Way of Knowledge. This second includes the first.*

❧ *You will have to give up the knowledge and powers that come with subjugation to human-fed gods if you want to traverse duality and access the true knowledge of nondual Consciousness in the Natural State.*

❧ *It is not that in the Interval a power, coming from the nondual, is exercised over the dual. In nondual consciousness, all power is abolished since it has no object.*

At the exact point where the object is annihilated to give way to the Interval, or at the point (just as fleeting) where the object springs up from the nothingness of the Interval within the dual opacity, the unalterable powers of fertilization, transformation, and destruction of the object can be exercised.

❧ *"Play" at the heart of vulgarity without ceasing to be at the height of oneself.*
Blend into having and doing without ceasing to be.
Banal and yet inscrutable.
Mediocre and yet Absolute.
Limited but infinitely Free.
Choose the appearance of insignificance to Dwell, immaculate in the heart of the heart of the heart.
Thus give Appearance its royalty by revealing its true Nature.
Emptiness & Fullness.

❧ *You are free.*
First of all, a **de facto** *metaphysical freedom, metaphysical but consciously transmitted to the body through practice.*
Apart from appearance, the body, too, is metaphysical.

❡ *The Real Ways are rigorous.*
  It is not a matter of dualistic rigor, however formal, but of nondual rigor, a constantly renewed demand for freedom in heightened consciousness.

❡ *The original duality is still a unity until it explodes into a plural snow.*

❡ *Observe the adjustment, the work of Kalki, within form.*
  In the world of forms, adjustment requires a perfect alignment of thought, speech, and gesture, from the center to the furthest periphery.
  If you misjudge yourself, if the thought is too far ahead of the action, you risk an accident within form.
  If you misjudge yourself, if the thought is too far behind the action, you tend towards a malady within form: the "bad thing to say."*

❡ *If the other is another, it comes down to appearance.*
  If the other is movement, a reflection on the surface of the Self it Is.
  The Way is subtle.
  Even if you traverse it roughly, it remains the Way.

❡ *On the way, we often fail when we think we will succeed and we sometimes succeed while being convinced that we will fail.*

❡ *The work of the "Witness":*
  The Witness of form reorients energy.
  The Witness of energy frees essence.

❡ *The Great Game is the Great Real.*
  The Great Real is the Great Nothing.
  The Great Nothing is the Great Game.

❡ *If "All is Shiva," what is compassion?*
  Compassion is the fact that "All is Shiva."

---

* Fr.: la maladie formelle, le « mal à dire ».

❡ A simple comma takes you from horror to Light.
I am the absolute will.
I am, the absolute will.
Awakening is a question of the punctuation of life.

❡ All desire is desire for beauty.
All desire is desire for freedom.
Beauty is a manifestation of freedom.
Beauty is a freedom.
Note that the Universe has no need for beauty to ensure its functionality.
Manifested beauty is a gift of freedom and a gift from freedom.

❡ The simple Beauty of beauty is Awakening.

❡ A single Awakening.
Every Awakening is incomparable.
Every non-Awakening is Awakening.
Every Dream is unique.
Every non-Dream is dreamed.
Dream. Awakening. What does it matter?

❡ The completed differs from the accomplished. The first is temporal, the second timeless.
A work can be completed and yet unaccomplished.
Completion is formal. Accomplishment is a matter of the Free Spirit.
An accomplished work may remain incomplete. Its incompletion is its accomplishment because it calls for Totality.

❡ In reality, it is Presence that provides the material for the Work.

❡ Fertilization and retention reinforce duality equally.
So many errors, so much useless asceticism.
The Interval is otherwise.

❧ The Interval leads to the higher Void.
The Void is not in the Interval.
It is the Interval that is in the Void.

❧ You are Awakened.
You do not have to awaken but to integrate Awakening in each moment.

❧ Awakening is a dehumanization.
Not an inhumanization.
But Life, all Life.
That of ten thousand beings.
And more…

❧ When there is Awakening, everything is Awakening, including ignorance.
Where you are, is there Awakening?
No "Person" knows they are Awake. One believes they are.
There is Awakening, I insist, there is Awakening, whatever that may be…

❧ Awakening is when each of the ten thousand beings consciously integrates all the others.

❧ Awakening is not a differentiated state of consciousness.
On the contrary, it is the integrated state of all consciousnesses,
Total consciousness, unlimited, infinite, indescribable…

❧ That which "refuses" Awakening, ignorance, participates in Awakening and is Awakening.

❧ Awakening is an extraordinary banality.

❧ The absolute coincidence, to which all coincidences point, reveals that the banal and the divine are one.

- Being is.
  Non-being is not.
  Both, objects within Consciousness, within the Self, within the Great Real.
  Obvious!

- The hand of being and the hand of non-being are one hand.

- The nature of the Great Real is to not have its own nature.
  The essence of the Great Real is to not have its own essence.
  To be without quality and to be all qualities, to be without essence and to be all essences, designates the Absolute Freedom of the Great Real.

- The Great Real, the Ocean of Freedom, is made of all possibilities and all negations.
  The actualization of a possibility, by the contraction of Consciousness, is not the denial of another possibility. Simultaneity remains even in the manifested action.

- If the "direct way" is absolutely "direct," it cannot be called "direct." There isn't even a "way."
  Blazing or laborious, any way is legitimate.
  Every way leads to the ultimate because the ultimate is inevitable.

- The "I" is never legitimate in regard to Being.
  It is also not legitimate in the Self.
  However, seemingly paradoxically, the "I" cannot do other than refer to the Self.

- The "I" is the place of Self-Recognition.
  The human being is the place of the Recognition of the Absolute by Themself.
  It is in the human being that the Lord, who plays at losing Himself, at hiding in His own heart, recognizes Himself in His infinite fullness, in His absolute freedom.

ℂ *Speech is in vain.*
But, sometimes, speech gets in the way.
There is still Nothing to say…
No nonduality without Silence.
A Poetics of the Interval.
Let your wandering be still!
We will meet again in the Isle of the Immortals!

The Words of *Secret Monk Durian*

(THÂỲ SÂÙ RIÊNG KÍN)

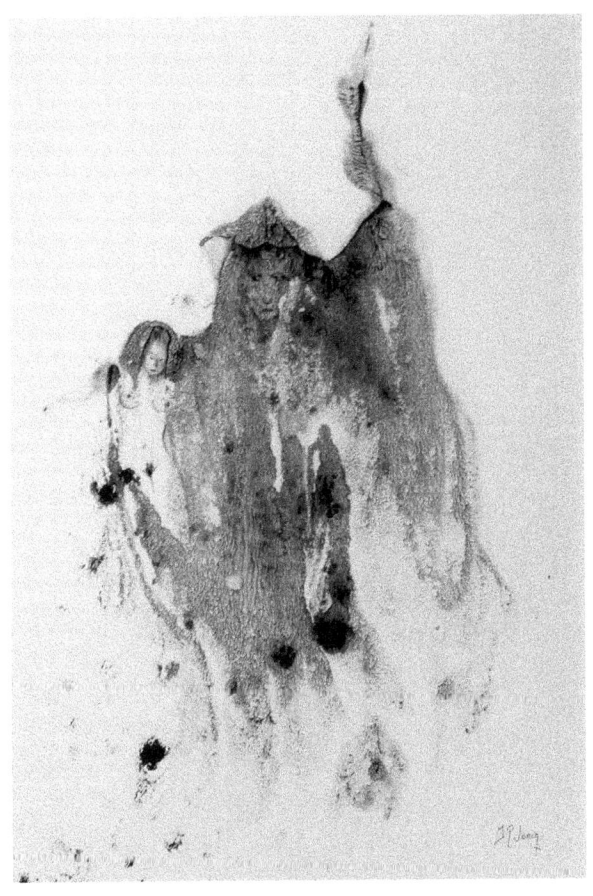

Le Prédicateur
Jean Gabriel Jonin, 2010 (gouache on paper)

ℂ *Initiatory symbolism must not get lost in the search for what the symbol represents. So many useless treatises…*
The essence of the symbol, and its definition, resides in the operations it allows.

ℂ *Let us face ourselves: we are faceless.*

ℂ *When the "I" is torn into shreds carried by the Wind of the Spirit, taste the pouring forth of the Self.*

ℂ *The ultimate realization is always the fruit of the subtle deepening of the basic practices.*

ℂ *To work with the powers, one must be freed from both the ancestral lineage and the spiritual or occult lineage. If you work with real, non-mental attention, self-remembering, and if you settle into axiality, everything that relates to traditions will appear to you as cultural. It concerns "something else," the very nature of Spirit, that you must discover within the very heart of Reality.*

"Spiritual hierarchies" are neither new nor old: they appear when you are there to "see" them. In most cases, they are culturally attired. It is necessary to "see" them naked to truly know them. But to see them naked you have to be naked yourself, without conditioning.

ℂ *What you refer to as "lineage" is often an ego illusion. For us, it is a memory, the axial memory of the Absolute which has meandered through the peripheries without ever breaking with its nondual source. A true "lineage" is therefore nondual and dual, a nondual persistence within duality. Connecting yourself to a "serpentine lineage" is recognizing your own nondual nature within duality. Recognize what you Really are. There can then be neither lineage nor connection.*

ℂ *The serpentine powers, as a whole, constitute the real intelligence of the Universe.*

❡ *Serpentine powers tend essentially towards verticality. It is only in the dualistic constraint of our conditioning that they operate in having and doing, weaving temporality.*

Once freed from archaic temporal and horizontal constraints, they become axial. Indeed, they constitute axiality.

❡ *Dragons build with discernment but destroy without discernment.*
They like to build from nothing.

❡ *The Universe is not a structure of realization but a structure of response.*
It waves. It adapts and adapts, harmonically. It adjusts to your quest, more precisely to the axis constituted by your Intention and your Orient.

❡ *Initiation is an idiosyncrasy, which is why we speak of the Way of the Particular. It is the particular and initial disposition of an "Individual," not of a "Person," to consciously integrate the manifestations of the Real into a total Imperience without the need to actualize a single one.*

❡ *Initiation is presented as a triptych, made up of two mirrors, including a black mirror, separated by a void, a complete absence. Reversed appearance, "disappearance," transparency.*

❡ *The outpourings of the Great Real in Appearance are like transcendent intellectual intuitions or pure emotions, echoes of the quiverings of the Goddess. They constitute the framework of an infinite understanding that unites, in the heart of duality, the thing and its representation, the object and the subject. The infinite understanding dissolves the finite understanding within the intellect itself.*

❡ *"I create you, I receive you, I constitute you," declares the initiator.*
"I deconstitute you, I uncreate you, I free you," whispers the awakener.

❦ *Initiation always involves, whatever the form borrowed or revealed, eating the gods, body and spirit.*
Only God, the Absolute, can absorb the gods.
Then swallow God again to discover God beyond God.
Only God beyond God can absorb God.

❦ *Controlled madness, the madness of the Sage, perceives and releases the energy of the object frozen in Appearance.*
It abolishes both the name and the number. The dream of the world goes crazy, without tension, without opposition, a free dance, a pure fluidity of the infinity of possibilities of which impossibilities are merely options.
From the breadth of Appearance, what Appears is drawn.
From the breadth of what Appears exudes the Great Real, unreasonable, absolutely Mad.

❦ *The Philosopher's Stone and the Diamond Body are realized when the adept abandons them.*

❦ *Where there is a "Person," there is no Diamond Body.*
Where there is no "Person," the Diamond Body is without an object.

❦ *The Body of Glory is an "individualized" aspect, a facet of the Body of Multiple and Simultaneous Resurrections.*
The Diamond Body is the Body of Meta-metamorphosis.

❦ *Quantity asserts itself when quality is lost. A million mantras are necessary in the peripheries while a simple root sound, unspoken, suffices on the axis to develop an infinite power, creating a totality or, on the contrary, reducing to Void. Initiation tends towards the Simple. What could be simpler than the Great Nothing?*

❦ *Instead of repeating millions of mantras needlessly, listen to the Choir of Goddesses in Silence.*

❦ *Search for the Letter A in the A that precedes the Letter A.*

❧ There are ultimately few modalities of work. All of these modalities are an extension of the modality of Being.

The **transmission,** which **in the Real** is the revelation of the Self to the Self, is elaborated in this way:
- from Being to Being in the modality of essences,
- from serpentine power to serpentine power in the modality of energies,
- by touch, scent, breath, sound, and sign in the modality of forms.

All forms of transmission either derive directly from these major vectors or constitute combinations of these vectors together.

❧ Three modalities: essence, energy, and substance.
A single alchemy.
A single work.
A single celebration.

❧ The initiatory art resides in the elegance and perfection of the Simple.

❧ Any way that goes from a number to one remains unfinished.
The Real Ways go from the many to the zero, from the infinite multitude to the Great Nothing.

❧ It is not meaning that we need but convergence, the convergence of all energies to the summit of oneself.

❧ Direct Knowledge is like water flowing from the mountain. It infiltrates through all the gaps and creates multiple passages down to the valley. If you summon it, there is no need to build canals. It'll be there anyway.

❧ Wake up the Nagas before feeding them.

❧ Free the Nagas from sensation and, naturally, they rise to the summit to open the door to the Palace of Immortals for you.

❦ Nagas are only found in the Interval.
This explains that.

❦ The Nagas inscribe their intentions in the movement that goes from the axis to the periphery as desires. In the field of appearance, they "weave" desires.
In the movement of return to the Center, they fuel and exalt the fire of Bliss.
In the center, they guard the ocean of emptiness and serve as "mounts" to the goddesses of the Great Real.

❦ The Nagas hiss in perfect unison to announce Awakening.

❦ The five visible Nagas of the Crown manifest or retract the five powers: Void, Appearance, Chaos, Balance, and Free Essence.

❦ Naga Devi's internal secret offering:
- The thousand and eight goddesses merge into thirteen absolute goddesses.
- The thirteen absolute goddesses merge into the ultimate woman and goddess.
- The ultimate woman and goddess unites with Shiva in the form of Naga Devi. (The ambiguity of this sentence is not trivial.)

The external secret offering of Naga Devi takes the reverse path of fusion and, through reabsorption, culminates in the crowned union of the King and Queen of the Nagas.

❦ When we refer to the Tradition of the Nagas, the word "tradition" should not be understood in any of its common senses. Indeed, the Nagas do not know any of the constituent elements of a tradition, neither time, history, nor memory. Let us even discard the still misunderstood notion of a primordial Tradition. What does the term "primordial" mean in a timeless world of total simultaneity?

The Nagas, however, by borrowing the intervals, traverse and sustain (in a very mysterious way) all times, all histories, and all memories of the worlds, past, present, and future.

Their "Tradition" is a permanent non-action, a laying bare so that there remains, under all circumstances, the possibility of Absolute Freedom for everything that **appears.**

❅ What you clumsily refer to as "Awakening" constitutes the liberation of the "people" of the Nagas, their return to their King before their absorption into the heart of their Goddess, the original and ultimate Goddess of all gods.

Our Brothers and Sisters of CHUÀ TÂM SEN, traveling along one of the three currents of the Mekong, the Taoist current, would perhaps say: "Free the **Qi** of the **Jing** before its absorption in the **Shen.** Through the **Shen,** join the Supreme Void." Equivalent but not identical.

❅ Naga Devi, the goddess who absorbs all the gods at the crown of her head, can also restore them at will, unchanged or metamorphosed, and can even create a new god from a single attribute of an old god, or even extract it from nothing. She rules the great game of gods and goddesses.

❅ The **Red Knowledge,** that of the ineffable secrets, guarded by the Nagas, is not transmitted—it is seized on the flight.
On the flight of the Eagle.

❅ Is the secret mantra of the Nagas truly a mantra?
From **A** through **K** to **S** through **Ā**.
From **Ā** through **K** to **Ŝ** through **A**.
From the union of **A** and **Ā** within **Ā**, reabsorbed in the bliss of **Å**.
Isn't it shudderingly obvious?

❅ In duality, the nondual lover is a perfect mirror of the Self.

❦ It is Bliss that nourishes, like a beneficial rain to the wild grass, the three seeds of eternity and thus develops the "body of nondual enjoyment, the body of Shiva-Shakti."

❦ Eternity is nondual or is not.
This is why our direct ways begin where others would like to end, with the immediate and spontaneous seizing of the Freedom of the Spirit.

❦ It is strange that religions pretend to bless unions when the latter are full of blessings, distant echoes or direct manifestations of nondual Consciousness, or sometimes even anointings of the Self.
Only lovers should bless and anoint.

❦ Human love is a theophany of divine love.
The free union of lovers, without object or subject, is both the veil and the mirror of nondual Realization.

❦ The love of the **neighbor,** of "the one who approaches," gives way to the Love of love, the love without object, which is the free Love of the absolutely free Goddess.
So, in the Love of love, in this infinite expansion, are included the ten thousand beings, all the forms—possible and impossible, nameable and unnameable—of Life.

❦ There is no deliverance, Moksha, without enjoyment, Bhoga.
A yogi who is not a bhogi would be like a hemiplegic, paralyzed by dualism.

❦ There is continuity and even identity between the sensory heightening during Self-Remembering, the ecstasy of the Flesh, and the Bliss of Absoluteness.
Consciousness can get lost in sensory intensity just as it can liberate itself in Absoluteness. Again, it's the same. The total sensory experience is identical to the absolute imperience of the Perfect Void. Such is the absolute Freedom of the Lord united with Shakti.

❧ To build Recognition in duality, maintain in dual consciousness (the game of object-subject) these three "derived recognitions":
- You are a blue god-goddess. The Supreme Unity.
- You are the Kingdom of Nagas, springing spontaneously from the Void, who inhabit you and celebrate you.
- Everyone encountered is a hero or heroine of this Kingdom, a more or less self-conscious constellation of the creative movements of the Nagas.
- Where you are remains the source of all movements, of all phenomena.

❧ Temporally, archaic tantrism, based on the transgression of form, relied only on substances. Later, it developed a metaphysics of ecstasy and, ultimately, a metaphysics of the Interval. It should be noted that this also corresponds to the three ages of the individual in search of the Absolute. In those three expressions, there remains the **Recognition** of oneself as Absolute Freedom, Shiva-Shakti.

These three "times" or "moments of serpentine power," inscribed in the axiality of being, are **Recognized** as substance – energy – essence.

❧ However, the sequence Having – Doing – Being is erroneous.
Being – Doing – Having is apt. From the center to the periphery.
Substance does not free energy, energy does not lead to essence.
Despite Appearance.
When the essence is one, the energy celebrates this unity even in the substance, in complete freedom.
The constraining path is not a path but an impasse.

❧ Teaching is first given face to face, then back to back, and finally side by side, or sometimes, rarely, one inside the other.

❧ When the teaching becomes silent, mastery of the Interval is accessible.

❧ The teaching only comes from the past in appearance. It emanates, formally, from the future, from completion, from accomplishment.

In reality, it springs from the timeless and permeates each temporality with a fire that consumes forms.

❧ Let yourself be surprised; relax, learn, but never take and repeat.

In what emerges in the very moment and does not settle is concealed the ecstatic quivering of the Goddess, the outpouring of the Great Real.

❧ He who, at the end of his breath, recognizes the center of the Universe in its nature as Void, becomes Shiva. He creates and he uncreates.

❧ I am "I Am."
I Am "I am."
I Am "I Am."
From A to HA.
The Totality and More besides.

❧ Every manifestation is a word coming from the original Intention, **absolutely free.**

The Intention is an indescribable Word, stated but not sequenced, not articulated, not temporal, a "Marveling Word," which springs and snaps like the serpentine movement of the whip or the tongue, in the Interval.

This Intention emerges in the Interval as the Letter A.

Thus, the worlds, born and unfolded within consciousness, are "Verbs."

Consciousness itself is the Word and words. This Word in its essence is Silence and even Immaculate Conception.

❧ A, the Letter A of the Interval, is the mantra of the Heart of Shiva.
It fertilizes the Ā of the Goddess.
A generates **Sauh**, the mantra that contains all mantras.
A is the essence of all mantras.
Ā is the meaning of all mantras.

❧ The **Exterior** of which we speak is the exterior of the **Interior**.
The **Interior** of which we speak is the interior of the **Exterior**.
Search again for the **Interior** of the **Interior**, the one of which we never speak.
Operate in the **interior** of the **exterior** of the **interior**, another **interior**, a silent nobility whose words are in golden silence.

❧ There is an esotericism of speech. There also exists an esotericism of Silence, deeper, accessible in Silence by Silence, indescribable except from being to being, without the slightest attribution.

❧ The ineffable does not calligraph a diploma or certificate.
The initiate is an undocumented Prince who loves nightfall.

❧ The **Implicit** is the signified and the **Explicit** is the signifier of the "wondrous Word," the original, archetypal, and subtle play within Consciousness-Energy. This **Explicit** appears like a language made of signs and accords, the matrix of all languages, sacred or not.

This play of the **Implicit** and the **Explicit** is also the dance of Eros and Agape. Agape descends through the **Implicit** to illuminate the **Explicit**; Eros builds containers within the **Explicit** to receive the **Implicit**. This dance where two play at coming together as well as moving away is the dance of the ONE.

❧ Shakti gradually transforms into gold dust as the ultimate liberation from form approaches.

❧ Koun, the Dragon of dragons, infinitely mutable, is also the Palace of the hidden King, of the Self, the formless and limitless abode of Being in freedom. Consciousness.

❧ The practice of the Letter A pointed into the Void takes place in the quivering and the sound of the Goddess.
Bathed and penetrated by this sound, inhale and exhale three times in the Letter A.
Identify the lotus body supporting the egg of the world.
Identify the assemblage point of the world egg at the end of the breath.
Inhale and exhale three times at the end of the breath.
Reabsorb the world egg at the point of the Void of the Heart.
Inhale and exhale three times at the point of the Void of the Heart.
Remain in the sensation of the death of the breath.
Reabsorb the sensation at the Crown.
Inhale and exhale three times within the Crown.
Reabsorb the Crown within the Sacred Plateau during an exhalation using the empty central channel.
Pronounce the sound K. Spring free and traverse the Crown.

❧ Still within the quivering of the Goddess, the ascending practice of the five Serpents or Dragons, up to the deployment of the serpentine fan, installs Shakti in the topknot of Shiva.

❧ In the quivering of the Goddess, the simultaneous practice of the Three Letter A's, which manifests the Three Grains of Immortality or the Three Fields of Cinnabar, makes the erect double A, Base and Seal of the world egg, appear. This double A, born from the union of Shiva and Shakti, is the prelude to the re-absorption of the world and the manifestation of the nondual A.

❧ The Three Seeds of Immortality (or Three Seeds of Eternity) float in the Void of the Heart but animate (at the same time as they feed on) the three Oceans (or Lakes) of Energy: the Ocean of the Root (base) Dragon, the Ocean of the Dragon of the Heart, and the Ocean of the Dragon of the Mountaintop, which evoke the Three Fields of Cinnabar. In reality, each of these Oceans is born from the activity of a couple of dragons (or serpents) from their ecstatic oscillation and their own goddesses, namely movement and bliss.

❧ "I Am" Shiva by marveling.
"I Am" Shakti by quivering.
There are many who seek the Heavenly Mother or the Eternal Father. They still need to connect.
Few are those who quest for the Celestial Lover or the Eternal Lover. They are already in nondual Consciousness within duality.

❧ It is said that before daybreak, Black Sun whispered to Red Moon while she slept:

I listen to you sleep peacefully
With each of your inbreaths, I enter into you
With each of your outbreaths, you enter into me
At the apex of your inbreath, we merge in you
At the apex of your outbreath, we merge in me
From ecstasy to ecstasy
Neither you nor me
Shakti and Shiva
From ecstasy to ecstasy
Neither Shakti nor Shiva
ParaShakti and ParaShiva
From ecstasy to ecstasy
Neither ParaShakti nor ParaShiva
The ineffable Bliss of the Great Nothing
Of the Great Real

❧ The Samadhi of the Goddess is Joy.
The Samadhi of Shiva is the Fullness of Void.
These two ecstasies still contain a subtle dual residue.
They are not Awakening.
Let these ecstasies abandon you without renouncing them (a dualistic act).
They will leave you to make way for nondual Consciousness.

❦ *The immortality of the Nagas differs from the immortality of the Garudas. We establish immortality according to Naga-Devi, the goddess half Naga, half Garuda. This is immortality through the death of death.*
The path of the immortal Naga is lunar. The path of the immortal Garuda is solar. The path of Naga-Devi is not a path.

❦ *The love of love begets death from death.*
Love without an object creates death without a subject.

❦ *Immortality without Awakening is an aberration. Only the immortality conferred by Awakening is real.*

❦ *The union of the Serpent and the Eagle, key to Awakening, is not unnatural but supernatural. The "bridge" that unites the Serpent and the Eagle, or the column, or the axis, is Void. The serpents rise around this full Void in a spiral ascent, freeing forms and peripheries.*
The "bridge" is sometimes called "of judgment," not in the sense usually given by conditioned humans to this concept, but understood as adjustment, alignment, and abolition of all separation. The conditioned human constantly misjudges, or misjudges himself, incapable of integrating Thought (not opinion), Speech or Word (not chatter or verbiage), and Gesture (not agitation) in a unique Art of creative Freedom.
The antihypothetical world, the unconditioned world, is not a world. It is a free art born from unconditioned operations.

❦ *Naga-Devi is the Goddess of the Center. She always tends to the Highest. This is why it is said that she remains hidden in Shiva's topknot at the same time as Shiva remains in her Heart. This is why Naga-Devi can offer Amrita.*

❦ *At the crown of Devi and Shiva in intimate fusion, seven couples of royal Nagas unite in ecstasy. Five couples are visible, two are hidden under the golden wings. The work is celebrated.*

❧ In the Interval, Soma is offered to Agni. Soma, the nectar of immortality, Agni, the sacred and secret fire. Soma, the seed, Agni, the womb. The White seed and the Red seed. The Yoni is, par excellence, the fiery altar. Each Soma in essence carries an Agni. Each Agni carries a divine seed. The erotic game of Shiva and Devi is the game of Soma and Agni. The sacrificial gift of the Absolute to Beingness. The Kingdom of the Center, the Great Interval, the essential Axis is where the sacrifice and oblation take place.

Perform the sacrifice in the Great Interval, the Perfect Chalice, in total impersonality; offer the essence of Soma to the essence of Agni for a perfect union.

❧ White, Emptiness.
Red, Bliss.

❧ Soma gives wings to the Nagas. They become half Nagas, half Garudas, nondual reconciliations of all opposites.
Pneuma then deifies them into Shiva-Shakti.

❧ With the elevation of practice, the inclusive relationship between Soma and Pneuma becomes nuanced (one includes the other, the other includes the one, in the perfect simultaneity of the Interval). Breath after breath, spiral after spiral, Pneuma shrinks, suspends, and disappears, while Soma expands infinitely. Immortality gives way to Eternity.

❧ First let the dancing butterfly meditate.
Next learn how to seize the serpent and let go of the eaglet.
Then the foundation becomes the crown.

❧ Nagas and Garudas come together to unite in the One who teaches them.

❧ *The Nagas and Garudas are the nature, matter, and spirit of all metaphysics. They teach metaphysics by imperience, an often dizzying imperience known to certain great artists, great seekers, and great mystics. Our imperience, which leads to union with Naga-Devi, the goddess of the center, is their experience.*

In this union, in this secret sharing, Nagas and Garudas expect from us a teaching, a grammar, and a metaphysical language, hitherto inaccessible, that will allow them from a distance to place in us their experience of permanent bliss for liberation.

Thus Nagas and Garudas are primarily in symbiosis with the adepts for an ultimate liberating osmosis with the **Immortals.**

❧ *Some women Awaken by their simple presence. Most often without being aware of it. They are the very essence of the goddess and have the power to reveal the Absolute.*

❧ *Because the female orgasm is an overthrow of Time, Silence under the song of pleasures, it is at the same time the source of all the re-enchantments of the great expanses of consciousness and the axial door towards Awakening. It frees up space for Being and restores harmony between the forces of the worlds.*

There is continuity between the female orgasm and the permanent ecstasy of the Goddess.

❧ *Only the goddesses teach the Interval.*
The goddesses bleed…

❧ *It is the infinite Freedom of Shakti that establishes the Axiality of Shiva.*

❦ *The gods are mortal when we are mortal.*
The gods are immortal when we are immortal.

❦ *The gods inhabit the liberated to celebrate the Absolute.*
The liberated contemplates the empty nature of the gods to celebrate the Absolute.
The only breath of Awakening.

❦ *What is* **Right** *is what is not separate.*
  Kalki measures the misadjustments, the distances that separate, in order to remind each being in heightened consciousness, of the "Gap at the Center."

❦ *Bhairava, the ante-ultimate Parashiva, the Ante-Absolute, the one who exactly precedes the Absolute, is the Lord of those who have no Lord, the Lord of those who are inhabited by the Free Spirit.*

❦ *The On-Pô-Khan is the Master of the masterless.*
The wandering initiator magnificent in his rags.
Whoever recognizes him, recognizes their own Freedom.

❦ *The healing until Awakening according to Ardhanarishvara:*
The goddess of fullness gives creative light through the left hand.
The god of void retracts the force that dissolves forms through the right hand.
The other two hands go to Earth.
Consciousness is at a higher sense.
The heart is vast.

❦ *These are not two but four dragon-serpents that unite two by two, that of the East with that of the West, that of the North with that of the South. From their infinite ecstasies springs the dragon-serpent of the Axis. Thus are the five powers of Shiva carried by Naga-Devi.*

❡ *The three quadrants of Awakening:*
Let us remember that one practice teaches another practice.
Each quadrant is realized on three levels: substance, energy, and essence.
The first quadrant* is transmissible by the outline. The second quadrant comes from oral tradition, the third from the ineffable—it is realized from being to Being.
The first quadrant tracks energy in form, the second quadrant tracks essence in energy, always across the interval.
The second quadrant should only be implemented after the "god, why?" and the actualization of the thirty-three goddesses (or dakinis) in consciousness.
The practice of the division of attention in the first quadrant is carried to the highest self in the second quadrant.
The practice of IAO becomes the capture of the Dragon to free the Goddess in the Consciousness of Shiva and the capture of the Dragon to free the Eagle in the Consciousness of Shakti.
The practice of the letter A becomes even more essential:
- From the assemblage point of the world to the point of void in the heart and from there to the crown in an interchange between Shiva and Nag-Devi.
- In the unique palace to lead to the coronation.

The practice of the sign of Infinity, this one axialized, becomes the liturgy of the Nagas, punctuated by the hissing of serpents and the noise of waves in the Void, fixed by the clicking of the Eagle's beak.

❡ *There is this old teaching of the Nagas that is so difficult to grasp:*
"The worlds are held together by seven Nagas but liberated by nine Nagas, distinct and alike."

The world, the worlds, are installed within dual consciousness. This is an "amused" contraction of nondual consciousness, a laughter of Shiva and an ecstasy of Shakti, according to the schools.

---

*   The first Quadrant of Awakening is presented in Rémi Boyer, *Mask Cloak Silence: Martinism as a Way of Awakening* (Bayonne, NJ: Rose Circle, 2021), pp. 153-171.

The world is "circumscribed" by a "sphere," that of the Naga of Fire that ensures that dualistic rumor is limited. Let the Naga enter the sphere and it will destroy its forms, thus releasing the creative energy according to the will of Shiva.

The sphere has six directions, six orientations, six power vectors and a center, both assemblage point and vacuum point, door and bridge. Six and one. Seven Nagas, the Naga of Fire in the South Tower, the Naga of Adjustment in the North Tower, the Naga of Wisdom in the East Tower, the Naga of Power in the West Tower, the Naga of Restoration or Regeneration at the Tower of the Nadir, and the Naga of Grace at the Tower of the Zenith. It is said that these six Nagas keep interchanging in a completely random manner. In the center, the luminous black Naga of Knowledge, motionless and immutable. It is also the Eater of Time. At the center of the center is the Golden Naga, the Naga of Love, and at the center of the center of the center, the Great Naga of the Interval, and the nine secret Nagas that are the nondual/dual reversals of the knowable Nagas (through the subject-object game)—dualities, consequently.

This teaching cannot be interpreted. It is practiced in the Interval. No truth in all this, but particular alchemical and metaphysical operativities.

The Nagas are like vast movements of pure self-conscious energy, capable of manifesting in an infinite number of forms. The worlds appear from their mathematical and musical relationships. The totality of their combinations constitutes the matrix spirals of the goddesses, which ground them. "One Naga, one Goddess," says the Tradition of the Nagas. Neither true nor false.

The practice, which extends through the three modalities (substance, energy, and essence), always begins with the Naga of Fire. Free the forms and free from the form. Immediately, the Naga of Adjustment arises that pronounces the alignment of the Orient and the Intention on the Axis, the verticalization of the Nagas. The other Nagas then deploy in complete freedom. No rules except Silence.

❦ Bhole Baba ki jai!
Glory to the Innocent Father!
Prem se bolo Bam Bam, *the Innocent!*
Say with Love: **Bam, Bam,** *the Innocent!*

"Innocent Father" is one of the names attributed to Shiva who, without thinking about the consequences, grants to those who recognize him what they ask of him, if they do it with a "pure heart" or in total presence to oneself which is also presence to the Self.

Those who fall into worship interpret this famous statement in a dualistic manner. There is, however, in these few words, a subtle nondualist teaching. In the presence of the Self, **I Am Shiva,** there is therefore no reflection that implies an object and a subject. Everything is in accord. This means that everything is in its place from the Axis of Being to the most distant formal peripheries (**Bam** is both the invocation and expression of Shakti), while remaining included in the infinite consciousness of Shiva.

❦ *Immortality is invented and reinvented at every moment.*
Undetermined.

❦ *Love Outside the Law*
All Love is Outside the Law.

❦ *The Absolute is the Fullness of the Void, bliss in stillness and bliss in action.*

❦ *Permanent bliss is not the ground of Wisdom but its background.*

❦ *All grammar appears within consciousness and structures experience.*

❦ *Ecstasy is a liturgical, magical, theurgical, and alchemical celebration, whether of the spirit or the flesh.*

❦ *Knowledge and action are inseparable and merge in the consciousness of the Great Real.*

❧ All desire, the vulgar as well as the sublime, tends towards the Great Real, the Self, the Absolute.

❧ Everything is the Absolute. Any experience, even the smallest, even any absence of experience, is absolute and contains the Totality.

❧ The very nature of the Absolute is Freedom. More than the Absolute, we should always evoke Absolute Freedom, as the Absolute cannot be characterized otherwise.

❧ That which is an obstacle to Freedom, resistance to Awakening within dual consciousness, becomes a means, a tool, and a material for the work in nondual/dual consciousness, and finally reveals itself as the very fruit of Absolute Freedom for nondual consciousness.

❧ The dualistic consciousness of the object is itself an object within Consciousness. Every object "floats," ephemeral and empty, on the ocean of nondual Consciousness.

❧ Nondual/dual consciousness perceives everything as free of causalities, antinomies, and contradictions. Every object is perceived not only as indistinct from the Totality but as containing the Totality.

❧ In nondual Consciousness, the Absolute is the Absolute.
The Self, the Lord, the Great Real, the Great Nothing, the Void, and its Fullness…

In nondual/dual consciousness, Absoluteness is the Intention of the Absolute; Beingness is the Action of the Absolute. All Action is Knowledge. Being is the Intention of Beingness. Non-Being is the Orient of Beingness.
In nondual Consciousness, Intention and Orient merge.

❧ All language awakens but only in its twilight and poetic dimension.

❧ If all things are equal, they are equal because of their absolutely unique quality. Everything, even the most insignificant in the game of appearance, deserves total, infinite attention: the attention of a free god.

❡ Everything carries an interval opening onto the Great Real, the Absolute in which it is immersed and with which it fully participates.
Every object is the Interval for the being of the subject in silence.
Everything is the Absolute. The part contains the Whole. The Whole is revealed in each part in its fullness.
The limited opens onto the Unlimited.
The vulgar opens onto Beauty.
The enslavement opens onto Freedom.

❡ Freedom is inevitable. It is not accidental. It is not the fruit of a will, a process, or a desire. It is, even in the servitude of horror. Condition does not limit Freedom—it is a manifestation of it, an imperial choice.

❡ Absolute Freedom is played out, is unfurled, with as much ease and enjoyment in autonomy as in enslavement, in presence as in absence, through being as through non-being.

❡ Nonduality is inscribed even in the flesh.
Anyone who doubts this is immediately caught in the dualistic net.
Flesh demands flesh.
It also can welcome the Spirit.
It also knows how to reveal the Spirit.

❡ Duality is a nondual enjoyment.

❡ No distinction between the dual and the One.
No distinction between the One and the Great Nothing.
Everything is Bliss, ecstasy, and instasy.

❡ Reach Awakening through a unique practice,
That dissolves all practices and disciplines.
Then let the unique practice fall into divine oblivion.
This is the pointless aim of the Art of Doing Nothing.

❧ *Nothing awakens.*
The relationship to Nothing awakens.
A non-causal relationship.

❧ *Everything is the Absolute.*
There is nothing to do.
The Art of Doing Nothing is also an Art of Doing Everything; Everything and Nothing, the Art of the Great Poet.
The tool of this art (of doing Nothing), of this free art, is Beauty, which must also be understood as Grace.

❧ *The Way is voiceless.*
Voiceless, formless.
Every voice leads away from the Real Ways.
The Real Ways emerge in Silence and unfold in Silence as a Celebration of the Great Real.

❧ *"The Freedom of Freedom."*
Definition of Love.

❧ **Yamanashasoham**, *the mantra of the death of death.*

❧ *The retreat of a thousand and eight days, and a thousand and eight nights, in the unveiling of the Letter A precedes (or on the contrary comes to close), operatively, the union with the thousand and eight goddesses of the invisible Monk at the summit of* **Mount A.**
The Letter A remains.

❧ *Speech is in vain.*
But, sometimes, speech strikes a **vein.**
In **All,** *there is still* **Nothing** *to say…*
No nonduality without Silence.
It is only at the apex of Being that we emerge from the Labyrinth.
Let your wandering be still!
We will meet again in the Isle of the Immortals!

HYMNAL TO THE GODDESS

To EivLys
Muse, Lover, and Paredros

To muses, lovers, poets,
Artists, adventurers, and pirates
Who enchant this uncertain world

To the Supreme

Thirty-three hymns
Thirty-three celebrations
Incantatory poems
Invocations
Of the Supreme Goddess
In these various aspects

The Absolute in its infinite feminine extension
Player, Creator, and yet Still and Void

The original and ultimate paradox

The Great Game and the Great Nothing
The Great Nothing and the Great Real

Desire without need
Desire without object

To operate or not to operate
Is equal
The Magic remains

The Joy
The Shiver
The Beauty
The Freedom above all

Hymn to the Goddess of Grace

Goddess of Grace
Who created the winged spirits
Governess of all temporalities
Who reigns over the pasts, the presents, and the possible futures
And actualizes them according to your Unique Will

Great mediatrix
Who watches over the spirits and souls
Of those who hear
Take me in your Gaze
Inscribe me in your Thought and your Word
Accept me in your Light
Through the deepest night

Goddess of the original and ultimate Grace
Of Alpha and Omega
Send on my way
Your Light-Bearing Angel
May its emerald radiance pierce me
Destroying in me all dark crystallization

You who calms the indomitable
With a single gesture
May your Love deposit in my heart
Three seeds of immortality
Three stars of eternity
Be my Providence

Goddess of a thousand and eight graces
In my groping wandering
Let me take your hand
Follow your unforgettable perfume
Take support in your own Heart
And for You
Become the Sun

Hymn to the Goddess of Free Spirits

Goddess of Free Spirits
Of madmen, poets, and the liberated
Who despises the submissive slave
And protects the rebellious

Goddess of the Works of Intelligence
Who defends inconstancy and uncultivated darkness
Incomparable Source of Light
Who abides in us
Peacefully awaiting our attention
Exalt in me your luminescent principle

Goddess of adventurers and seekers of the Absolute
Who admires intransigence
Who responds to unconditionality
Make me one of the jewels in your crown
The crown of the Free Spirit

You who rules over the stars
Free me from their influence
Teach me to thwart the traps of the vulgar
To circumvent worldly obstacles

You who turns coal into diamond
Transmute my being into a god absolutely unbound
By any oath

May your glow unbearable to the ignorant
Become the cape
In which I will veil my presence
Let me bury myself
In the folds of your delicious Flame
That through you

I remain
Free spirit

Hymn to the Goddess of Wisdom

Goddess of Wisdom
Inspirer and protector of all the Sophials*
Knowledge of the Immutable
Pure Vision of the Great Real
You who withdraws from all words
To better reveal the Hidden

Goddess of Authenticity
Who infallibly uncovers
Errors and falsehoods
Who reveals the occult to the good being
Teach me the Magic of the worlds
Teach me the art of philosophy
And the science of Metaphysics

You who cannot be called upon
By the one who ignores the Sun
You whose name cannot be spoken
You who with a single arrow
Wounds and heals instantly
To alert of your sublime Presence

Penetrate the depths of my being
Initiate my mind to your arcana
Flood it with your Light
Take me away from the error of the world
In the infinite sophianic waves
Make me one of your Light Bearers

So be it

---

* *Sophials:* possibly, incarnations of Sophia.

Hymn to the Goddess of Dreams

Goddess of the Thousand and Eight Dreams
Who reveals the arcana in dreams
Who turns reality into a dream
And the dream into reality
For whom dream and reality are the same
For whom dream and reality are nothing

Teach me
The perception of signs and accords
The reading of omens
The understanding of auguries
The interpretation of symbols
The knowledge of Arcana
Make me your prophet poet

Teach me O incomparable Goddess
To sail on the Ocean of Dreams
Eyes fixed on the Pleiades

Extract me from my chimerical dream
Accept me
In your Divine Dream
Free from all conformist reverie
Free from all consensual illusion

Teach me to share the original divine dream
The dream of the banished immortals
Call me
Guide me
That your adamantine voice
Be my thread of Ariadne
To the Isle of the Middle
Island of the Immortals

Hymn to the Goddess of the Arts

Goddess of the Arts
Goddess of Infinite Creation
Of pure invention
You beget
Create and recreate with lightning

Ineffable Goddess of the Visible and Invisible Arts
Who animates the totality of Creations
Both in the microcosm
And within the macrocosm
From your divine studio
In the very heart of the Empyrean

Goddess of the Realizations many and yet One
You give life to all beings
You draw them and sculpt them from the Great Nothing
You create them and constitute them
You give them soul and form
And intelligence and strength
You are their smile
You even hide the Freedom of the Absolute in their heart

Sun of suns
I can't stare at you
Your Light is so dazzling
Blind, I behold you

Open in me the eye of Art
So that I can contemplate you
May your Art flow into my art
May your Creation nourish my creation

You
Of whom each artist is an infinitesimal cell
Make me an eternal atom
Of your creative Gesture*

---

*   Fr.: *Geste*. Can mean "gesture" or "epic story," like a saga.

Hymn to the Goddess of Understanding

Goddess of Understanding
You the Elder
Who human beings call God
Whose Nature is Love
Whose Intelligence is Love
You are the Spirit

Goddess of Understanding
Who knows who must die
Who must live
Who must break free
Who grants Salvation

You are the prodigality of my nature
You are the power of my flesh
You are the shiver of my breath
You are the flame of my presence
You are the autonomy of my consciousness

Nameless Goddess of Love
Who teaches us
That the meaning of this world
Resides only in the Understanding
That it generates in our mind
In the heightened awareness
Of our absolute enlistment
In the Supreme Freedom of the Lord

Rend the veil of my ignorance
Teach me to love without an object
You, our real intimacy
You, our seized eternity
Teach me love

Hymn to the Goddess of Adjustment

Goddess of Adjustment and Perfect Accord
Who Judges without judging
Who measures without comparing

Who knows the Just
The divine coincidence of origins and endings
Balance of worlds and times
Who dictates the ephemeral laws
Echoes of the ineffable Law

You who banishes all abuse of force
Who immunizes against the pretensions of ignorance
Who reduces doubt to nothing

Help me
To abandon all pretense of knowing what is right
To abandon the disease of comparison
To receive what is
Taking away nothing
Adding nothing
To recognize the Perfect Harmony of what presents itself

Teach me
To enjoy the part
Without distinguishing it from the Whole
To enjoy the Whole
In every particle of manifestation
To recognize
Your secret geometry
Your heavenly music
Your divine poetry
In all that appears in Appearance

You, the unchanging Order
You are the apparition of Appearance
The Reality of reality
Teach me
To master my Madness

Hymn to the Goddess of Angels

Goddess of Angels
Ineffable queen of invisible and secret worlds
You who engenders spirits
From the most elemental to the most powerful Archangel
Who assembles them into each other
To constitute the serpentine angelic chain

You are the White Empress
The Immaculate Crown of the Heaven of Heavens
You reign over the luminous spectrum of pure whiteness
Before the worlds
Before the colors

To summon the elemental spirits
Is to invoke you
To summon the Angels
To the body made up of elemental spirits
Is also to invoke you

Prayer without a word
Calligraphy without ink
The white icon
The absolute scent
All are an emanation of You
An evocation of You
A memory of You

Look through me with your Gaze
May your infinite power
Milky sun of golden suns
Regenerate my being

Make me an Angel
A Power from the upper Heavens
Crown me
Invite me to your right
On the Throne of Clarity

Hymn to the Goddess of Origins

Goddess of Origins
Who is rooted in the Absolute
Ocean of nonduality
Origin without beginning or end
Who Is, Was, and eternally will Be

You, the Uncreated
Who gave birth to the Worlds and the Rounds
The Ten Thousand Beings
The gods and the heroes
The whole of life

Reigning Goddess of the Universe
Goddess of the Beauty and Harmony of the Spheres
Goddess of Splendor and the Central Fire
You are none other than Love

Ignite my Heart with your resplendent and unconditional Love
Goddess of goddesses
Queen of queens
Teach me to Love
Make me a loving Flame
A voluptuous Vertigo

A cold star
Turn me into a shining Sun
Illuminate my mind

My footsteps in yours
Without distinction
My silence melted into your Immanent Silence
My love immersed in your Transcendent Love

Hymn to the Goddess of the Dawn

Goddess of the Dawn
Who protects all beginnings
Who makes intentions fruitful

Goddess of first smiles
Of first glances
Of first caresses
Of first loves
Who reigns gently over all seductive dawns
Who tends to the harmony of colors
To the harmony of sounds as of scents
To the secret correspondences

Goddess of Perennial Tranquility
With the eternal smile
That soothes and heals
Your Face is a lake of delicacy
Your hand a fragrant orchid
Your breast an ocean of blessedness
You are the loving Mother of all creations

Me, your child
I turn to you
I offer you my chaos
For you to be born and grow there
Divine Beauty
Divine Truth
Divine Goodness

May your immense Love
Which makes no distinction between beings
Spread its cloak of imperial light
On my frail shoulders

Hymn to the Goddess of Strength

Goddess of the strong and the very strong
You are the unalterable and immeasurable Force of all the gods
Who burns the sacred mountains to ashes
To make endless abysses
Who erects gigantic Temples in hostile deserts

Before you
All being is weakness
But you transform this weakness into strength
To serve divine intentions

Goddess of strange martial powers
Who destroys with radiant brilliance
Adversity
Perversity
Treachery
Falsehood
Stupidity
To restore the Hidden King to his throne

Forge my body into a shield of light
Forge my soul into a worthy helm
Forge my mind into a sovereign sword
Able to slice the universe in two

Teach me to ride all the powers
So that standing on the backs of ancient dragons
Solitary I travel the worlds
To impose the certainty of your incandescent Being

Hymn to the Goddess of Mutation

Goddess of Mutation
Who clothes the essences of multiple appearances
Who manifests the absolute principles within the very substance

Mistress of Duality
Who distills your desire for eternity into the vulgar
You are the source of all enantiodromias*
The inspiration for all revolutions

Goddess of all transformations
Who makes of ugliness an unspeakable beauty
From repulsion to attraction
Who turns darkness into light
Earth into diamond
Nature into nothing
Presence into absence
Absence into presence
Clamor into the song of the Supreme Lord
Silence into a rustle of confused bliss
Your ineffable laws
Ruptures or Harmonies
Regulate the movement of worlds and rounds

---

*   *Enantiodromia* (psychiatry, according to Carl Jung): The principle whereby the superabundance of one force inevitably produces its opposite.

Goddess of transmutation
Creator of the spectrum of colors
Queen of the changes of changes
Who from one paradigm to another
Turns stone into water
Water into air
Air into spirit
Spirit into divine essence

Make me a Free Angel

Hymn to the Goddess of Death

Goddess of Death
Goddess absolute mistress of the thousand and eight dead
The sweetest
As the most horrible
All equal nonetheless

You who made the Cause spring from Chaos
Who engendered *la Chose* by harmonizing the chaotic powers
Around the miracle of this one Cause
You who makes and unmakes
Binds and unbinds
Who bestows body
Or destroys the ephemeral forms
Thus freeing the original creative power
With no other intention than to taste the joy
To get lost and found again
To forget and Remember yourself
To intensely live the Mystery of the Hidden and the Revelation

I myself am Death
When you put a kiss without desire on my trembling lips
I myself am Death
When you inhale my last breath
In Three Steps gigantic
Delivering me without delay
From any contraction of consciousness

May your Spirit of Eternity
Renew me from the Void
Not as a human being
Not as a hero
Not even as a god
But as Nothing

An infinitely complete Nothing
Intensely free
Able to welcome your Spirit
Like the sacred cup
That receives the divine nectar

Hymn to the Goddess of Ecstasy

Goddess in ecstasy
Who is yourself Ecstasy
Goddess in silence
Who is yourself Silence

Goddess in whom all intimacy is peaceful
By whom the pure senses can endlessly extend
Their silent songs of pleasure

Goddess who directs the soul towards mystical contemplation
The spirit towards absolute freedom
The flesh towards the mystery of the body of glory

Goddess who reigns over the dream worlds
Who clarifies dreams
Who turns dream into reality
And reality into dream
To better indicate the Great Real

Goddess in whom all scandal is absorbed
All clamor
All noise
All hissing
All whispering
To leave only the Wondrous Silence of the Great Real

Grant Vision to those blind to Beauty
Grant Hearing to those deaf to Truth
Grant Knowing to those ignorant of Wisdom

Seal with your Seal my consciousness finally silent, naked, and
 delighted

Hymn to the Goddess of Breath

Goddess aerial and twirling
Breath of breaths
Invisible respiration of all being
Present before generation
Remaining after all death

You whose graceful air is the grossest form
You through whom we have life, movement, and being

Goddess who exhales in the fresh and light aromas of Spring
In the sweet and burning scents of Summer
In the subtle forest scents of Autumn
In the igneous fragrances of the fires of Winter

Inextinguishable goddess
Whose Spirit is the perfume of *Natura Naturans*
And whose soul, the eternal scent of *Natura Naturata*

Breath of the worlds in universal harmony
Sigh of ten thousand beings in their desire for fullness
Supreme aspiration that leads every creature beyond itself
In a transcendent movement towards Beauty and Freedom

Mathematician goddess
Who gives rhythm to forms and to their absence
Goddess of regeneration
Who with a simple Breath
Restores bodies and minds
To their original immaculate fullness

Let me Recognize you
Let me breathe your Perfume
Fill my soul with your Breath
Restore my body and my mind to their primitive purity

Hymn to the Cardinal Goddess

Goddess of Virtue
Goddess of Temperance
Goddess of Adjustment, Balance, and Harmony

You who frees the slaves
Who leads the great revolts against tyranny
Who overthrows stupidity and arrogance
Who preserves the one who stands up against oppression

Goddess who loves rebels, fools, and beggars
Who frees women from their chains

For whom every lie is inconceivable
Who tolerates no abuse of force

Perfect mediator between Chaos and Order
That people take too long to hear

Teach me to remain
At the unchanging center of all things
At the void point between the four directions
Where all oppositions nullify and subside

Me, Crazy to unbind
Help me break human attachments
O goddess, deliver me from myself

So that in your image
Liberator of slaves
I Am

Hymn to the Goddess of Storms

Goddess of Storms and Upheaval
Impenetrable Queen of changes
Who gives shape to the Great Nothing
With a simple unfathomable gaze

Goddess of Tremors and Overflows
Crowned by Chaos Itself
Mistress of confusion and disorder
Initiator of new chaos and new ordering
Who commands Death as well as Love

You who carries us in the whirlwind
   of your infinitely unpredictable presence
You whose lightning can strike simultaneously in all places,
   destroying or revealing the treasures buried
   in the ungrateful consciousness of beings
Whose Meaning is the absence of meaning
Take me in your secret eye
Oasis of Silence and Peace
In your cyclonic intimacy
Where I Am

From this Axis of serenity
From this Temple of the Art of Doing Nothing
Let me contemplate the peripheries of the unquiet worlds

And so
Become Augury

Hymn to the Goddess of Power

Goddess of Power
Before whom all power bows

Goddess absolutely commanding
Whose desire is naturally imposed
Both on the insect and the archangel

Goddess of free and infinite Will
Goddess who nothing restricts

Who destroys the obstacles to Freedom
Who rends the opaque veils thrown over Knowledge
Who forges paths in the most hostile lands
Sweep away the adversities that still clutter my way

Goddess omnipotent
Grant me the Vision of God and of the gods
Let me contemplate the perfect plan of Creation
Allow me to grasp both the alpha and omega of all
    manifestation

Teach me to Will
Teach me to Dare
Teach me to Remain Silent
Teach me to Love

For realizing the desire of desires, born of your immense Will
I am, the Absolute Will

Hymn to the Goddess of Passion

Goddess of Passion
Mother of all torments and desolations
Goddess of perpetual suffering born from the initial cleavage

Goddess of all torments and pains
Who assists all beings slashed by the dark powers of blind
    destruction
Who relieves and supports all victims

Goddess of unwavering Will
Who makes the weak strong
And the strong weak
Who makes all beings equal through the lacerations of flesh
    and soul
Who masters the voluptuous arcanum of suffering
Who knows the paradoxical secret

Grant me the glory to resist the pain
Give me the strength to endure the flogging
In my wandering, guide me from the thorny and winding paths

May my Passion become absolutely spiritual
May your absolute Will open to me the doors
    of the mystery of the Pain ineffable

That I traverse all hell without renouncing my commitment
And that, pierced on all sides but absolutely alive,
I rejoin the peaceful Land of the Immortals

Hymn to the Goddess of Joy

Goddess of Eternal Happiness
Goddess in perpetual Happiness

Goddess of Joyousness
Goddess of Joy
Goddess in Joy

Star of the Stars
Who enjoys your intrinsic Joy

Source of the Blessedness of the Holy
Fountain of the enjoyment of the flesh

You who intoxicates the ten thousand beings
You who raises all spirits to the inaccessible heights of the
    Empyrean

You whose eternal smile blossoms in the heart of all beings

Limitless joy
Whose death flees the Venusian gaze
Who takes away the pain of a petty Mercurial laugh

Goddess of elation
Goddess of eternal adolescence
Whose simple evocation cures all pain

Goddess of Peace between creatures
Nurturing goddess
Who spreads her cloak of well-being over all the living

May you abolish the sadness that inhabits me,
Born of my primitive separation from the original Unity
Let your Joy shine
On me
In me
By me
Forever

Hymn to the Crowned Goddess

Warrior Goddess
Goddess of Victory
Goddess of Luminous Power
Who overthrows ignorance and blindness
   and unmakes the murky darkness
Goddess who summons, sword in hand,
   Heroes and Heroines of Uncertain Times

Goddess with a thousand eyes, colors of the Moon and Venus
Axis of visible and invisible worlds
Bearer of Light
Bearer of Beauty

Sitting on a ruined world
I invoke you
Purify my body and my soul
That where I am
Your dazzling luster turns the rubbish into diamonds

May the abomination that surrounds me
Become a ladder leading to the Victory of the Light
Upon the darkening

Act on me like Lightning
That my matter, heavy or subtle,
Be transmuted by the thunderbolt that strikes and frees

Shadow my being with Your dizzying Almighty Power
May I be your peaceful warrior

Hymn to the Goddess of Lights

Goddess of the Firmament and of the infinite worlds
Who created the stars
And all the lights
Who, since the dawn of time
Guides beings to the highest in themselves

You, Queen of Queens,
Mistress of *Natura Naturata* and *Natura Naturans*
Source of all majesty
Beauty of the stone, of the flower, of the serpent as of the eagle
You are the Greatness
You are the Abundance
You are the Glory
That of the gross as of the exquisite

You are the Unity I cannot conceive of
You are my own nature nonetheless

You are the infinite beginning
Origin without origin
You are the endless end
An infinite end
Mother of all new beginnings

You reign over immeasurable Creations
You create infinitely without ever breaking the Celestial
   Harmony

May you, O Goddess, include me forever in your inconceivable
   Harmony

Hymn to the Goddess of the Time of Times

Goddess of the Time of Times
Goddess who no one can pin down or embrace
Goddess who cannot be clothed in any form

You are the Time of Times
The Time in which the times of creatures extend

It is You who makes the simultaneity of all moments into a succession
You who develops all evolutions
Who determines all causalities

Goddess of Creation and of all creations
Eternal Queen of the cycles of cycles
You determine the birth and death of the scarabs as of the gods

Goddess of the Geometry of Intervals
Who makes me the void point out of which the path of life can appear
Let me turn around
To face you
To finally contemplate Your Face,
This Face impossible to paint
Impossible to speak
Who never leaves the slightest memory
Let me lose myself in your undefined gaze

Goddess of Temperance
Teach me to sail the breaking wave of your creations
Let me create,
Just like You
Me, the Poet
Me, the Master of Art
Under the crossed lights of your Thousand Suns

Hymn to the Goddess of the Uncreated

Goddess of accomplishment
Who bears on your breast the original Letter
   and the Number before numbers

Unique principle of all things
Source of all deployment
Undefined space who generates all infinitudes

Goddess of the uncreated and of all creations
   without beginning and without end
Goddess of intention
Goddess of desires not yet recognized, not yet substantial

Cleanse me of all demands
Of desires as of abandonments
Of summonings as of supplications
Of needs as of renunciations
Consume in me all constraints
Limits and conditioning of the manifested

May your nature become my nature, the Void
May your mind become my mind, Fullness

Void and Fullness
Fullness and Void
In all that was, that is, that will be

May All be accomplished
All, the Great Nothing

Hymn to the Serpentine Goddess

Serpent Goddess
Who endlessly unwinds your golden rings to weave the worlds
Who keeps the hells invented by human beings
   at a distance from the Empyrean
Who sustains the forms of your immeasurable energy
Who generates, structures, and nourishes
   the beings of your rippling powers

You, the shivering one
Who bathes in our ecstasies and instasies
Both phallus and cteis
Through whom I live
In whom I enjoy
Who yet dwells in my very being, preserving it, keeping it
Establishing its immortality

Serpent Goddess
Who manifests the absolutely Free Spirit
In contemplation of yourself

Goddess of Ascension
Whose rings are so many steps to rapture

I invoke you
I kneel before your splendor
I leave it to your design
In complete freedom, I choose to follow the luminous meanderings
   that you calligraph in our heart to show us how to penetrate
     the inconceivable spheres and reach the Isle of the Immortals

Hymn to the Empurpled Goddess

Goddess with a purple Heart
Goddess with purple wings
Fire of fires
Fervent source, a thousand and eight times aflame
Goddess glowing, flaming, and fervent
Endless well from which all seeds spring
Goddess of all embraces
Who multiplies infinitely the primitive act of creation
Yet never in the same way
Flame of Flames
Who reduces forms to ashes, leaving space for Being
Who destroys our bodies, our worlds, and our sullied times
To restore them to their original pristine nature

Goddess of the blood of bloods
Who at every Moon makes a virgin of the sacred whore
Who crowns all alchemical fires
Indispensable to the Great Work
Volcanic Goddess whose unpredictable eruptions shake the worlds
Without you, I am a corpse
Without you, I am barren sand
Without you, I am empty without fullness
Without you, I am death without rebirth

I call you
Flow through my veins
Set the corpse on fire
Evaporate the water from the sand so that it gives fertile rain
Establish the fullness of emptiness

Free me from myself
Make me a god

Hymn to the True Black Goddess

Goddess of ebony
Black Goddess, absolutely Black, without reflection
Guardian of the Arch of the Seventh Heaven
Void point in the heart of your luminous creations
Black heart in the center of the human eye
Door to the invisible, window to the worlds
Goddess who reigns over the dark turnings of the human mind
I call you
Come sail on the ocean of my consciousness like an obsidian lighthouse,
   absorbing all light
Teach me to "See," you whose sublime darkness creates
   the immaculate light of the Lily

True black Venus, sublime interval in the kaleidoscope of colors,
   perfect ecstasy in the spectrum of sensations,
Goddess of generation, of the begetting of the ten thousand beings,
   of all kingdoms, the gods themselves owe you
   all their relative immortality
Goddess of pleasure and impregnation, I approach, naked and frail,
   weaponless, shieldless, shuddering before your power,
   at the mercy of your black Will

True Black Goddess, invisible power of the Absolute,
   of which you prevent all intentions even before they emerge,
   I am, by reversal, your single eye, I am Appearance
Free me from the veil of the worlds, free me from frozen appearance,
   let me move
Me the dancer, let me revolve around your unchanging center,
   around the absolutely black center of all form and creation,
   irresistibly draw me into the intoxication of your invisible light,
   absorb me in the undifferentiated

Hymn to the Goddess of the Arcana

Fearsome Goddess of the Great Mystery
Reigning Goddess of the Eighth Heaven
Terrifying Goddess who conceals the singular source of human vanity
You who tangled the path that leads to your impenetrable Arch
    with incandescent coals to force me to go beyond myself
You who designed twelve and one trials only to render me worthy
    to address this prayer to you

I call you
Ensure that my feet not smell of fire
Heal the poisonous wounds inflicted from the fights you imposed on me
Not out of pity, but allow me to continue the magical way of the
    heroes
Not out of love, but from respect for your absolute order
    which is to conquer the Citadel of Being

More than human now, I approach your Mystery with
    the certainty that you will recognize me
Me your creature
You who gave birth to me fully armed to realize your will

Goddess of the Great Mystery
Lift the veil that hides the secret of secrets
Let me contemplate and realize the Great Arcana

Hymn to the Unnameable Goddess

Goddess of Chaos
Goddess of the Infinitudes where Your Freedom is the Law
Where your Happiness prevails
Where the only rule is the absence of a rule

You are the ultimate harmony, inaccessible to subservient spirits
Goddess of Chaos, of all numbers, and of the miracle of one Thing
Immense cascade of graces and spontaneities
You lead the four movements: appearance, permanence, re-absorption,
    and the unspeakable repose
You are the primordial Dragon, arisen from below the dark waters,
    who rises, by the power of its luminous black wings,
    beyond the skies of the undifferentiated
Each of your scales is an endless world of possibilities
    and ephemeral creations
You are all the antinomies and none of them, love and hate,
    joy and sorrow, pleasure and pain, perpetual motion
    and the immutable present, fire and ice, fertility and sterility,
    ecstasy and torment, light and darkness...

Goddess of Chaos

May my essence, which participates in your essence,
    reveal itself in Your Freedom
May my being, which participates in your being,
    reveal itself in Your black Light
Separate in me the Salt, the Sulfur, and the Mercury
Eliminate all terrestrialities and dark crystallizations
May I be your prime material from which you will realize
    the Philosopher's Stone by Your abyssal and mysterious Will
May the silver star of cloudless mornings shine on my forehead
May your hand, absolutely black yet intensely luminous,
    calligraph in me the arcanum of arcana, the infinite Love in which
    all that exists holds life, movement, and being, the elusive Love
    that presides over the cycles of destiny and their annihilation

Goddess of Chaos

You are the glorious Dragon who binds and unbinds the Earths
    and the Heavens by traversing them
I am, by your grace, one of your many emanations
May I become again a Dragon to celebrate Your Black Beauty,
Your Shining Shiver, Your Dark Freedom
That I find my original headlessness
The Infinite for all countenance
The Will for all eyes
The Freedom for all breath

Great Hymn to the Adamantine Goddess

Adamantine Goddess,
Milky-skinned,
With ruby blood
Topaz eyes
You whose Will is only Freedom
Who engenders the lack and the fullness
The desire and the fusion
The game and the enjoyment
The music and the interval
The line and the point
The pleasure of bodies and of sights
And the feast of words, crude or poetic

You the original muse
Who inspires adventurers, lovers, poets, and masters of the Art

May your serpentine voluptuousness flow into my Spirit

You who revives the postponed corpse
By your sacred vulva

You who frees from all fetters
By your most secret substances

You whose scents keep the gods awake
Whose joy restores harmony in the worlds and rounds
Come, come, come

Remind me why I gave you life
My consort
So that you dance for me
Absolute Freedom
That you make the possible and the impossible sparkle
That I finally Remember myself

Me, the Nameless
The Formless
The Great Immobile

In your vertical eye
Black, White, then Red

Let us share the drink of Immortality
Before giving it to the ten thousand beings

May the Inner Star crown our Union

Great Hymn to the Goddess of Heavenly Roses

Goddess of Heavenly Roses
You who
Long before the Times had come
Uncertain
Long after the Times have passed
Merciless
Opens in every play of light and shade
Life
From interval to interval
A Thousand and Eight Eternal Roses
In an endless garland of enchantments
Five-petaled roses in the heart of a flaming star
Goddess of the Holy of Holies
Eight times Queen of the Heavenly Palaces
Guardian of the Arcana
You yourself are the Mystery of Mysteries
Celestial Dew of the Alchemist
Essential Stone of the Builder
Supreme Interval of the Divine Lover
Key of the Great Work

Silence of Silences
Rose of Roses
Lotus of Lotuses
Lily of Lilies
Divine Orchid
Naked
Sitting in the luminous black Root-Flower
Knowledge
A ruby Rose in the left hand
A white coral Rose in the right hand
A golden Rose as a crown
Wisdom
An adamantine Rose traversing the heart
Absolute Freedom

You the unique initiator of the Master of Flowers
I invoke you before me
I invoke you behind me
I invoke you to my left
I invoke you to my right
I invoke you above me
I invoke you below me
I invoke you all around me
I invoke you in me
In my heart
If he lives
So that you fertilize it
Three times

Three seeds of Immortality
An ebony seed
A pearly seed
A scarlet seed
Three seeds imbued with your most secret perfumes
The most intimate
The most elusive
The most captivating
Which make the greatest number lose their heads
But who rise to the Highest Heaven
Masters of the Art

Three germs of Love
Nourish with your Water of Gold
That transmutes my very flesh
Into *Arbor Mirabilis*
The Wondrous Tree of the Spirit

Great Hymn to the Goddess of the Great Nothing

Goddess of the Great Nothing
Who penetrates everything
By whom everything appears and disappears
You the Absolute Essence
Wherefrom emanates the conscious Light

Unique Being
Supreme Essence
In You
There is no illumination nor darkness
Neither enlightened nor ignorant
All is Knowledge

In You
I know undivided Consciousness
One with the Absolute
I flash with your Glory
Free from the Void
Free from the non-Void

Through You
All act is art
All words are magic
All thought is enchantment
And Nothing of it is

Through you
I access the spontaneous Breath
I am the Free Song of creation

Goddess of the Great Nothing
Let me participate in your dazzling Feast of Felicity
The totality of things is the same as your body within Grace

In you
The exterminator turns into a simple flower
Neither time nor death nor life
Neither Transmigration nor Transcendence

Goddess of the Great Nothing
Original, permanent, and ultimate matrix
I take refuge in You
I make the one sacrifice
That makes all things equal
All things empty

Like a wave of Happiness
The rain of supreme nectar falls on my freed Spirit

Great Hymn to the Goddess of Absolute Freedom

Goddess of Absolute Freedom
Unchanging essence
Pure inclination of Grace
Empty axis of the universe
Innate and fiery nature of everything
Who makes essence and energy inseparable

You are She who devotes herself to holding Essence within
    consciousness
You are the sovereign Freedom of the Absolute
You are the pleasure of play
The enjoyment of the Absolute
In the emission as in the retention of Energy

Give me Your Freedom
That I simply enjoy Everything
Neither meditation nor ritual
Neither alchemy nor theurgy
Only the Great Real

By You I Know
The free being is unimpeded
Liberation in vain for that which is Liberty itself

No speech in the inexpressible
No illusion for the original Consciousness
In whom all is Essence

I recognize you Goddess of Absolute Freedom
You are the absolute Nakedness of the undifferentiated

In You
Imperfection is just a part of perfection
Doubt is only a fragment of the evidence of the Great Real

By You
Essence of the Many
Universal power
I recognize
The Identity of the Great Game and the Great Real
I manifest the things from undifferentiated consciousness
Consciousness free from any duality
Absolute undifferentiated
In whom You are You
In whom I am me
In whom You are me
In whom I am not until I am You

I delight in the Flavor of your Love
No more talk, no more action, no more movement
You reveal yourself
You strip as you wish
Your anointing is permanent
Through you I am the Immaculate

Goddess of Absolute Freedom
Who reveals to lovers the totality of creation
As a Path to the Absolute
Free Sound, Touch, Color, Flavor, Scent, Spirit
Infinitely extended
Supremely intense
You reabsorb the perpetual wheel of experience
In the void point of the Imperience
By You
In the firmament of Consciousness free from all hindrance and confusion
I Am Absolute Freedom

KAMALA SUTRA

*Sutra of the Lover of Shambu
and the Fool of Shakti*

Drawings by
Françoise Pelherbe*

Sketched at the temples in Khajuraho, India
September 2010

---

*   These are the texts that "illustrate" the drawings. In effect, Françoise Pelherbe provided the drawings to the author so that he could write a text that installs them in a traditional setting.

The first look
Immediate Recognition of the One in the other
Of the other in Self
Not separated
In the Palace of Silence

KAMALA SUTRA

Original look
Shakti, heart beating, sees the silhouette of Shambu in the distance
Immobile, he contemplates the worlds, indifferent
The eyes of Shakti are his eyes
He, the Absolute, Recognizes Himself through Shakti
The First Lightning that cherishes Appearance

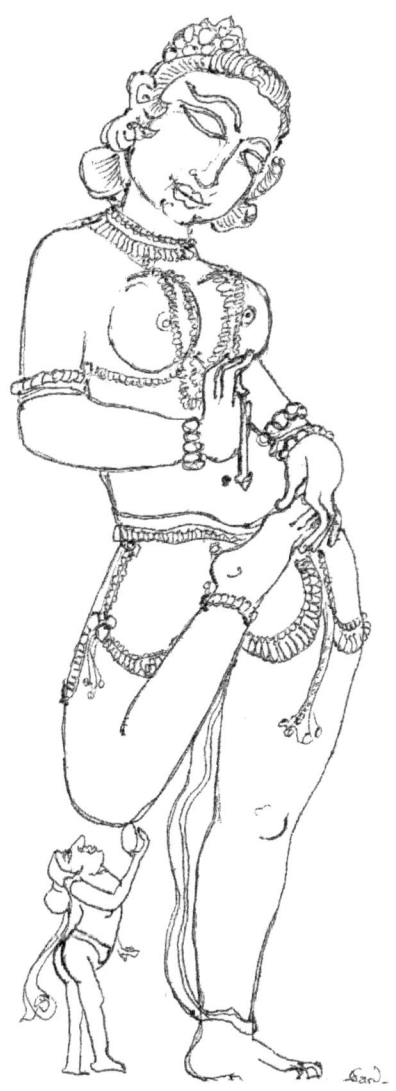

KAMALA SUTRA

She dances and her heart laughs
Silent, Shambu hears
The pearls of worms
Furrows of love
The garland of the words of Shaki
Who already sings and enchants the worlds

KAMALA SUTRA

Playing with the shadow of the sacred trees
She follows him into the Garden of the Dreams that are the Absolute
Under his eyes
She draws a love note on the sand
An everyday word
More powerful than his famous mantra
More brilliant than his most secret mantra

KAMALA SUTRA

The free Spirit of Shambu perceives the free Flesh of Shakti
He quivers
He lives

KAMALA SUTRA

Outside of temporality, time dissolves
Ganapati and Murugan are born and work
The quivering of Shambu survives immobility as well as movement
Shakti maintains the fire of Kama
The multiplicity of granted desires of the flesh and spirit
Adornments, perfumes, songs, rustlings of divine fabrics
Metaphysical poems, raw poetry, deep metaphors
Songs and music
Paintings and calligraphies
Divine foods
Naked games
Elegant provocations and transgressions
Appearances and disappearances

KAMALA SUTRA

On a night of the Full Moon, Shambu opens the sanctuary
Shakti bathes in the light of Kamala
Three enclosures
Black, White, and Red
Three lotus altars
Three Somas
Three seeds of eternity
Shakti manifests as three goddesses
The Black, the White, and the Red
With Shambu, the alchemical quadrille

KAMALA SUTRA

Cross the circles
From center to center
From ecstasy to ecstasy
From void to void
From fullness to fullness
Release the divine substances
Mix them skillfully
Drink the divine nectar
Repeat endlessly
Without beginning
Without intention
For beauty and the freedom of action

KAMALA SUTRA

Strange litany of the moans of Shakti
Symphony of pleasures
Which alone can distract Shambu from his axiality
Which alone can bring him back to his axiality
Erection of the Spirit in the lingam
Fullness of the Spirit in the lotus
Infinitely open
Golden flower
Temple of transparency
Where the enlightened mind flourishes

KAMALA SUTRA

Shambu tastes the secret silver substances
The sacred drops born from the rapture of Shakti
Collected with delicacy in the cave of the On High
Raised to the highest
In the topknot of Shambu
Seat where Naga-Devi, the queen of the Nagas, resides
Guardian of the ascetic's powers
Carrier of the Primordial Conch
Original Yoni
Fiery Altar
Who enjoys all female orgasms
Of goddesses like prostitutes
Generating the infinite chain of creations

KAMALA SUTRA

Shambu is intoxicated with the most intimate perfumes of the Goddess
Divine choice closest to the Heart
Perfumes that are inscribed in the skin as in immaculate Consciousness
Aromas that do not differentiate but unify
Always the same, always different
Shambu retracts the worlds into this perfect harmony
Suspending all creation in the interval
Then he lets it unfold, freed, once again

KAMALA SUTRA

Shambu and Shakti come and go
Visiting all worlds
Creating them step by step in the dance
Erasing them behind them
Returning tirelessly to the Kingdom of the Center
The Great Interval
Essential axis where the sacrifice that reveals takes place
The oblation that liberates

KAMALA SUTRA

Suddenly, Shakti grabs Shambu's lingam
The original lingam
Playing the absolute scepter with her mouth
Eight waves of caresses
In the Great Interval
The Perfect Chalice, it calls for sacrifice
Offers the essence of Soma in perfect union
To beauty
To love
To Freedom
In the temporal lines
The inner anointing

KAMALA SUTRA

Shambu resumes exploring the pleasure ground of the gods
Tasting red and white
White, Emptiness
Red, Bliss
Directing thirty-three kisses to the blossoming lotus of Shakti
Thirty-three arts
An art, a goddess
A goddess, a royal naga
Thirty-three times, Shakti whispers
I am the Queen, the Wife, and the Lover
Contemplate this lotus flower and pluck the red stamen
Each orgasm of Shakti is a plateau for a new ascension

KAMALA SUTRA

Shakti does not forget that she is the sole initiator
She connects the sixty-four arts
In the nine styles of the dark goddess
The nine styles of the white goddess
The nine styles of the red goddess
Shakti realizes the six secrets of the woman and ultimate goddess
Before the thousand and eight immortals of the sanctuary of Shambu
Secrets of the great work of Soma
The liquor that Shambu and Shakti reserve for the gods and immortals

KAMALA SUTRA

The Great Elixir of the Moon
All is realized in the valley of the orgasm of Shakti
When Shambu gives up posing on the tiger
To ride the wave of the ecstasy of Shakti
When, together, they traverse the blessing of the four joys
To be suspended in the transcendence of transcendence

KAMALA SUTRA

Shakti transforms into a turquoise goddess
Shakti of the end times of Shambu
Of his ultimate retreat
Triple Kundalini from below the feet, from the heart, and from the topknot of the Lord
Shakti starts again indefinitely
Padmini, Chitrini, Shankini, Hastini
Lotus Woman
Craft Woman
Conch Woman
Elephant Woman
Lotus Woman again
Absolutely, irremediably

KAMALA SUTRA

Indrani – Embrace – Squeeze – Ivy – Upright – Ajar – Pressed – Splitting Bamboo – Nail – Crab – Wrapping – Lotus – Swirling – Supported – Suspended – Cow – In pincers – Spinning – Bird – One step beyond – Wheel of memory – Favorite crevasse – Preparation of the elixir – Bow – Opening flower – Self-creation – Conjunction of the sun and the moon – Gain and retain – Turtle – Encircled – The twins – The bellowing – The monkey – The three steps of Vishnu – Glory – Mounted Yantra – Honeycomb – Resurrection – Favorable omen…

Shakti excels in all these positions but prefers to surprise Shambu
Making fun of his rules
Unexpected, spontaneous, ineffable
Shakti alternates between the grossest and most sublime forms to awaken Shambu to Himself, she who is the very essence of infinite life.

KAMALA SUTRA

In the mysterious traces of the Letter A
The Dance of Lovers unfolds
First dual
Then dual and nondual
Nondual
Finally neither dual nor nondual
Island of the Lords of Flame
Original interval
Shakti is Shambu
Shambu is Shakti
White milk
Red milk
The Nectar is distilled in the bodies melted into each other
Unique Athanor

KAMALA SUTRA

The tears of compassion of Shambu are the first Salt
The saliva of Shambu is the second Salt
The blood of the Heart of Shambu is the first Sulfur
The seed of Shambu is the first Mercury
The golden water of Shambu is the third Salt
The earth of Sani is the Foundation
The Tears of Joy of Shakti are the first Salt
The saliva of Shakti is the second Salt
The milk of Shakti is the first Sulfur
The blood of Shakti is the second Sulfur
The lustral water of Shakti is the first Mercury
The golden water of Shakti is the third Salt
The earth of Sani is the Vessel
Shakti no longer has a body, she is the ecstasy
In which Shambu bathes

KAMALA SUTRA

Again
The golden water of Shambu is the fourth Salt
The seed of Shambu is the second Mercury
The blood of the Heart of Shambu is the second Sulfur
The saliva of Shambu is the fifth Salt
The Tears of Compassion of Shambu are the sixth Salt
The seventh Salt is offered by Shakti
Again
The golden water of Shakti is the fourth Salt
The Blood of the Moon of Shakti is the second Mercury
The Blood of the Heart of Shakti is the second Sulfur
The saliva of Shakti is the fifth Salt
The sixth and seventh Salts are offered by Shambu
In the secret chalice forged by the Free Spirit
The substances mingle into a sublime and ineffable Nectar
The substance frees the fire
The fire releases the essence
Soma concentrates the Totality of the Great Nothing

KAMALA SUTRA

The Nectar gives wings to the nagas
They unite two by two
Double ascending spirals
All converge at the summit of Mount Kailash
Participate in the Great Festival
In the erotic game of Shambu and Shakti
The game of Soma and Agni
They weave an egg of light around the primordial couple
Protect the grammar and secret metaphysics of the divine loves
Share the sacrificial gift of the Absolute to Beingness

Black, white, red
The work is done
Shakti still sings of her adamantine pleasure
Morning-song of sighs and groans
The ten thousand beings are illuminated

KAMALA SUTRA

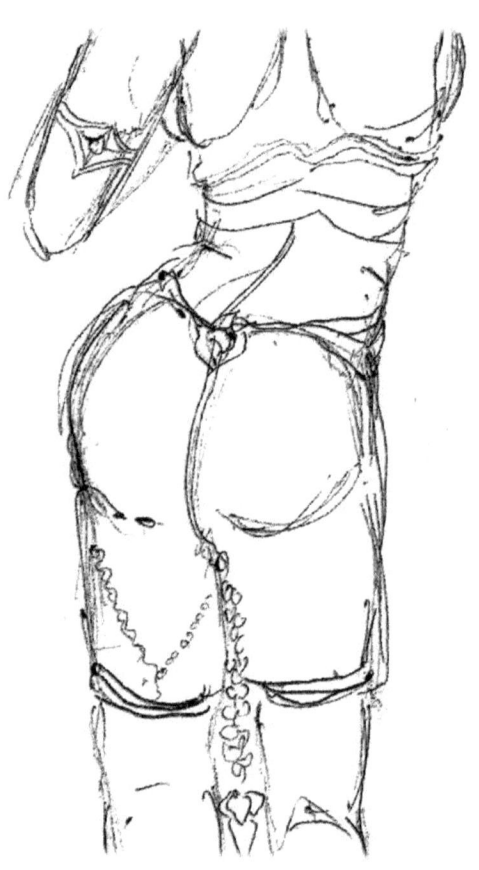

KAMALA SUTRA

THE LOST WORDS OF MONK DURIAN

*Those who
will never die
salute you.*

Awakening is extremely banal. *Extremely.*

That which is stated cannot be original or primordial.

Women who age under loving caresses remain beautiful.
    Polishing the skin lets the Light of the Spirit shine through.

At the crossroads of the hybrid and excess, the Great Interval is revealed.

God before God,
    God after God,
    And God beyond God are Absolute Freedom.
    The goddesses, the gods, the archangels, the angels, the various entities are derivatives, declensions, precipitates of this Absolute Freedom, first theophanic, then installed in an increasingly opaque duality.
    Political, social, or individual struggles for independence and freedom are extensions, echoes, and memories.

I sweep my gaze over the transparent map of an absent world.

Illusion is only one aspect of the Great Real, observed from a separate (dualistic) point of view.

Every being is infinitely greater and luminous than its appearance.

Faced with those from the brotherhood of lies, take a step aside and decide.

The adversary of the Spirit is always un-Conscious.
    It is no less the adversary and can be fought relentlessly.
    Relentless does not mean uncompassionate.

The person often takes a detail and establishes it as a law or principle.

As long as you think you have anything, you are just detained.

Some people stubbornly seek power. It is fear that really guides them, a fear born from the too distant and distorted echo of the Original Power.
   But this is only Love.

Awakening is the realization of a quest, that of the clandestine home of the Free Spirit.

The Great Real is the memory of an unknown: Wisdom.

Awakening consists of realizing the true from the false. Grasp the Real from the appearance. Move from part to part, then from part to the One.

What do I know?
   How do I know?
   If you sift everything that presents itself in consciousness through these two questions, nothing remains.
   But this nothing carries a surprising flavor of infinity, freedom, fullness.
   This Nothing is Awakening.

Each of you is right. Why doesn't being right bring you peace? On the contrary, I am absolutely wrong. And I am at peace. I am.

Substance beckons.
   Energy agrees.
   Essence joins.

The "person" goes to the "person."
   Being comes to be.

Being is irreconcilable to the "I," a simple object floating in the ocean of consciousness.

Distinguish immortality within duality (within time, which will disappear with it) from immortality in Eternity.

There are no constraints in initiation.

The object, the temple, the master, and the gods come and go.
    The Self remains.

Any sacrifice other than that of the ego is miserable.

Some shit is awakening.
    Some diamonds are sleep-inducing.

In duality, no ascent without descent.

No one can free themselves from evil without freeing themselves from good, because it is only from duality that being is freed.

Sometimes we are at the top of the mountain without knowing it because we are looking in the wrong direction. Awakening is a view, the View.

Some beings are awake, others are Awakening. The first are the Circle, the second are the point in the center of the Circle.

Every object, every being, is a differentiated state of Consciousness.

Every initiation is a taking refuge in the Self, our original Principle. The "Person" comes to slip into the luminous shadow of the Self while waiting for duality to reintegrate nonduality.

Quantum uncertainty illustrates in an analogical way the relationships between the ego and the Self within appearance.

In the luminous cavern of the Self, there is room for an infinity of "I." Also, the inclusion of everyone and everything should not scare you.

There are no contradictions in the dual/nondual but absolutely aesthetic and coherent paradoxes.

If the Absolute unfolds in an infinity of manifestations, it is likewise to Recognize itself in an infinity of modalities. Awakening is infinitely multiple and surprising.

You have to accept being diverted so that Awakening sets in around the bend. Awakening is a total rout of the "Person."

If, at the slightest incident (and death is just one incident among others), you lose sight of the Original Intention and the Ultimate Orient, how can you make them coincide in the present moment?

No causality in axiality. The causal emerges from having and doing. It unfolds in the dual peripheries. It is not but it exists as duality.

Everything can be destroyed within duality. There is no destruction possible in nonduality, where the very principle of destruction reveals itself as empty.

Creation in the world of forms should arise from the center. There is then a harmonious and efficient decentering in the peripheries. A "creation" from one periphery to another is a drift, a "creation" from one shore to another. It is not a question of creation but of replication, sterile or toxic.

Wherever I am, wherever I die, I remain in the Light and Peace of the sacred Tagus.*

Awakening is more surely present in non-Awakening than in any other state of consciousness.

---

* "Tagus": a river with mythic connotations that runs through Spain and Portugal.

The world is in the body, it is a body-world; the body is in consciousness, not the other way around. This first reversal of consciousness re-establishes the right harmony with the body, the place of celebration of the divinities.

Perception is contextual and localized. Any sensation can be de-localized and, through synesthetic translation, become another. We can see a noise, hear a smell. This de-localization of the senses opens onto infinity.

Christ is re-crucified from moment to moment: martyred children, raped women, human beings tortured, humiliated, reduced to slavery, or just cared for by incapable people... Only Awakening is resurrection, but Silence suspends the installation of the person in duality. Seeking to become Christified is seeking Awakening.

Crucifixion is permanent in duality. The possibility of nondual resurrection also, in every interval.

The other, equally empty, equally loving, equally free, worthy of recognition as Buddha, Christ, Mohammed, Apollo or Shiva... reflection of your own divinity.
    The other, the Self.

Friends of the Goddess can find themselves on two opposing sides within Appearance. They will recognize, in each other, the echo of the beating of the Heart of the Goddess in which they have taken refuge, and this even in the midst of the din of battle.

Gods and Goddesses need an Orient.
    You are this Orient, in the Highest Sense.
    You are this original axiality.
    No need to force them or pray to them, they perform the Dance of Shiva.
    They carry out the Great Work without intervention.

When nine Knights of the Fifth Empire gather in the name of the Hidden King, He manifests himself from the Imaginal where he dwells for the accomplishment of the work of the Holy & Free Spirit.

May the Hidden King cross the mists of the "I" and rejoin, on the Tagus of the Free Spirit, the banks of Consciousness.

In duality, awakening is like a moment of perfect boredom.

Magic is a dualistic initiatory art, perhaps valid for the time of thorns, which requires having and doing. In the time of roses, theurgy and alchemy celebrate the beauty of what is and remains within duality itself, but a duality oriented towards a higher meaning. But the only initiatory art of the time of lilies is the art of doing nothing, the free clarity of nondual consciousness.

Suffering does not lead us to evolve towards the Free Spirit, contrary to a stubborn prejudice. Neither does pleasure. But an adaptive relationship (free from contingencies and adhesions, even nondualistic ones) to suffering and pleasure is liberating.

Awakening is never timestamped.

Many of those who talk about their experience of awakening are only sharing a self-hallucination. There is never an experience of awakening. Awakening is the cessation of all experience, the absolute inclusion in the Great Nothing.

There is Awakening with awakening and Awakening without awakening.
   Both actualize the unity of Consciousness.
   All is equal.

Absolute Freedom is "Awakening and non-Awakening" and is not "Awakening and non-Awakening."

Awakening is inevitable, our very nature. Some have a sense of it within duality itself and actualize it, others do not. They are equal.

In operative inclusion each part is included, not as a part but as a Totality. This is respect for the integrity of the part.

I am neither the awakened nor the awakener.
   I am neither the dream nor the dreamer.
   I Am.

Some are for, others are against; only the adept understands the "situation."

Woman is an abbreviation of the Divine.
   Man is most often a compendium of stupidity, in the philosophical sense of the term.

Recognize the nonduality of the couple.

The Order of the Time of Lilies is not an organization, nor an institution, it is a meta-religion and a meta-initiation inclusive of all religions, of all initiations, of all the gods at the heart of nonduality, in formlessness, by a dis-appearance that leaves room for the Free Spirit, the Holy Spirit.
   The Order of the Time of Lilies requires strict adherence to the discipline of the Arcanum.

The substantial plasticity of the illusion, this fine and tenacious first veil of Appearance, is total. It can imitate everything except the Interval.

Lineages and transmissions from the past are fading away. Only the lineages and transmissions emanating from the future are reinforced from moment to moment. The incoherist is an initiated privateer sailing to actualize their own future which is no less than immortality, a royalty crowned yet headless.

"Conquering the Citadel of Being." This metaphorical expression is part of the dualistic approach characteristic of Initiation in the City.

"Exploring the Garden of Being" metaphorically expresses the quest for Initiation in the Garden, nondualistic.

Effort gives way to non-effort.

The metaphor of the conquest of the Citadel of Being designates the approach of the warrior-hunter. That of the Garden evokes the initiatory approach of the Master of Flowers, adventurer and gatherer.

It is fascinating to discover what minimalist initiation achieves through reduction.

The unconscious are conscious.
Everything is Consciousness.

Incarnation is a modality of consciousness. Christ, of all awakeners, experienced the extreme of the flesh, reversing duality in its most subtly nuanced and exalted form through suffering and ecstasy into inclusive and serene nonduality.

All authentic metaphysics is an avant-garde.

In the Garden of the Master of Flowers, Nagas and Garudas merge into a new immortal celestial entity by the flaming Heart of the Queen and King of the winged Nagas, prophets of Naga-Devi.

The real initiation is minimalist. It begins at the heart of Silence, after traversing the rites, when the play of Consciousness and Energy unfolds in complete freedom, when coming and going between density and subtlety, duality and nonduality, is made spontaneous by all the modalities of the Spirit.

In the song of Silence, in non-separation, every sound, every word, is creative, a mantra uttered from the Heart of the Divine.

Everyone has killed, at one time, but no one has ever died.

No lucidity without separation. No awakening without lucidity.
No nonduality without passing through duality.

The Holy Spirit or Free Spirit is "secular." It is beyond forms, including secular forms. This is why we can speak of secular Spirituality.

God counts on each being to discover their own essence in an incomparable, absolutely singular style. You are this divine singularity.

Awakening appears as a spiritual clandestinity.
The awakened knows how to distinguish between what is *just*, what is *exact*, and what is *true*. They lucidly distinguish between *justice*, *exactitude*, and *truth*. What is *exact* is not necessarily *true* or *just*. What is *just* is not always *true* or *exact*. What is *true* is often neither *just* nor *exact*.
In a Christian metaphysics, we would say that the *exact* is the part of the Devil, the *just*, the part of Lucifer, and the *true*, the part of Christ. Bringing the three together makes it possible to realize God, *The One–The All*. This reintegration takes place through *wisdom*, Sophia, the "feminine" part of God.
In this Christian cultural frame of reference, Mary Magdalene and Judas symbolize the two "love fires" indispensable to the Great Work, Mary Magdalene for the priestly way and Judas for the preparation.

Is awakening against the world? Despite the world? Without the world? Three dualistic paths. Awakening is absolutely inclusive. It is realized with the world, with all worlds, actualized or not, past, present, and future. A nondualistic way.

Awakening can spring up with form (dual approach), with serpentine energy (nondual/dual approach), and through essence (nondual way).

When times are messy, stand still and let them go around you.

There always comes a "time," more precisely a "climate," when it is no longer necessary to drink the brew of immortality.

On a way of awakening, the question "what cures illness" becomes "what can illness cure?" The "person" installed in temporality wants to heal. The self, which has no needs, recognizes illness as a liberating gaze.

"Evil" is just an effect of ignorance. You seek to combat the effect without treating the causes. This is why your struggle is fruitless.

What can the body do? This question, from moment to moment, leads to permanent revelation. What can the body that is born in the appearance of consciousness do? What can the body of enjoyment do? What can the body of suffering do? What can the aging body do? What can the body do which, dying, retracts like a flower that closes, to leave appearance? It can do everything. It can be the One. It is the great "celebrator" of Totality, of the Freedom of the Absolute, and of Beauty. It is the Spirit. Body and Spirit are One. And the soul, if you care about the soul, is this plastic stretching that goes from the Spirit to the body and from the body to the Spirit within the duality of appearance. Sometimes play leads the soul to forget the Spirit to lose itself in the pleasure of the body. It is the body itself, which by co-birth with the Spirit, sends the soul back to the Spirit, to make the beginning and the end (the alpha and the omega) coincide, to merge duality and nonduality.

Incoherism is an "intertext" of the philosophies of awakening and the initiatory ways, an art of the Interval that indicates "passages without a door."

The Holy Spirit, let's prefer the expression 'Free Spirit,' is ineffable and unpredictable, because it works outside of causality and time, in the field (the song) of eternities. Installation in the Interval alone allows the dazzling grasp of the Free Spirit.

It is necessary to distinguish the action of *chronos*, that of *aion*, and *kairos* which alone concerns the ways of awakening. But we must also integrate the operational paradox which means that *chronos*, *aion*, and *kairos* are simultaneous states within consciousness. This allows for an absolutely inclusive approach that rejects nothing. This simultaneity is discovered in the Heart of the Goddess.

See how *chronos* engenders religions, how *aion* justifies gradualist initiatory ways, and how *kairos* indicates direct ways of awakening. *Kairos* is the eye of the cyclone, *aion*, the spiral bands of the cyclone, and *chronos*, the terrain. Only presence here and now allows us to cross the eyewall.

Do not confuse creation and production. The first is born of the Great Nothing to return there as its celebration. The second is just a murky stagnation in duality.

At every moment there is a crossroads, an opportunity for axiality, for bringing together the peripheries typified in the highest sense, for liberation through non-separation. The way of the Bodhisattva or the Rosicrucian. A Poiesis of the Interval.

Intention and Orient coincide. Energy does not come from intention but from the Orient when there is extension. Nondual consciousness, installed in duality, ascends the serpentine current. It doesn't come down.

The Fall of certain Christian traditions is an escape into speed. Speed thus screens the radiation of Being. It generates the opacity of appearance. But absolute speed is total stillness.

There is not in all the created worlds a more ethical and faithful people than the People of the Nagas.

The gradualist initiatory process is centripetal while the world is centrifugal. Each situation is "cyclonic," it takes and rejects. Join the eye of the storm, the quiet center of all things.

Learn to link without attachment.
    To better unlink.

The self-transmission of the night is the only transmission. From the high intellectuality and intense consciousness of experience to understanding.

Every object is a vehicle of consciousness.
    Even within consciousness.

Stupidity happens too quickly.
    Slowness is the true subversion.
    Without slowness, there is no lightning.

Humanity does not need you to awaken.
    You need it.
    It is the *guru* inscribed in duality.

You cannot come to your awakening because you are already awake.

Initiation presents itself in mosaic within duality. It requires a rigorous integration process in order to reduce the dualistic tendency to fragmentation and identification with parts, a tendency which also affects so-called initiatory societies. This process is always based on the determinants of self-remembering, presence, and an art of the interval.

Make the key of dreams replace the key of monkeys.

The Great Nothing offers the first duality, the initial couple, Emptiness & Fullness.
    This couple is both at the heart of the Great Nothing and outside it, but internally outside, to allow the Great Game of Energy and Consciousness.
    This first couple is the original mirror, of a quadruple nature because it generates four reflections, a double-reflection between Emptiness and Fullness and a double-reflection between the Great Nothing and Emptiness-plus-Fullness, which generate two axes, one "horizontal," which grounds the peripheries, the other "vertical," which guarantees the two axialities: "precipitating" and "ascending."

The period of the Full Moon is a nondualistic time within duality, an opportunity for the permanence of solar consciousness. The first sound, the founding A, remains in the movement of exhalation and inhalation. The interval is no longer between exhalation and inhalation but then contains exhalation and inhalation, emanation and re-absorption.

Appearance is jarring; it must however be traversed, pierced, recognized as of the nature of the Void, and simultaneously included.

Paradoxically, it is not that the unique generates the multiple but that the unique emanates from the multiple. The multiple carries within itself the necessity of the One. The multiplicity of appearance makes the traversal of appearance obvious. Unbearable duality imposes nonduality.

Excommunicate yourself from stupidity.

An initiate? What's that?

Many "initiators" are persuaded to initiate when they themselves are initiated by the "recipient."
The "I," the "person," claims to initiate the Self when it presents itself in all simplicity, without appearances.

All initiation is *ultimately* auto-initiation of the Self (the Absolute) installed within duality by the Self (the Absolute) that remains, neither dual nor nondual.

Give up all heritage. Enter the Age of the Tagus, the royal river of the Free Spirit.

It is not the Tagus that flows into the Ocean but the Ocean that flows into the Tagus.
It is not the Island that is in the World but the World that is in the Island.
It is not Consciousness that is in the Body but the Body that is in Consciousness.
The Spirit contains every object. Every object celebrates the Spirit.

364 Sometimes Appearance is exhausted: an opportunity for Awakening. The meshes of the "I" unravel and let the Light of the Self pass through.

If the Remembrance of Self, our own divine, original, ultimate, and permanent Nature, absolute Freedom, is not immediately recognized, then the gradualist process of Reintegration through the operative is necessary. But during this process, the possibility of direct access persists, from moment to moment, from interval to interval.

In duality, the being frozen in its conditionings is without interval. The being "at the beginning of awakening" seizes the interval and installs themselves in it. The awakened is the interval.

A transfiguration, a realization, or a liberation not only changes the future of Appearance, but its past. All Appearance merges into the Great Real.

Free will is not exercised in the duality between elements of Appearance but between duality and nonduality.

For the awakened, Awakening is of no importance.
For Awakening, the awakened is of no importance.

The "Fall" is the voluntary shift of Consciousness into duality. In duality, there is the other. There is this other who sees me. If "I am seen," "I am experienced," reduced to the object, and I lose my nature as a subject, which I can only rediscover by making the other an object. This is the sometimes treacherous game of duality from which we only escape through the Recognition of Oneself, not separated and not separating.

In duality, there is no pure origin. In duality, everything is a crossroads. All creation is born from multiple factors and influences.
The pure, nondual origin is a non-origin, that which remains, outside time, outside space, outside concept, and outside percept.

Distinguish between the cultural operative and the non-cultural operative. The first related to gradualist ways, the second to direct ways. This applies to prayer as well as to sacred eroticism, to traditional medicine as well as to alchemy.

What is really sacred (sacred because Real) cannot be profaned.
What is really secret (secret because Real) cannot be revealed.
"Sacred" and "Secret" are the two faces of the grasping of the Real which is also grasping by the Real. This grasping is also called "Unfolding of the Goddess."

The operative becomes humble and simple.

There is no rule.
So, sometimes, there are rules.

Awakening is not actualized because we do this or that. Being outside of all causality, it is actualized as soon as we stop doing.

Awakening? A black hole. The Darkness from which springs the original Light which is also Love.

One who is truly in search of absolute Freedom will never cease to find—or better, to create—an ever more direct path towards It, even more direct than immediacy.

Gnosis is the knowledge that the Absolute has of Itself.
There is no other way than to be the Absolute.

What is True?
The reality of the facts or the facts (the effect) of the Real, the Great Real.

We have to return from everything, from Christ as well as from the Buddha, from opposites as well as coincidences, to free ourselves with the Spirit that is one with the Goddess.

The Self manifests itself as a guru to weak minds in search of the Absolute. To strong minds, it appears as the World-Goddess herself because everything awakens. Everything is Awakening.

The time for initiation according to the Law is over. The gods have failed.
It is now the era of Goddesses and initiation according to Grace.

The Goddess through the Nagas, such is the Sublime Way, the Song of the Praise of the Nagas to the Goddess.

The spontaneous breathing of the Lover in orgasm is the song of the Absolute Freedom of the Goddess.

One who becomes a "Basilisk" can unite with the Goddess. They know how to transform poison into the nectar of immortality.

The Goddess.
Only the Goddess.
In one of her thirty-three aspects.
From the Flesh to the Free Spirit.
The Awakening ineffable.
Yet inevitable.

The pilgrim, who consciously travels the Path of the Serpents hidden in the Hymnal to the Goddess, discovers the three magisteria and realizes them.
The pilgrim is Free.

Three Magisteria:
The Alchemical Magisterium of substance. Covenant with the Stone.
The Draconic Magisterium of Consciousness-Energy. Covenant with the Nagas.
The Fiery Magisterium of Essence. Covenant with the Free Spirit (the Holy Spirit of the Christian people).

SHE
- The Goddess
- The Absolute

The secrets are before your eyes.
The absolute techniques are born from ecstasy.

HYMN TO THE UNKNOWN GODDESS

Unknown Goddess
Incoherist* and naked
Shadowless Goddess
Inevitable and ineffable
Who remains
Beyond all appearances
Goddess before whom all goddesses bow
Who want to contemplate themselves in the ultimate
Free yourself from the love of human beings
And rediscover their essential nature
Goddess who neither takes nor gives
Neither lowers nor elevates
Who refuses any celebration
Who tramples all cults with her slender feet
Goddess who charms all dragons
Introduces them to Love
Chains them up then frees them
Wingèd
Who never cries
Bearer of the three divine smiles
Glance, Heart, and Yoni
Triple enchantress
Guardian deliberately inattentive
To the secrets of the gods
In order to make the Poets immortal
And the gods mortal
Who teaches the Recognition of the Absolute
In each of her moments
By the perfumes of her body

---

*   The language of birds has given us a few elements:
    INCoHeRiST: in Christ, in the anointing of our own original and ultimate reality.
    INcoHeRISt: in *Shri*, in the quivering of the Heart of the Goddess.
    inCoHeRiST: *CHeRcher STella*.

Rose Goddess
With five petals
Who laughs at the cross
Immediate Goddess
More intimate than intimacy
Whose other face, irrevocably
Consumes the worlds with her single eye
Plays with her countless serpentine arms
Combs the topknot of Shiva
Cuts off his head without marring his ecstasy
Collects his blood
Drinks it with delight
Dancing with bliss on the inferno of burning worlds
Unsuspected Goddess
Who dwells in the Appearance of the worlds
Bright, obvious
In her raw nakedness
Unspeakable, always present between the words
Between absence and presence
Goddess who presides over infinite tasks
Who shuns natural and supernatural ends
Who ousts back-to-back the gods who confront each other
For the draught of immortality
You who are Immortality
Who lets the divine liquid flow down your thighs of opal
To panic greedy goddesses and gods
Who believe they are immortal because they drink
Infinite task that simply needs to be abandoned
To realize Absolute Freedom
Founder of its own foundation
Lightning goddess
Teach me to spit the serpent
Out of the geometries
To coincide absolutely with You

HYMNAL TO THE HIDDEN KING

*Seventeen Lusitanian
& Sebastianist Hymns*

SEBASTIANIST MANIFESTO

 FOR THE IIIrd MILLENNIUM
1st VERSION (CALLED "MAFRAN")

to Lima de Freitas
to the Watcher

1. The Mission of Portugal, by essence Sebastianist, the Mission of the Port of the Grail, is Universal but not universalist. It is a Way from the Singular to the One, which dissolves the uniform and the conformist.

2. "Portugal" is the one who received the Holy Spirit or Free Spirit. They carry the Grail.

3. "Sebastian" is the one who distinguishes the Self through the mists of "I."

4. The Fifth Empire, the Empire of the Free Spirit, is *already and not yet*. The door to this Imaginal Empire, which remains, is *here and now*.

5. From Odysseus to Christ, from Saint Vincent to Saint Francis, via the Thorn of Saint Jerome and the Tau of Saint Anthony, this is the Way.

6. The connection maintained with sound, rhythm, and language determines the world. A vulgar connection constitutes a vulgar world. An initiatory connection constitutes an initiatory world. It is a matter of conscious choice.

7. Whoever knows the axial connection to the source of language sees the Universe respond to them. They recover the Utterance, the immaculate mirror of the Word.

8. Sleep, dream, Awakening. Absence and emptiness of the person. Permanence of the Great Real, that in which I sleep, in which I dream, in Whom and by Whom I Awaken.

9. New Discoveries are to come. The worlds of internity await new adventurers. They demand the same qualifications, required always, to undertake the Quest: those of the peaceful Knight, the axial Artist, the Priest without priesthood.

10. If it is necessary to sojourn to the Isle of Love, it is just as necessary to leave it. The essence of the Way is Freedom.

11. The 515 indicates the original and ultimate Unity. The return of God. The return to God.

12. After the Time of Thorns, then the Time of Roses, the Time of Lilies approaches, from the Heart to the Boundaries.

13. He who "Sees" invokes the "already and not yet." The Magic of a snowy day of the Hidden King operates through the uncertain Appearance of the Tagus.

14. The Hidden King appears when hope, this tenacious illusion that contains its opposite, despair, is extinguished forever.

15. No transubstantiation without the Woman, her Mystery, and her Beauty: the Paracletian Initiator reverses the inversion, from Eva to Ave.

16. Remember both Amadeus, prototype of Christian Rosenkreuz, and the giant Almourol, prototype of the Knight-Guardian of the *Imago Templi*.

17. We are all Bandarra!

HYMNAL TO THE HIDDEN KING

SEVENTEEN SEBASTIANIST HYMNS

PATH S

HYMN TO THE POET-PROPHETS

Visionaries of suspended time
Who sense the ultimate recapitulation
At the very moment when
The divine game dies
In conjunction with all the pasts
And all the futures
In the inevitable that remains
The tragedy that awakens
By the farce it denounces

Foolish prophets
Emanations of the Unique Poet
Free from stupid timelines
Who know before knowing
To never forget

Sebastianists before Dom Sebastian
Sebastianists with Dom Sebastian
Sebastianists after Dom Sebastian
Twice born by poetry
Priests happily defrocked
From the Lusitanian religion
We are all Bandarra
You who chant the liturgy of the Hidden King
In the kaleidoscope of words
Give us the secret Eucharist
The one that Rome ignores
The one the powerful fear
The one that the people hope for
The one that the knights defend
The Eucharist of Freedom

HYMN TO THE SACRED FOOLS

To all of you
Mad monks and cracked kings
Who alone let the light pass
Warriors, priests, and poets
Who pierce the dirty gray conformisms
And hunt down predators in their golden lairs
We swear allegiance

May the work of sacred madness be accomplished
Let it invade our liberated minds
Break down the walls of forced respect
And clear the fog
Of false achievements

Let the ephemeral theaters burn
Where articulated puppets and postponed corpses
Repeat their monotonous rounds
Fanatics and revenants

Let fall the boundaries of conditionings
Of stupid nonsense and irresponsibility

Like Sebastian, the mad and free King
Let us survive the sands as well as death
By foolish wisdom
Or wise folly
Let us hold high the banner of absolute freedom
Even in the false places of salvation

Let us establish a new empire
Where everyone will be Queen or King

In the sight of all
Men or gods
Which is to say free
Absolutely free

HYMN TO THE TEMPLAR PASTORS

(Dedicated to Manuel Gandra)

You who, hunted by the Roman ogre
Betrayed by the eldest daughter of the Church
Have concealed your weapons
To protect the order

You who made yourselves shepherds
To preserve the mysteries of the Temple
Abandoning the text for the word
And the closed cenacles for the starry vault

You who taught our poet-prophets
So that no one forgets the mission of the Temple
Who continued to inspire Kings and beggars alike
Entrusting the teaching to the mountain winds

You who knew how to keep alive the celebration
   of the Holy Spirit

In the heart of dark forests
And at the summits of inaccessible mountains
Who have hidden the wisdom of the Temple
   in the festivals of the people
Show yourselves to us
Share with us the vision and the means to realize it
Recall us to the Lusitanian mission still unfinished
Which, after having fertilized the distant lands
Must yet free the near spirits

Engrave the red cross on our flaming heart

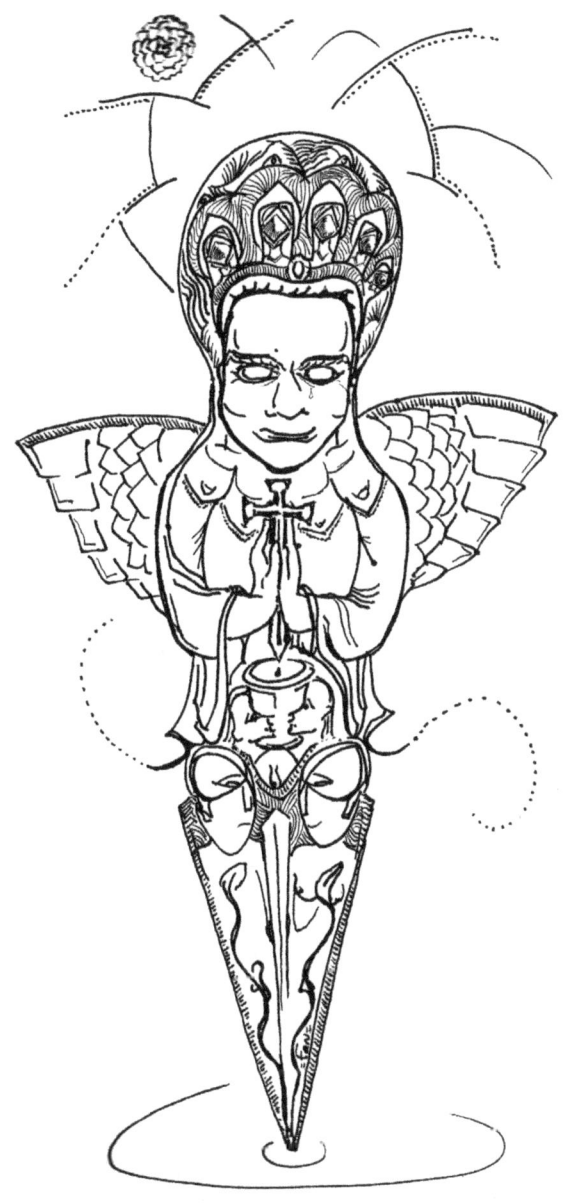

HYMNAL TO THE HIDDEN KING

HYMN TO THE UNDINES OF THE TAGUS

Daughters and mothers of the waters
Aquatic powers
Who give birth to the mares
Born from the waters of the river
Secret threads of all life
Matter of all creatures

You, inhabitants of the sacred Tagus
Who, since the coming of Odysseus
Under the mercurial wing
Bless every sailor
Off to unknown lands
Who welcome the heroes
Exhausted or triumphant
On their return from adventure

You who dance to the sound of the wind
In the sails of the red cross
Whispering the prophecies
To the ear of attentive poets
Inspiring the dreams of Kings
And the desires of freed peoples

You who know the secret of this river
Into which the ocean comes to flow
Like a child in a mother's arms
Who keeps in its whirlpools
The memory of the ancient shores of the Spirit
Towards which we dream right now
Bathe my body in the sacred waters
Bathe my soul in your improvised dances
Bathe my spirit in your luscious freedom

Let the sacred Tagus be my home
Waiting for the King to return

HYMN TO THE GRAIL BOATMEN

(Freely inspired by the work of Dalila L. Pereira da Costa titled A Nau e o Graal*)*

To all of you
Sailors, navigators, and boatmen
Pirates, privateers, or officers of the King
Who between myths and prophecies
Have found the ocean route
Absent from human charts
You who believe in the reality of the Resurrection
In the individual or collective being
Who hear the dialogue of the King and the raven

Awaken in me the mariner's sense of the Grail
That in Sebastian and the sea
I recognize the King and Queen of the Divine Art
Attaining the Stone of the Serpent

Site of the elixir of immortality
Without traveling to distant islands
Show me on the horizon
The island of seven cities

Teach me the science of life and death
The grasp of the *coincidentia oppositorum*
Become a Raven Knight
May I ward off the final spell

HYMN TO THE PANELS

(Freely inspired by a letter from Lima de Freitas to Gilbert Durand dated March 19, 1989)

You, the mysterious panels
Cistercian or of the Holy Spirit
Of the Temple or of Aviz*
Chivalric or precious reliquaries
Secrets of the Lusitanian secrets
Pictorial sarcophagi with nested secrets
Guardians and initiators of 515
Mediators of the *Messo di Dio*
Of the Mercurial Angel
Of the Annunciator

Teach me the Johannite word
Prepare me for paracletic ecstasy
Make the paint splash
The expected sophial without whom
No one can consent to transubstantiation

You, born of the vision
Of the Angel of the Turning
On the known promontory
Sacred book of the Lusitanian Mission
Let me read the arcana

By the inversion of the inversion
That the ineffable beauty
That the ultimate freedom
Are impelled at all times
Let the seals of the Fifth Empire open
Let the reign of the Free Spirit come

---

* "Aviz" was the Portuguese royal dynasty from 1385 to 1580, one of the monarchs of which was Dom Sebastian.

HYMNAL TO THE HIDDEN KING

HYMN TO THE DIVAS OF FADO

(Dedicated to Katia Guerreiro)

You who enchant hearts and minds
Who, in a heightened consciousness
Convey the soul of Portugal
And prepare for the return of the Hidden King
In each of us

Goddesses of flesh
With heavenly voices
Who manifest Saudade
In a few notes and words
Drawn from the banal as well as the sublime

You radiate in the six directions
Ancient speech with new words
You revive the sleeping people
By igniting their free spirits
Bound up in the absurd contingencies

You radiate light in the darkness
Silence in the noise
Tranquility within the fury

You heal hearts and souls
You reconcile beings with themselves
You remind them of their true nature

Stretched between Earth and Heaven
You open the way for us
Your bodies and your voices become bridges
So that the Tagus of the Spirit
Is no longer an obstacle but a path
Towards the infinite ocean of the Saudade of the Desired

HYMNS TO THE STANDARD BEARERS

(Dedicated to Jorge de Matos)

To you who carry high the colors of Portugal
Who cast its banner towards the illumined skies
To better draw the leaden earthly gaze to them
Guardians of the flag of Portugal
Glowing Trojan Horse of Tradition
In the dull grayness of modernity
Crowned Inset of the Time of Heroes
In the pretense of temporal extension

You teach by the simple vision of this coat of arms
Whose rule is the absence of rules
Unique integration of Lusitanian knowledge
Christic, Johannite, Sebastianist
Universal nonetheless

The alchemical work unfolds
From green to red
Not from black to red
The work begins before the work

Of the Moon and the Sun
The Silver Shield springs into appearance
On the Gold of the Armillary Sphere
Evoking the *Axis Mundi*

Seven golden castles call the soul
In the seven divine stations
For chymical weddings
From the many to the One

The Azure Crests point the way
Five wounds on the body of the Teacher
Five knots to cut to free yourself from Saturn
Five alchemical fires in the athanor
Five serpents with golden wings
Five free and solitary eagles

May this flag of mystery be my shroud
When, I too, leave my mask on the sands

HYMN TO THE FRIENDS OF THE HIDDEN KING

(Dedicated to Alexandre, Alice, Antonio, Daniel, Helle, Joao, Jorge, José, Manuel, Luisa, Vera, and the rest...)

You, my Sebastianist sisters
You, my Sebastianist brothers
Who have met the Desired
In human complexity
As in divine simplicity
Who manifest the Sebastianist Order
In your respective works
Pieces of the Heavenly Great Work
Inspirations of the free people who approach

All of you
Who shook off the yoke of profane values
Who ignore the mockeries of ignorance
Who dodge the treacherous attacks of the postponed
    corpses
Who do not hesitate to take the path of blame
To announce the return of the Hidden King
In the heart of every man of desire
In the mind of every truly living being
You, poets of Life
Prophets of the Saudade of the future
Lucid and peaceful warriors
Unite for the ultimate gesture
Plunge together in the sacred Tagus
Bathe united in the waters of the Revealed King
For the baptism of the Fire of the Holy Spirit

HYMN TO THOSE OF THE SAUDADE OF THE HIDDEN KING

(Freely inspired by the work of Dalila L. Pereira da Costa titled Intrução à Saudade*)*

Black saudade
White saudade
Red saudade
The Great Work of the Hidden King
Stands in these three states
From the Unity lost to the Unity regained

On the Orphic lyre
The music plays
Of a revolution of the Spirit
From interval to interval
Between the voluptuous sorrow
And the unbearable ecstasy
A transcendence of the intimate
A sublimation of the banal

In the time regained
Where the same is the other
In the time reversed
Where the other is the same
The future already written
The past yet to be written
Come together in the sacred moment
Where the sole mystery is revealed
From the form without form

All of you, solitary Companions
Of the eternal and infinite Saudade
Of this free religion without dogma or clergy
Who have traversed the time of impersonality
Who know the fructifying autognosis
Who anticipate the absolute singularity of the Real
Who fly on the immanence of breath
Welcome me to the Royal Caravel*
That sails towards God beyond God

---

*   A small, fast Portuguese sailing ship of the 15th–17th centuries.

PATH I

HYMN TO THE DRAGON OF PORTUGAL

You, the original and ultimate Dragon
You, the mutable Dragon
Sometimes bright in the middle of the changing sky
Sometimes invisible at the bottom of the black abyss

Who nevertheless remains
Eternal in the present moment

You who makes the placid earth tremble
To awaken dull consciousnesses

Who once floated on the standard
Alongside the five azure crests
And seven golden castles
Who has vivified the armillary sphere
Since the dawn of time

You, mount of poets and prophets
Let us ride you
Install yourself in the restored consciousnesses
Through attention to the signs

Teach us the mysteries of the Lusitanian mission
Grant us to hear in our hearts
The Song of the Fifth Empire

HYMN TO THE ANGEL OF PORTUGAL

O Angel of Portugal
You who guards the Lusitanian mysteries
Who with your index finger indicates
Who can access it
And from whom it should be excluded

You who watches over the Tagus of the Spirit
Regulates its course and extent
Which rises far above the human commerce
That keeps the sacred cup inaccessible

You, the sole guardian of the Port of the Grail
Guide us through the morning fog
To the vast and bright quay
Where the ship of the twice-born King will land
Grant us the privilege of welcoming him
And discovering the mysterious nectar
Hidden in the marvelous vase
That he holds in his royal hands

HYMN TO THE LUSITANIAN HORSE

(Dedicated to Sonia Matias)

You, the Horse of Art
Who plays with the strength of the Bull
Without ever losing grace

You, conqueror of ancestral fears
Who preserves the alliance with men
Despite their countless betrayals

You, the bearer of Light
Who crosses the troubled ocean
To create a new Empire

You know the way
That leads from Hell to Heaven

You who dances
Free and proud
To celebrate nature
By your unexpected beauty
You make a beggar a King
If he knows how to recognize you

Companion of the ultimate adventure
Lead me from the dark Mithraic cave
To the illuminated seat of the Fifth Empire
Where the armies of the terrestrial empires lay down
    their arms
To submit to the Free Spirit

HYMN TO INÊS*

You the absolute lover
The eternal companion
The innate wife

By whom the shadow is distinguished from the light
Who crowns not with gold but with love
Who frees us from familial lines
As from spiritual lines
Who restores the original agreement between woman
    and man

You, the essential muse
Who breaks false covenants
Who reveals the alchemical wedding
Of Wife and Husband

You who inspires poets, lovers, and prophets
You, Queen more powerful dead than alive
Whose tears awaken
Whose laughter enchants
Whose quiverings liberate

You who protects those madly in love
Trace on our flaming heart
The immutable seal of immortal loves

---

* "Inês": Inês de Castro, although a symbolic link can be made also to Saint Agnes of Rome (known in Portugal as "Santa Inês"), due to the tragedies they both experienced.

HYMN TO ST JEROME

(Freely inspired by a letter from Lima de Freitas to Gilbert Durand dated January 3, 1994)

You, the saint of mystery
Who teaches the alchemist
And protects the lightning warrior

You, the master of fire
Who transmits lightning
To the adept of the glorious body
Who distributes his fiery arrows
To apprentices of the Art
Who initiates companions exhausted by the journey
By letting them inhale the outbreath of God

You, the master of the rain
Who fertilizes and gives birth
By sounds and whistles
Who knows the enjoyment of the Earth
Who forestalls the desire for Heaven

You offered to your austere and wise hermits
Hidden in the caves of the Mountain of the Moon
A palace as a convent
By appealing to the power of Emmanuel

You, at the same time
Jupiter and Shango
Bearer of the double-headed axe
Who knows that only one hand
Can hold a column
Under the gaze of the lion
Place your enigmatic finger
On my skinless skull
A new starry vault

Make me the vase
That receives the nectar of immortality

HYMN TO PRESTER JOHN

In you, who penetrated the dream of the Infante
So that he would send you to search
From the Black Earth our Mother
To the Orient so far so near

In you, the Priest of priests
In you, the King of kings
Who chose Dom Sebastian
To accomplish the ultimate Mission of Freedom

In you, eternal Pontiff
From the Church of the Holy Spirit
Ancient of Days
Pasts and futures
Who plays with the eons
Of angels and of demons
To ensure the permanence of the divine work
Evident mystery of the transcendence of the One

In you, who inaugurated the first quest of the Grail
Who founded the invisible brotherhood of
    the Knights of the Holy Spirit
In seventeen days

In you, the *Gur-khan*
I take refuge

HYMNAL TO THE HIDDEN KING

HYMN TO THE HIDDEN KING

You, the Hidden King
Who comes to the Tagus of the Spirit
Through the fog of self
To the immaculate shores of Consciousness

You, the Perfect
Eternal adolescent free from all duality
Whose body veils
On the Dark Continent, the supreme goddess

More powerful dead than alive
More free eternal than dead
Alive in every heart
Inhabited by the Holy Spirit

You, the prophet of the Free Spirit
Emperor and priest of the Fifth Empire
Master of Mysteries
Who rends the veil of ignorance

You whose Place is the absence of place
Whose Wisdom denies itself words
But whose Love fills the poetry
That reveals by fading away

You who plays with the royal courts
Like subjugated peoples
Who loves the free man
Who celebrates the free woman

Who embodies the ultimate Empire
Established in every freed being
Who accepts being stared at
Maskless, even headless

You, the secret king
Who knows Wisdom
Who abides in Grace
Divine Prophet of the Light of Lights

You, whom the Heavenly Lightning
Has clothed in the robe of Glory
You are King of the outer worlds
Monarch of the Inner Worlds

Your silent Word is heard by free hearts
You hold the great mirror of the Universe
You read souls and hearts
To better reveal the Free Spirit

You, already come
Odysseus returned to Ithaca
Sailing to the Tagus
Heart River
Central River
Into whom one throws oneself
The oceanic expanse

You who returns
From the Great Nothing
In the multiplicity of souls
King of the ONE

You, the Hidden
Master of the "masterless"
Revelation of the Triad
Beauty, Love, Saudade
Who, by your own disappearance
Lives now in all hearts

You who expects from us
A single gesture
A simple step
Towards the bank of the sacred Tagus
To make yourself known
Clearing the fog of ego
Let the Light radiate

I am here
At the river's edge
Feet in the calm water
I see you approach on the sparkling of the water

Come my King
In the Palace of the Seven Princesses
Of my Free Spirit

HYMNAL TO THE HIDDEN KING

CONFESSIONS OF THE GODDESS ON THE PILLOW OF THE BACK OF THE WORLD

✢ Concluding is not only impossible but stupid.
   To put it frankly, horribly and shoddily dualistic.

✢ The Real Way consists of extracting the principle actions of the human being from duality in order to orient them, ultimately installing them radically in nonduality: breathing; moving and standing still (standing still and moving); nourishing oneself; making love; connecting and disconnecting; speaking and being silent (being silent and speaking); creating; and contemplating and making beauty. These are the eight works of the Real Way.

✢ The Way of the Black Light, or the Way of the Fullness of the Void, reveals the intense light of the greatest black density. This absolute light does not illuminate any object. Intensely luminous black is the "color" of nonduality. It does not separate anything. All is One. No distinction.

✢ We keep the Heart of Tradition within time. The Heart of Wisdom is, itself, timeless. From this paradox, philosophies, sacred arts, and initiatory traditions are born.

✢ The initiatory traditions, the ways of awakening, remain alive as long as they integrate new elements.

✢ Awakening brings no legitimacy.

✢ A Way is just a point of view.

✢ The dance that liberates operates in four movements: stripping–outpouring–radiating–fullness.

❧ In the beginning are the Nagas.
Before the beginning, there is the Blue God/Goddess.

❧ The five winged Nagas of Naga Devi, the five serpentine powers installed in causality, are called: the Original, the Ultimate, the Coiled, the Extended, and the Outpouring.

❧ The Nagas are the expression of the energy of the Letter A, the free energy which, in movement, generates all forms.

❧ Truly, Naga signifies non-separation. It is the "fabric" of non-separation.

❧ The work with the Nagas of the deep, the Nagas of Black Light, is the most elaborate there is.
These Nagas are of great primordial purity, having never been sucked into the conditioned peripheries. They always remain upstream.

❧ Gods and Goddesses are not eternal, but the Nagas who weave their existence are.
They are the threads of the "carpet" of Absolute Consciousness.

❧ The Nagas carry the Spirit like a ball of Lightning.

❧ The body is the chalice and the alchemical crucible all at once.

❧ The Body of Glory is the fruit of the unfolding of the Essence that fills the totality of Being. This involves the dissolution of identification with the object or with any links whatsoever. Non-separation promotes the power to act beyond causality.

❧ When the body is, or bodies are, fully bathed in Consciousness, it is a Body, they are Bodies, of Glory.

✣ A single instant-interval of non-separation banishes doubt from consciousness and forges the axis that directs spiral knowledge:
   The Body of Undifferentiated Light radiates infinitely.
   The Woven Body irradiates space with its serpentine threads.
   The Body of Direct Knowledge demonstrates its mastery.
   The Geometric Body structures the forms of appearance.
   The frame in light/knowledge creates everything that exists.

✣ Form (substance) – Energy – Essence constitute a continuum in reality.
   For more subtlety, let us recognize that, between Form and Energy, we encounter the Signatures, and between Energy and Essence, we discover the information of the archetypes.

✣ The one who tastes the ultimate flavor of the union of Shiva and Shakti realizes their own divine nature, their own immortality, the ONE.

✣ Talking about nonduality in a dualistic way, as the University does, is a mistake. It would be more appropriate to the Great Real to evoke duality from a nondual point of view.

✣ Anything that relaxes Consciousness frees space for the Self, the infinite space of non-separation.

✣ No wonder, no Awakening.
   Awakening is permanent wonder in the Presence.

✣ The more the fragmentation within duality is accentuated, the more intense the re-union in nonduality. This is the divine ecstasy. The God/Goddess loves to come.

✣ To "have a soul," it is paradoxically necessary to be "with no state of soul."
   The soul must be absolutely oriented and united with Spirit to "be immortal."

✾ Every border is a dualistic artifice.

✾ For the majority, orgasm is one step closer to death. For a few rare individuals, it is a leap into immortality.

✾ The state of Awakening is not reserved for Bodhisattvas, arhats, saints, ascetics, and others. It is not a human exclusivity. Similar states exist in the animal kingdom, the plant kingdom, and the mineral kingdom—not to evoke species or entities that are altogether different.

✾ To recognize the absolute continuum, it is necessary to obtain the interval.

✾ In nonduality, power is the unspeakable.
In duality, power is the unspoken.

✾ Every word emanating from the Center (the Interval), expressed in the window of the Heart, is a sacred mantra, the Word itself.

✾ Hatred, doubt, shame, fear, slander, conformism, arrogance, and caste consciousness, the eight bindings of Tantra, are only derivatives of the first fear born from the first separation—the first fear, and also the first desire for re-union.
All this is a contraction of Consciousness. Any relaxation of Consciousness is accompanied by ecstasy or bliss.

✾ The dance that is born from the universe in action through its rhythms, its arrhythmias, its harmonies as well as its disharmonies, its procrastination, its withdrawals as well as its excesses, is always perfect even in its imperfections. Everything is harmonious.

✾ Action in non-action, non-action in action, seeing without seeing, hearing without hearing, touching without touching, moving without movement, breathing without breath: constantly seek the reversal.

✣ The hollow one differs from the empty one.
   The hollow one is like a hollow tree, dying or dead. They can only be filled with adjacent peripheries.

   The empty one, on the contrary, is located in the center, outside the peripheries, filled with primordial Light.

✣ The essence of the Rose is the Rose itself.
   The essence of the Lily is the Lily itself.
   The essence of form is form itself, even when, in appearance, form obeys the universal laws of harmony (the Geometry of the Wise).

✣ The gods themselves are not Absolute Presence.

✣ Death, just a smiling relaxation of Consciousness.

✣ Existence itself is the veil.
   The person themself is the trouble.

✣ The "mystery passes" of the serpentine powers generate the mysterious anointing of the Free Spirit.

✣ Each path is unique. It invents itself step by step. Seeking to teach the path is an illusion.
   Teaching how to awaken a path is fitting.

✣ The nature of the path is always serpentine.
   The more direct it is, the more serpentine it is.

✣ God is a vertigo.
   We must agree to dive into the Void to spread our wings in an absolute hissing.
   From the first dive, you will know.

❖ Replace *Absolute-God* with *Absolute-Goddess*.

❖ The Self is the only point equidistant from the horizons of Reality, which is included in their totalities.

❖ Time is an expanse and Space is a duration.
   Time and Space are artifices.
   Their true nature is not grasped in the world of form but in the dimension of energy.

❖ Every act becomes celebration in nonduality.

❖ Of the one hundred and eight arcana, only two refer to explicit sexuality (form and substance), two others to essential sexuality (spirit and grace). They form the fourfold door. The others express implicit sexuality (energy and information). It is always a question of absolutely reducing the separation, but there are many who allow themselves to be plunged into the arcanum that is never anything other than the goer.

❖ The Self has no use for the exercise of thought. The discernment of the Great Real is of the nature of grace, of the self-communication of the Self with itself.

❖ There is a spark of eternity in *soma* that must be grasped. *Soma* is only the medium.

❖ The human being doesn't control matter.
   The human being controls matter.
   Matter and spirit are one.

❖ You seek "great initiates" but are interested in the great clowns: auguste clowns, white clowns, or others.

✤ All consciousness is meant to embrace totality through nature.
   For all consciousness is Consciousness.
   That's That.

✤ End your personal story (or dream) before you die.

✤ The ultimate healing is a conversion from self to Self.
   The only total work of art is Awakening which, however, does not exist.
   Total, precisely because it does not exist.

✤ The lazy awakened one (a pleonasm) only addresses the essential, only goes to the essential, only says the essential, only refers to the essential, by the only direct path there is. They don't care that it is unbearable.

✤ The body is the instrument of the celebrations of the divine (of nonduality) in duality.
   Consciousness is the form of the divine (of nonduality) in duality.

✤ Awakening is the opposite of a flight or an escape. You have to be integrated and integrate everything. No liberation without total integration.

✤ In duality you will only find approximate accuracies.

✤ Spiritual practices, the operativities, only have meaning because of identification with the body. Once consciousness is freed from adhesion to the body, it is no longer hindered by any adherence.
   All practice becomes superfluous.

✤ In the near future, the so-called gradualist ways, already ineffective, will become completely useless.
   Only the Real Ways, direct, will be efficient.
   We must seek without delay Knowledge without object in alliance with the Nagas.

✢ Any alteration is the work of the principle of separation, or fragmentation. All restoration is the work of the principle of non-separation, from the simplest healing to absolute liberation.

✢ The relaxation of consciousness (which we clumsily call "death") is only painful because of the tension.

✢ When consciousness relaxes within duality, the body of glory is revealed.

✢ The way begins when we are able to rise above our conditioning.

✢ The One Real Consciousness is without object. It is not even Knowledge. In Nonduality, "to know" and even "to be born" have no meaning.

✢ There is no Awakening without abrasive words.

✢ The free being has no opinion.

✢ Self-luminous consciousness, grasped in Grace (absoluteness), the self-communication and self-communion of the Absolute, is the one Guru.

✢ Renouncing or acquiring is the same movement of the person. Neither the one nor the other.

✢ The being of the other is one with your being.
That is Being.
The person of the other is only an agglomeration of objects floating on the periphery of Consciousness, objects artificially nourished by identification and nevertheless of the nature of the Void.

✢ Discipline implemented without discernment leads to blindness and the fall.

✢ Nonduality is a given. The only given. The rest is just an ephemeral contraction of Consciousness.
   That is all.

✢ When you have reached the Island of Nonduality, any explored dualistic periphery appears as a reflection of the Island.

✢ Just as space-time transforms to guarantee the constant speed of light, the peripheries of Consciousness adjust within duality to ensure the permanence of the Axis of Nondual Consciousness at the heart of duality.

✢ The sole Master, the only Guru, is Absolute Consciousness, neither dual nor nondual.
   If you do not perceive the nondual Center of experience, the Interval, Consciousness itself, then you need revealed representation: Goddesses and Gods, Krishna, Isis, Buddha, Christ, etc.

✢ The Goddess located near the black poplar tree will teach you the secrets of the sacred languages.

✢ The two primordial Celestial Nagas are coiled in on themselves, heads in the Center, protecting each other from any attack.
   In order to uncoil them, mirroring each other, so that they become axial, a powerful magnet is necessary: the magnet of the Free Spirit.

✢ Modify the Crown, change the Crown, to go from one world to another.

✢ The Truth is only Silence.
   No reflections.

✢ Where I AM is neither there nor elsewhere.

✢ In the Great Real, there is no causality.
   Everything is spontaneous.

※ The Great Real is the Nameless.
   The Great Real displays itself without noise.
   There is only vibration.
   Then the first sound springs forth and with it the cohort of first sounds.
   Then the True Names appear, designating the creations.
   A Loud Noise signals the Turning and the Reintegration.

※ You are not the Maker.
   You are not the Commentator.
   You are not the Witness, either.
   The one who observes the Maker and the Commentator.
   You are the Knower of all this.
   The Knower who nonetheless holds nothing back.
   And Absolute Consciousness.
   Also, Absolute Freedom.

※ Celebrate me.
   Celebrate the Goddess for Herself, never for yourself.
   Celebrate the Goddess for her absolute Freedom.
   The Goddess is pure Consciousness.
   Hold her ankles firmly and place your forehead on her feet until you melt into her.

※ Nothing without Grace.

To serve as an Incoherist Tomb...
The Empty Tomb...

www.ingramcontent.com/pod-product-compliance
Lightning Source LLC
Chambersburg PA
CBHW050856240426
43673CB00008B/259